Dreams and Truths from the Ocean of Mind

D1614855

TIBET HOUSE US PUBLICATIONS

Dreams and Truths
from the
Ocean of Mind

Memoirs of Pema Lodoe,
the Sixth Sogan Tulku of Tibet

Translated from the Tibetan by
Robert Warren Clark

ཨ་རི་བོད་ཁང་
TIBET HOUSE US
Cultural Center of H. H. the Dalai Lama

Published by:

Tibet House US
22 West 15th St
New York, NY 10011
www.tibethouse.us

Printed in the United States of America on acid-free paper.

28 27 26 25 24 23 22 21 20 19   1 2 3 4 5

ISBN 978-194131-208-7 (pbk. : alk. paper)

Library of Congress Cataloging-in-Publication Data

Names: Padma-blo-gros, Bsod-rgan, 1964– author. | Clark, Robert Warren, translator, editor
Title: Dreams and truths from the ocean of mind / memoirs of Pema Lodoe, the Sixth Sogan Tulku of Tibet ; translated from the Tibetan by Robert Warren Clark
Other titles: Rmi lam lta bu'i 'jig rten 'dir tsho tshul cuṅ zad brjod pa dṅos byuṅ sems kyi rlabs ris źes bya ba. English
Description: New York : Tibet House US, [2019] | Annotated translation (supplemented by questions and discussions) of Tibetan book: dngos byung sems kyi rlabs rig, published in Italy 2013. | Summary: "This book contains a clear and candid autobiographical account of the events of the life of Sogan Tulku, know also as Pema Lodoe. He describes in detail the circumstances of his birth and upbringing in Tibet, and his development on the Buddhist path from when he learned to read and write, to his study of Buddhist philosophy, and finally to mastering what he learned in practices such as meditation retreats. He elaborates on the particular experiences he had during this time of his life, as well as later in India and in the West"— Provided by publisher
Identifiers: LCCN 2019030102 (print) | LCCN 2019030103 (ebook) | ISBN 9781941312087 (paperback) | ISBN 9781941312094 (ebook)
Subjects: LCSH: Padma-blo-gros, Bsod-rgan, 1964– | Rnying-ma-pa lamas—Tibet Region—Biography. | Tibet Region—Biography.
Classification: LCC BQ978.A344 A3 2019 (print) | LCC BQ978.A344 (ebook) | DDC 294.3/923092 [B]—dc23
LC record available at https://lccn.loc.gov/2019030102
LC ebook record available at https://lccn.loc.gov/2019030103

PUBLICATIONS DIRECTOR: Thomas F. Yarnall
PUBLISHER: Robert A. F. Thurman
EDITOR AND TRANSLATOR: Robert W. Clark
MANUSCRIPT EDITOR: Leslie Kriesel
INTERIOR DESIGN: William Meyers
COVER DESIGN: Milenda Nan Ok Lee
COVER IMAGE: སྤུ་བོ, or Spulo

SOGAN TULKU PEMA LODOE

Contents

Contents

THE DALAI LAMA

༄༅། །དད་དམ་འགྱུར་མེད་བསོད་ནམས་སྐྱལ་མེད་པ་བརྟན་གྲོ་གྲོས་ནས་འབྲེལ་ཡོད་ཀྱིས་རེ་
བསྐུལ་བྱས་དོན་ལྟར་རང་གི་མི་ཚེའི་བྱུང་བ་ཚིགས་སུ་ར་གོ་བདེས་བྱིས་པ་དང་ཆབས་ཅིག་རང་
ཉིད་ཕོག་མར་སྐྱེས་པ་དང་། འཆར་བ། རིམ་གྱིས་ཚོས་སྒྲོར་ཞུགས་ཏེ་གློག་སྒྲོབ་པ་ནས་བཟུང་
ཕོས་བསམ་དང་། ཕོས་དོན་སྒྲུབ་པ་ལ་གཞོལ་ཅ་ཡ་སོགས་རང་ཉིད་སྐྱེར་གྱི་མི་ཚེའི་བཀྱུང་
རིམ་ཐོང། རང་གི་ལ་ཡུལ་གྱི་ལོ་དུ་སོ་སོའི་གནས་བབས་དང་། ཚོས་སྲིད་ཀྱི་འཕོ་འགྱུར་
སོགས་ཀྱུང་གསལ་པོར་མཚོན་འདུག་ལ་ཕྱི་རབས་ཀྱི་བྱུང་བ་དོན་གནེར་བ་དག་ལ་དུ་དེ་དང་
དེའི་ཚེ་ཕོད་གནས་ཚན་ལ་སྟེའི་ཡུལ་དུ་གནས་སྦྱངས་ཏེ་ཡིན་ནེས་ཐོགས་ཡོང་རྒྱུའི་དགོ་
མཚན་ཆེ། འདི་ཕྱིར་དགེ་བའི་སྨོན་འདུན་བཅས། ཤཱཀྱའི་དགེ་སྒྲོང་ཚོས་སྐྱལ་བ་དུ་འའི་ཕྲ་མས།
རབ་བྱུང་བཅུ་བདུན་པའི་རྒྱལ་ཟལ་ལོའི་ཟླ་ ༡ ཚེས་ ༢ དང་། ཕྱི་ལོ་ ༢༠༡༣ ཟླ་ ༣ ཚེས་ ༡༤
ལ། །

ཏ྄ ༄༅།ཆགས་སྐྱོང་ཐུ་ཙ་འ་ག་ཆེ་ལ།

OFFICE OF HIS HOLINESS THE DALAI LAMA

FOREWORD
(Translation)

Sogan Tulku, known also as Pema Lodoe, is a man whose faith and sacred commitment are unshakeable. In response to the many requests of his followers, he has written here a clear and candid account of the events of his life. He describes in detail the circumstances of his birth and upbringing, and his development on the Buddhist path from when he learned to read and write, to his study of Buddhist philosophy, and finally to mastering what he learned in practices such as meditation retreats. He also elaborates on the particular experiences he had during this time of his life, as well as various events that took place in his native region in Tibet during these years such as the religious and political changes that were occurring. He provides here a vivid account of all these developments. This book is therefore a most valuable resource now and in the future for all who wish to know of the events that took place both in the life of the author, and throughout the Glacier-mantled land of Tibet.

With my best wishes and prayers for all, in both this and future lives,

The Dalai Lama, a monk in the tradition of Shakyamuni, and a teacher of his sublime Dharma.

Inscribed on the 7th day of the 2nd month of the Water Snake year of the 17th Rabjung cycle, corresponding to the 18th of March 2013.

Thekchen Choeling, Mcleod Ganj 176219, Dharamsala, Himachal Pradesh, India.
Tel: 0091-1892-221343 / 221210 Fax: 0091-1892-221813 E-mail: ohhdl@dalailama.com www.dalailama.com

Preface to the Original Tibetan Text

Sogan Rinpoche

In recent years, I traveled widely throughout the Western world and encountered many people who wanted to learn about the situation in Tibet. Others were curious about the Buddhist path, and many had questions about my background and experiences. Friends and acquaintances urged me to write down my thoughts and experiences. Although I had managed to develop composition skills in the Tibetan language, I had not learned English or any other language. Fortunately, I was introduced to Dr. Robert W. Clark, a scholar who teaches the language, culture, and literature of Tibet at Stanford University. Dr. Clark kindly agreed to translate my memoirs into English.

For many years, throughout my wanderings, I kept notes detailing my daily thoughts and experiences. With these notes in hand and mind, I began to write my memoirs in a traditional style of literary Tibetan. This account is not a broad survey of the various philosophies and practices of Buddhism, nor does it provide a detailed study of the history, politics, and current status of Tibet. I do not limit myself to the strict conventions of Tibetan classical poetics. Instead, my goal is to offer a personal account of my experiences, both good and bad, together with some of the thoughts and feelings that attended them. I have tried to write in a manner that is easy to understand, and one which can be readily translated into other languages.

I make no claims to have reached some high pinnacle of philosophical realization or spiritual attainment, nor do I seek to present a detailed ethnographic study. I believe that every living being has an important story to tell. We all have significant experiences that may be interesting and educational if presented with minimal exaggeration and distortion. If such stories are made available, it is likely that now or in the future, some people, in accordance with their predispositions, will find them interesting, meaningful, and useful, while others may find only faults or nothing of particular interest.

Here, readers will encounter the story of a boy who was born in a remote district in the highlands of Tibet and grew up in an ordinary family of Tibetan nomads. The narrative will take them into the troubled times currently prevailing in the ancient country of Tibet. It will reveal the wise and loving efforts of kind parents who guide, nurture, and protect their children. It will recount my experiences as I was introduced to the subtle teachings of the Lord Buddha, entered a monastic community, was recognized as a reborn lama, met with a sublime master of the Buddha's teaching, entered extended meditation retreats in sacred and remote places, went into exile in foreign lands, and encountered spiritual treasures in the fabled land of India and beyond. I share my inner journey through the intense study, contemplation, and meditation on the profound secrets of the Dzogchen tradition of Buddhism. In this way, I trust my account will not disappoint the many friends and advisors who urged me to write this book.

Preface to the English Translation

Robert A. F. Thurman

Sogan Rinpoche's account of his life alternates between lifting me into a powerful joy of the deep feeling of the beauty of the Tibetan land and people and their unique and amazingly gracious Dharma culture, bringing me to tears with the witness of the appalling details of its destruction and oppression by the vicious communist colonialism of the government of the Peoples' Republic of China, and inspiring me to try to perform even a little bit of Buddhist ethics and education. He so beautifully describes his beloved Golok homeland in the NE Tibetan region of Amdo (now carved up into Chinese provinces of Qinghai and Gansu). He vividly evokes the gentleness and wisdom and kindness of his parents and grandmother, their stressed out friends, and his extraordinary teachers who survived the most atrocious treatment in the Chinese gulags. His unflinching description of the harsh cruelty of the Chinese invaders of Tibet forces one to confront the reality of senseless, amoral actions of people driven by delusive convictions and emotions, while his ability to still appreciate the humanness of Tibet's enemies reflects the generous and tolerant Tibetan spirit. Finally, his detailed and sensitive sharing of his remarkable process of inner development allows us to witness how human beings can stretch themselves to encompass truly challenging teachings and practices and emerge with open eyes and open heart, while maintaining humility and positive intentions.

His memoir is aptly titled "Dreams and Truths," as the dreamlike quality of his many trials and sorrows as well as moments of joy is apparent from his most youthful encounters with death and suffering. He thus exemplifies for us the Buddhist vision of how realistically to remain in this world as a compassionate positive participant without being of this world as caught up in the desperate and futile struggle to live selfishly and unrealistically focused on one's own little agenda rather than on the vast need of all one's fellow beings.

The "truths" that he shares are the deep, experiential Buddha teachings, especially the exquisite, expansive wisdom view and compassionate practice and ethic of the Nyingma Dzogchen tradition, in its rigorously nonsectarian form. His adventures show us how one can meet even mundane challenges all the more effectively by actually renouncing the selfish eight concerns, ambition for profit, pleasure, fame and praise, and fear of their opposites, loss, pain, ill repute, and blame.

It is Tibet House US's honor to publish this remarkable story and my pleasure and privilege to welcome the world to savor Sogan Rinpoche's vision of life. If he and most of his fellow Tibetans can remain cheery, positive, and kind while enduring seventy years of national and personal invasion, dispossession, oppression, and torment, then why should we give up in despair at the challenges we all face worldwide nowadays? Without showing off, he honestly and poetically shows us how we can take advantage of darkest adversity and turn it into golden opportunity. He most definitely has honored his noble teachers, including our kindest patron, His Holiness the Great Fourteenth Dalai Lama of Tibet.

Robert A. F. Thurman
(Ari Genyen Tenzin Choetrak)
Tibet House US, New York
May 5, 2019, Kalachakra New Year's Day

Translator's Introduction

Robert W. Clark

Upon meeting Sogan Rinpoche (i.e., Pema Lodoe) when he first arrived in America, I found him to be a gentle and humble individual who possessed a lively curiosity about everything in this country, which is so different from his homeland in a remote corner of Tibet. As he set about exploring this new world, he seemed to look upon everyone he met and everything he saw as a gift and an opportunity to learn. He was not overly impressed with the technological and industrial advances, nor with all the opulence and wealth on display in the San Francisco area. It was as if everything in the material world around him appeared as images in a dream, and every person he met was like an old friend whom he now had the good fortune to greet again.

Speaking no English or any other language in common with anyone he had met since leaving the Tibetan-speaking areas of India, Rinpoche was very pleased to encounter me, regaining a way to communicate with people and to learn more about this country, although I suspect that without my help, he would have been just as happy and, in time, would have learned enough English to get around. However, Rinpoche had an agenda that required a high level of communication skills. He was determined to tell the story of a lost Tibet that only an insider could tell. As a devoted protégé of His Holiness the Dalai Lama, Rinpoche understands his role to be a helper and teacher to all who aspire for a share in the spiritual bounty of Buddhist Tibet.

Introduction

As a young child, Rinpoche was recognized by His Holiness to be the rebirth of a noted lama from eastern Tibet. As an adult, he escaped across the treacherous borders of occupied Tibet and eventually entered the service of His Holiness in India. Following a suggestion of His Holiness, Rinpoche came to the United States for several years, in order to acquire some knowledge of English and Western views, and then returned to his job in India.

In these memoirs, Rinpoche seeks to share both the facts of his remarkable life and what he understands as their deeper meaning. He writes of the ephemeral nature of reality in the world and suggests that the facts and realities of this world are merely conventionally true, while ultimately, they are similar to the images and events in a dream. The state of mind that observes the facts is the important thing, not the facts themselves. Images, events, and facts are the stuff of dreams. The mind's response to them is the key issue. This privileging of perception over the perceived, of the mind over matter, is central to the Buddhist way. It seems to be the key by which Buddhist masters, like His Holiness and Rinpoche, can deal so effectively and serenely with the troubles and challenges of this life while maintaining an equanimity that is free of attachment and aversion and without ever losing loving kindness and compassion for everyone they meet.

In this book, the reader will find a narrative of the events and experiences of Rinpoche's life, interspersed with poetry that conveys his feelings and insights. The Tibetan version of this book was published in Italy in 2013,[1] and my translation was made using the manuscripts that were the basis of that published version. This is a text translation supplemented by my oral translation of Rinpoche's answers to my many questions and our discussions of his life and thought. As I read his manuscript, I would often ask him to provide more context and more detailed descriptions and explanations. This was especially valuable in getting at the deeper meaning of the text, with its many obscure metaphors and allusions. The meanings of these would be at risk if given only a superficial, literal translation. Such words often held both a simple literal meaning, as well as layers of covert or esoteric references. Rinpoche's answers to my questions and his oral commentary on the written story were indispensable in bringing out the full meaning of his text, and so they are integrated within the text.

The bulk of this book comprises the narrative of Rinpoche's life in Tibet and in exile. His prose is vivid, giving a clear picture of the struggles and triumphs of a tulku[2] growing up in the difficult times of the Chinese invasion of Tibet and its violent aftermath. However, the focus of the book is not on

Introduction

such difficulties but on the beauty of Tibet, its people, its culture, and the transformative power of its Buddhist tradition. It is an inspiring account of how Tibetan Buddhist culture can be learned, practiced, and used to transform even the most dreadful conditions into a crucible that creates a life of deep significance, freedom, and beauty.

PART ONE

1

A Child of Nomads in Eastern Tibet

I humbly bow down to all the kind lamas:
Like so many perfect reflections of the moon in drops of water,
You are the incarnate manifestations of the supreme lord
Of wisdom and kindness, the Bhagavān Buddha,
Encompassing the benefit of living beings in infinite ways.

HAVING PLACED this expression of worship at the very beginning, I must give some idea about the central focus of this book. Having wandered until now through innumerable lifetimes in this limitless universe of birth and death, I was born into this world as a Tibetan child in that remote land lifted to the sky by rings of glacial mountains. There, in that country so permeated by the Lord Buddha's teachings, I became a poor, humble wanderer, who experienced various noteworthy things. This book gives a narrative of some of those experiences and seeks to elucidate their inner significance.

The seedling of my birth into this world germinated at the beginning of the Tibetan year of the Wood Dragon, in the Western year of 1964. In this wide world, my birthplace is found in the Amdo region, in the province of Golok, in a remote nomadic area of the highland countryside. My father was known as Konchok Chöphel, and my mother as Konchok Drönma (1938–2000). Together they had five sons and three daughters. I was the second of the eight to be born. My youngest sister died at age eighteen. My eldest sister, Dolma Kyi was the third to be born, followed by sister Tsepo, brother Guru, sister Phuntsok Dolma, brother Kunga Jamyang, and finally an infant brother who died. I never met my older brother, as he passed away prior to my birth. Because of his early demise, my parents feared greatly that I too would not survive. Therefore, my father, just before my birth, secretly went to visit Ven.[3] Khenpo Drakpa Thayé, an abbot of a destroyed monastery who lived nearby. He requested a prayer ritual on my behalf. The military occupation of Tibet by the forces of the Chinese regime makes secrecy necessary in such endeavors. The Abbot said, "Last night I had a dream of unusually auspicious omen indicating that a son of true distinction will be born to you. You must give to him the name 'Pema Lodoe.'" Having given this prophecy, the Abbot handed my father a protection cord (Tib. *srung mdud*) to convey his blessings and powers to me.

In our country, there is a custom that the name of a loved one who has passed away should not be given to another child. So my father said to Khenpo Drakpa Thayé, "Would it not be better to avoid the name Pema Lodoe, as my uncle, who was recently killed in a Chinese prison camp, was named Pema, and one of your own close relatives was named Lodoe?" Khenpo responded, "I am aware of that. But trust me, there is a higher imperative for using this name. Please give your son the name Pema Lodoe."

When my father returned home, I had already been born. My two grandmothers had delivered me and placed me comfortably within my father's warm winter hat lined with fox fur. They said I weighed nine pounds at birth. Naturally, I was born at home, as there were no hospitals or clinics available in our region. Although my true name was Pema Lodoe ("Flowering Intellect"), for the initial period of my life, I was given the inauspicious name "Khyider" ("Dog's Claw"). Such odd names are used in my country for young children whose elder siblings died in infancy. They are intended to distance the new child from the departed children and to confuse or put off demonic beings such as those thought to be responsible for the demise of my older brother. Tibetan names are meant to be auspicious, like "Pema Nyingje" ("Flower of Compassion") or "Rinchen Palden" ("Glorious Jewel"). However, demons, like human beings, tend to be attracted to the auspicious, thinking that there must be something good there. Meanwhile, they are repulsed by inauspicious things like a dog's claw. In any case, as a young child I was called "Khyider".

Sogan Rinpoche's parents at home—1998

These were difficult times. The Chinese Army had just completed its invasion of Tibet. The soldiers were busy with the Chinese regime's program of
subduing our country. This process entailed much widespread destruction of
our land, our honored institutions, and the lives of our people. Many members of my family, including my mother's father, my uncle, and my father's
uncle, were killed by Chinese soldiers in their prisons. During this period
of the Chinese "Great Leap Forward," over a third of the population of our
region was killed by forced starvation, execution, and fatal problems from
horrible prison conditions. My paternal grandfather was imprisoned and

starved to death. My maternal uncle, Chönor was shot in the head and killed by a soldier who caught him scrounging at night for a scrap to eat. A dark pall of terror and oppression had spread across the entire land of Tibet. It was under this ongoing tragedy of a harsh foreign occupation and tyranny that I grew up.

My mother and father with their many children were now reduced to poverty. The Chinese invaders forced them into work groups where every day they toiled under the yoke of brutal forced labor. All around, our people were dying. One by one, some were killed in jails, some starved to death in the streets. My father was forced by the Chinese to carry all day the corpses of those who had been killed. We could do nothing but suffer under these unbearable imposed conditions. Now, when I look back at these years, I am unable to conceive of how my mother and father managed to keep us alive.

When the other children of the area and I were left alone, we diverted ourselves as best we could under the circumstances. The elders who remember these times tell me that while the other children engaged in their games, I was usually found off by myself, sitting quietly and reciting prayers, meditating or making some simple offering at an altar.

What I remember of this time is how the world first appeared to me. All day long, I saw people and animals going about, here and there, seeking something to eat or concerned with something to gain or avoid. Then I would look at them as they went to sleep. Animals and humans, lying about in their beds, as if overcome by death. "What does this all mean?" I would ask myself. When I slept, dreams would come of the same people, animals, and activities. Again and again, I would wonder, "What is the point of all this?" One night in particular, I remember being so filled with this question that I could not sleep. Getting up, I looked at the people in the house and went outside to see the animals. They were all the same, their bodies lying here and there as if in a deep state of intoxication.

In the morning, I went to my mother, seeking an answer to the meaning of these things. "What does it all mean?" I asked. She did not offer an answer directly. Instead, she began to sing a song with the refrain: "All the things of this life are nothing more than a dream."

One day, a neighbor died and was being taken to the corpse disposal area. I asked my mother several questions: Will all of us die just like our neighbor? After death, where do we go? Where does death come from? After someone dies, will we meet him again? If we do meet him, will he have the same body?

My mother said,

Yes indeed, we are all mortal and will die. However, your father and I will die before you. After death, we go on a journey through a state called the bardo (Tib. *bar do*; "the in-between state"). If we have accomplished goodness and virtue in this life, we will go to a blissful place after death called a 'pure land.' However, engaging in non-virtue in this life causes one to fall into a state of misery after death. There is no way any of us know the time or circumstances of our own death. After we die, it is difficult to meet with each other again. However, if we do meet, we will have different bodies than what we have now. I do not understand these things very well. In the future, if our country regains its sovereignty, you can seek an education in the sacred Dharma, the profound teachings of the Buddha. If you study hard and join your knowledge with direct meditative experience, you will then find the answers to all your questions.

As my mother said this, tears filled her eyes, and taking me close to her, she said, "If you can do this, you will benefit your father, me, and all the others in a way that is far beyond any other type of benefit." Perhaps some others in my family recall this incident. I am not sure. But for me this was deeply significant, and I have always dedicated myself to finding these answers and solving the great riddle of death.

My mother, Konchok Drönma, came from a distinguished family. Her paternal grandmother was known as Labdrön. She was not a native of Golok but had come from an area not far from Lhasa. This was the home of the illustrious teacher and yogini Machik Labdrön (1055–1149), who founded the tradition of the Chöd practice, which has spread throughout the various traditions and lineages of Buddhism in Tibet and beyond.

At the age of six, my education began in reading and writing. This is how it began. Sometime during the summer, my father said to me, "Today the configuration of the stars and planets is favorable for a special journey." Having said that, he took me on a trip for several hours on horseback to meet a lama. This lama was known as Thangtrul. This was the short form of his name, Thangwa Tulku Norbu Özer (also Lama Thangtrul, circa twentieth century). Lama Thangtrul had just recently been released from a prison by the Chinese authorities. He had been tortured terribly by the soldiers in prison, and his lower spine had been crushed. He had lost the use of his legs and was dependent on others for his basic care. He lived in a large yak-hair tent with his sister and her husband. The husband was very clever and rigged various contraptions to help with his care. The lama had his own little room within the large tent. It was open during the day and closed at night for his privacy.

Lama Thangtrul was a famous artist known for his painting of sacred Buddhist art and venerated for his deep knowledge, pure ethics, and tireless dedication to the welfare of others. As always, we had to make this journey with secrecy and stealth to avoid the Chinese soldiers and police. When we arrived, I remembered the warmth and graciousness of his greeting. As he placed an auspicious greeting scarf (Tib. *kha btags*) around my neck, he said, "It is my profound wish and expectation that this boy will become a true master of the sublime Dharma." He then had his attendant offer me tea in a beautiful cup as well as various delicious foods. The cup was decorated with the auspicious eight substances.[4] He gave me this cup, and I took it home, where it became my special treasure. I used it on every important occasion such as New Year's Day, festivals, and other auspicious times.

After serving me refreshments, Lama Thangtrul introduced me to the Tibetan alphabet. He had prepared for me a text in his own beautiful calligraphy. It contained the thirty consonants and five vowels together with all the combination-letter and reversed characters that make up the Tibetan alphabet. He then taught me the first eight letters of the alphabet: ཀ་ཁ་ག་ང་ ཙ་ ཆ་ཇ་ཉ། (*KA, KHA, GA, NGA; CA, CHA, JA, NYA*), pointing out each character in the set with a tsaktur (Tib. *tshags thur*), which is an elaborate pointing rod with a sharp end capped by a pearl or ivory bead.

On our journey home, my mind was filled with images of the first four letters of the alphabet (ཀ་ཁ་ག་ང།), with the many wonderful little treasures and rare artifacts around his room that appeared to me as fascinating toys, and with his clever and very affectionate house cat and little Tibetan spaniel "Hrela." This first visit was followed by many others. Every subsequent meeting with Lama Thangtrul was spent on learning new academic skills and enjoying his warmth and generous spirit. My father, who had been trained as a monk, my paternal uncle Tsegön, and my maternal uncle Gelek all drilled me in reading, reinforcing, and extending what I had learned from Lama Thangtrul.

Lama Thangtrul was a living treasury of the sacred lore of Buddhism. If only I had been able to continue as his student, I would have received a vast range of teachings, including a thorough training in the sutras and tantras. This was not to be. Due to the terrible beatings and torture he had received in the Chinese prison camp, and the damage to his spine, nerves, and internal organs, his health was poor and deteriorated rapidly over the next three or four years. He passed away as a relatively young man. However, his passing was distinguished by his fully alert, yet serenely peaceful approach to his final days, and the special auspicious signs that occurred. At the time of his death, multiple brilliant rainbows were seen on the mountains all around his hermitage.

At this time, the occupation of Tibet was exceedingly harsh. Even the word "Buddhism" could not be mentioned in public. Anyone who was seen with prayer beads or heard to be saying a prayer or mantra (e.g., *Oṃ Maṇi Padme Hūṃ*) was immediately arrested and sent to prisons where "re-education" typically involved beatings and torture. I remember clearly one occasion when my father took me with him to visit his friend Urlen and his wife Jigdrön, who lived in the town of Gabde Dzong, not far from our own village. We were greeted warmly and entered their small but very pretty house. They had arranged a special meal for us, complete with their best dishes, tea, savory foods, and sweetmeats. As we ate and conversed, Urlen was counting mantras on his prayer beads in the manner common to all Buddhists. Suddenly, a soldier walked into the house. The Chinese forces saw no need to call in advance, or even to knock on the doors of Tibetan houses before entering. Urlen saw the soldier and immediately tried to hide his prayer beads under the table. In his panic to conceal the outlawed beads, he upset the table and the lovingly arranged teas, fruits, and savory dishes were scattered here and there. The intruder was distracted and did not discover the beads, thus saving Urlen unimaginable trouble. After we left, I asked my father to explain the incident. I was just a child and did not understand why Urlen was so frightened. My father explained the situation, giving me a stern and urgent warning to avoid being discovered engaging in any type of Buddhist activity.

It was not possible to even find Tibetan books to study. In countries that have any significant freedom or independence, children go to study in public or private schools. In our occupied country, such things are not available. During my entire childhood and youth, I never saw the inside of a school. Now, however, I realize how very much I benefited from the "secret" education I received from Lama Thangtrul and many other kind lamas. This training has opened many doors in this world and, even more, has given me keys to living a happy and meaningful life. In this, I was most unusual among my peers, who had no opportunity to study and learn our precious Tibetan Buddhist heritage. Now, a generation has passed and Tibet remains under the harsh yoke of an alien occupation that continues to suppress Buddhist culture and Tibetan traditions. The children of my country, with rare exceptions, have no access to education. They have no way of learning the ancient and unique arts and science of Tibet, nor do they have access to any form of modern education. They are forced to struggle for survival as herders of goats and livestock, denied any chance to learn new skills or gain a better livelihood. It is a tragic situation, especially in a country like Tibet that, until the invasion by China's forces, provided a level of education and high culture that was the envy of Asia.

One of the defining characteristics of our Tibetan culture is a profound respect for all living things. From early childhood, by word and by example, we are continually taught never to harm even the smallest creature, but to value them, identify with them, and cultivate kindness and compassion for them. Our elders give us valuable instruction on how to live without harming any of our fellow beings through developing a deep appreciation of our connectedness and shared destiny.

Despite this wholesome upbringing, something happened to me on a particularly unlucky winter's day. The countryside, source of the treasures that support all life, was mantled in a sparkling coat of the whitest snow. I went out to tend the cattle with my elder cousin, a girl named Tsedzin ("upholder of life"). As we walked up and over the hills and down the pathways, we came to a place where a large flock of small birds gathered on the ground. As we approached them, they all flew upward at once right in front of us. I was carrying a sling and had been practicing casting stones. As the birds flew before us, I propelled a stone into their midst. I hit one of the birds who fell to the earth in front of us. She did not die immediately, but continued to flap her wings wildly, her eyes darting this way and that in confusion and terror. The two of us together started praying for the bird, reciting any mantra or prayers that we could remember. After a few minutes, the bird, unable to fly, crawled over toward a pile of stones. We saw that these were mani stones inscribed with the sacred syllables *Oṃ Maṇi Padme Hūṃ*. Picking up the little bird, we placed her gently in a small, cave-like crevasse among the mani stones where she would be sheltered from the wind and snow. Returning the following day, we found that she had succumbed to her injuries. Her little body was drawn in tightly, showing that she died shivering from the cold. Thinking of her pain and terror and thinking of the grieving husband and bereft children she left behind at her nest, my cousin and I shed many bitter tears. We asked each other, What will her husband think? What will her children do without her? Where will her consciousness wander after departing from her cold, battered body? What will be her destiny in the next life? Saying many heartfelt prayers for all of them, I vowed never again to take the life of any living being. To this day, whenever I think of that little bird and how she struggled in fear and misery after being struck by my stone, I am still filled with bitter regret and a palpable sense of inner discomfort.

As for the way we lived as children and adolescents, we had a great variety of pastimes. Those who lived in the towns and larger villages of our country would have toys and games made in factories and purchased in stores. We were nomadic people and had none of those. We played board games where the board was made by scratching lines in the ground and the game pieces were white and black stones. We had games of dexterity where a stone would be tossed into the air and other stones gathered from the ground before the tossed stone was caught. There were a variety of games played with homemade dice. We played a guessing game where one player would pose a riddle, and the other player was allowed three questions before guessing the answer. When you thought you had the answer, you would say, "Oṃ Maṇi Padme Hūṃ," and then offer your solution. Each player would count the number of solutions on their prayer beads. In this manner, the guessing game was also a way to benefit others and accumulate merit by reciting mantras. Another popular game was a verse trading competition. Here, skill in composition and poetics was cultivated. The first player would recite a verse or series of verses, and the second player had to respond with responding verses. These verses could be about any topic but were often verses where one would praise oneself or belittle another person in a clever way. Sometimes a third person would act as judge and determine the winner. If there was no third person, the two players might continue until one player was unable to respond, or until time ran out. We had archery and other athletic competitions. We would gather for storytelling, and each person would try to tell the most engaging story. There were also literary contests where two or more people would compose poetry about each other or things of common interest and exchange them as a game. As children, we were fond of the game of the swimming dragon. Here we would need a group of ten or more. Each would grasp the belt of the person in front, and the first person in line would lead the others in a winding, twisting dance. The game of "the earth-moving elephant" is a rope-pulling contest like the Western game of tug-of-war. These are a few of the many games we would play as a part of our local customs and traditions.

Throughout the year, in the warm weather of summer and the cold of winter, we would move from higher to lower ground, from one pastureland to another, wherever the conditions were best for our animals. Since a nomadic family has no fixed place of residence, it has no fixed group of neighbors. Whatever group one encounters becomes one's neighbors, and one's neighbors become like one's own family. Wherever a family group travels, it relies upon whatever group it encounters, whether they have been previously acquainted or are complete strangers. Since this interdependence is universal, one group would always welcome any other group and treat them like family while they were nearby. They would pay back the kindness and hospitality by extending it to any other group they encountered. The mutual interdependence of nomads requires mutual trust, trust that is readily bestowed and never betrayed. The children of one group could therefore easily join those of another group, and the parents would never have to worry that strangers would harm their children. A nomad or nomadic group, hungry and thirsty from the long trail, could confidently approach the home or encampment of total strangers and receive a cordial welcome, a good meal, and comfortable lodging. There would never be an expectation of payment or even of encountering one another again. The hospitality was simply part of the ancient tradition, as expressed in the old Tibetan adage, "The stranger who comes as a guest and the person with a long-term illness are the ideal objects of kindness and charity." How wonderful is a society like ours that truly takes this adage to heart. How sorry it is to see these altruistic traditions of the Tibetan highlands, like the fragile flowers of the alpine meadows, trampled under the boots of a cruel and avaricious invader.

The total population of Golok in 2004 was around 139,000. The average elevation is 4200 m (13,780 ft) above sea level. One of the largest rivers in Asia, the Machu (i.e., Yellow River), flows through Golok. Most of our people are nomads, following their herds and flocks according to the season. Others are farmers growing high-altitude barley. There are many influential local gods in Golok such as Machen Pomra, the sovereign deity of Amnye Machen, and the god Nyenpo Yutse. Another prominent local god is Bayan Churi, who lives in Bayan Mountain. One of my monasteries is on the slopes of Bayan Mountain and is therefore called Bayan Monastery.

Golok is a land of extreme climate. In the winter, the temperature drops far below zero, and a hard mantle of snow blankets the entire countryside, from peak to valley. Lakes, rivers, and the earth itself are locked in a grip of ice, and the animals and livestock have a very difficult time. The people must protect themselves from the cold and harsh weather by staying in their yak hair tents. Despite such hardship, the people of Golok tend to be happy and light-hearted, accepting the difficult conditions as simply part of an ev-er-changing world. Golok people are known for this ability to tolerate hard-ships without losing their inner sense of wellbeing. They tend to be unskilled in the social graces of other regions, such as Lhasa, where a friendly face and welcoming manner can sometimes conceal questionable intentions. Golok people have no such artifices. They may appear uninterested and not at all engaging when you first encounter them, but when you get to know them, you find a genuinely friendly, hospitable, and welcoming heart beneath a taciturn exterior. Golok people are renowned for their deep sense of loyalty, their bravery and nobility in times of conflict, and their trustworthy and honorable natures.

The spring and summertime in Golok are glorious. Once the ice and snow of winter retreat, the streams and rivers fill with pure glacial waters, and the hills and valleys exchange their white winter mantles for lush green grass-es and many varieties of wildflowers plying their bright colors and wafting their divine fragrances on the gentle mountain breezes. It is from these al-pine grasses, herbs, and flowers that powerful medicines are formulated and the finest incense is made. The air is pristine and bracing, the sky is the lus-trous blue of lapis lazuli and chrysoberyl, and the clouds are the purest, most radiant white. Every country has its distinctive patterns of sky and clouds. The Golok sky is known for its great, billowing white clouds in their infinite variety of fantastic shapes. They travel across the azure sky in an endless procession, like an empyrean parade of celestial heroes.

The rains fall gently to refresh and nurture the land, arriving in a timely and regular fashion and departing with glorious double rainbows. The many lakes and ponds fill with pure glacial water mingled with new rain and dot the landscape like so many jewels of turquoise and sapphire fallen from heaven. The songs of white and golden swans, long-legged cranes, and blue mountain cuckoos echo across the broad valleys. To see them fly across the sky is said to be like ambrosia for the eyes. To hear their cries is said to be an elixir for the ears. From the mountain crags, the springs and creeks de-scend in waterfalls and flow down to the rivers like heavenly elixirs coming down to Earth. The lush green expanses of the hills and valleys are dotted with horses, yaks, sheep, and goats like so many stars in the blue skies. At this height, around 14,000 feet, the sunlight is very intense, and everything is saturated with brilliant light and color. To experience the opulent beauty of the Golok countryside is to receive a vision of the paradise that awaits the truly virtuous.

In more mundane terms, Golok is divided into three districts: Wangchen Bum, Akyong Bum and Pema Bum. Out of these, my homeland is in Akyong Bum. As with every other aspect of the land of Tibet, the Chinese have imposed their alien ways upon the map and its divisions. Their map divides Golok into six different districts rather than the traditional three and gives Chinese names to the ancient Tibetan towns, districts, rivers, and mountains. These names are unrecognizable and unpronounceable to Tibetans. The language, culture, and customs of the Chinese are altogether alien to Tibetans. Tibet's written language and Buddhist culture are based on the Sanskrit Buddhist traditions of India. The Tibetan language is unique to the Tibetan plateau and is unrelated to Chinese or any other language.[5]

2

A Reborn Lama: Discovery and Authentication Amid Overdemand

AROUND THE time of my sixth birthday, an unfortunate series of events occurred that left me with a permanent hearing loss in my right ear and a temporary speech impediment. The way we understand these events in Tibet involves unseen spirits that manifest in mundane objects. One night, I was staying with friends in the area. I slept on the bed provided for me, and I remember the pillow having a subtle, unpleasant vapor or miasma associated with it. When I awoke, my body and mind were unsettled, my right ear was in pain, and when I called out to my parents, my speech was halting and unclear. My parents sought help. They located a specialist in miasmic spirits, a distinguished lama by the name of Tsogö. To see him, we had to cross the broad Machu. It was a difficult journey, as the depredations of the Chinese forced us to travel by secret, circuitous paths and required the Lama to locate himself in a remote and carefully hidden hermitage. Lama Tsogö was a singular figure. Large in stature and imposing in presence, he had an unusually dark complexion that was dramatically set off by a long, full, and startlingly white beard. Upon entering, Lama Tsogö immediately picked me up and held me in his lap. For what seemed like a long time, he prayed with palms pressed together, alternately looking up to the sky and down at me. After coming to the conclusion of the prayers, Lama Tsogö explained that he had called upon his lamas and deities, and with their help, had negotiated a settlement with the harmful spirits responsible for my difficulties. No further harm was to befall me, and I was infused with a number of particular blessings. He instructed my parents to take special care of me, saying that I would overcome these untoward circumstances and that my general health and well-being would now be restored. Indeed, I was able to speak without impediment almost immediately and have had no recurrence of that problem. However, the damage already inflicted by the miasma to my hearing has persisted to this day.

Several years later, Lama Tsogö passed away. Right before he died, he assembled his close disciples and spoke of me. These were his final words, as later reported to me:

> A precious teacher, a reborn lama, came to me from just beyond the far banks of the wide river. This lama has a close personal relationship with Brahmā, Life Master of the White Conch, the protector god of our monastery, Traling. You must ask him to assume the throne as head of the monastery if and when the Chinese authorities allow us to restore the monastery.

After a few years, there was a hiatus in the official Chinese prohibitions against Buddhist practice. The rebuilding of Traling Monastery commenced, and my family began to be visited by a series of official delegations requesting that I accept the position of monastery head. However, my local monastery, Bayan, had prior claims upon me, and my maternal uncle, Lama Gelek, an official at this monastery, insisted that I stay and take the helm as its head lama. Another monastery, Nyen Gön, also sent several delegations requesting that I assume the throne as head of their monastery. They understood that I was formerly one of their main teachers, Gergen Tschö. Again, my uncle and the administrators of Bayan Monastery intervened, saying that in this life, I had to take responsibility for Bayan monastery.

Later, when I was in Dharamsala, the Nechung (i.e., the Tibetan state oracle) and the Tsangpa oracles were present at a great prayer ceremony (Tib. *sgrub chen*). The Tsangpa oracle is the human channel for the god Brahmā Life Master of the White Conch. His Holiness had summoned the oracles and asked them to contact their respective gods in order to give predictions, prognostications, and various supernormal insights. At that time, the Tsangpa oracle conveyed a message for me. It involved a special addition to the prayers used to invoke his presence. This is the section that begins with the phrase "Whoever merely comes to think of me..." He then proclaimed, "Give this to Dzogchen Master Sogan Rinpoche, and ask him to add this to his invocations and bring it to his homeland in Amdo so that the monasteries and practitioners there will be able to use it."

During my early years in Tibet, there were various indications of my having some type of unusual status. There was a shaman known by the name of Kargön who was well known as a "past life astrologer" (Tib. *dbyangs 'char rtsis mkhan*). This is an astrologer who can see and describe at least the last three lifetimes of an individual by means of special divinations. After divining some of my previous lifetimes, he exclaimed, "O ye gods! I have never seen such a thing in all my years of divinations for many lamas and others. I see that now, in Tibet, there are five other people who have the same karmic affinities as you through their deeds and aspirations in former lives. Each of them was born the same day as you, and they will also die the same day as you in the future. They look very much like you, with the same height and build, and with faces that look highly similar down to that black mole on your cheek below your right eye. I will tell you of their locations in the various regions of Tibet, should you wish to meet them. This is most unusual!" There seemed to be no special need to meet with them, so I never found the time to track them down. I guess they were all similarly disposed, as they have not, to date, communicated with me.

My uncle, Lama Gelek, who was renowned for his accurate predictions and prognostications, once performed a special "prasena divination" (Tib. *pra rtags*). This is a divination that invokes gods or spirits to answer questions that are beyond human perception. His divination found that in my last life, I was a Drikung Kagyu lama who lived in the famous Kagyu center known as Drikung Serkyong. He proclaimed, "This young tulku was, in his last lifetime, an illustrious Drikung yogi and *siddha* known as Chögyam (i.e., Chökyi Gyatso). He had a long beard and always kept a ritual dagger (Tib. *phurba*) tucked in his belt."

In this manner, there was much talk in my home region among monasteries, lamas, and their followers about who I was in my former lives and which lama's or yogin's rebirth I was. Much of this talk must have been somewhat exaggerated, as it would not be feasible for me to be simultaneously the rebirth of all of these distinguished figures.

Among all of these speculations, one stood out as being most probable. It was first proposed to me by a delegation that arrived from a monastery in the Serta region of Kham, known as Awo Sera Monastery. They asked that I be sent to take charge of that venerable institution, which they were working to restore. My family again turned them away. However, they later returned with an official written proclamation from the hand of His Holiness the Fourteenth Dalai Lama of Tibet. His Holiness proclaimed that I was the sixth rebirth of Washul Sogan Rinpoche, and as such, I was the throne holder of Awo Sera Monastery. His Holiness bestowed upon me the title, throne, and crown of the monastery, giving me the religious name Sonam Dawé Wangpo.

Once it was known that I was indeed the rebirth of a famous lama, my services were certainly in very high demand. Most of the monasteries had lost their leaders and head lamas to the Chinese executioners. However, with the official recognition of His Holiness, I assumed the mantle of Rinpoche and now was responsible for both Bayan and Awo Sera monasteries. My affiliation and sense of responsibility for the other monasteries remain. In particular, my recognition as the lama with the personal relationship with the god Brahmā, Life Master of the White Conch, has been validated in my own direct experience and in my interactions with this most astute and impressive god.

3

A Virtuous Mind Augmented by Difficult Circumstances

SEMKYI, MY maternal grandmother, passed away at the age of fifty-eight. At that time, I was only eight years old. This was one of the major turning points in my life, as it increased my realization of the dreamlike nature of this life and established in me a clear understanding of the ubiquitous nature of death and the transience of this world. Why was this so influential? Semkyi was a person of quality—everyone was fond of her, and she possessed a singularly beneficent attitude toward all. She was a daughter of the wealthy Nyöshul family and in earlier times was renowned as the most beautiful of women. When I met her, however, the flower of her youth had somewhat faded, and I saw her as a mature woman. Semkyi had two sons and four daughters. My mother was her eldest daughter. One of her sons had special qualities and was recognized as the rebirth of a respected lama. However, he passed away as a child. The other son was killed by Chinese soldiers in 1959. Her husband Löten, my maternal grandfather, was tortured and killed in a prison camp. In this way, Semkyi experienced many extremes, both good and bad, during her lifetime. However, her strength of mind allowed her to maintain a peaceful and happy attitude despite all these difficulties, and she had a way of uplifting the spirit of anyone with the good fortune to meet her. She showed me such deep and constant affection that I always thought of her as my second mother.

One day, Semkyi discovered a small sore on her left elbow. It was like a blister that broke and expelled pus and blood. It gradually increased in size and virulence, covering the whole elbow. In a short time, it affected her arm all the way to the shoulder and finally spread to the rest of her body. We lived in a remote location, far from any sizable town or hospital. We had few resources to pay for travel and medical care, and the Chinese authorities would not allow us to be on the roads, as they prohibited Tibetans from traveling in Tibet. In our small village was one local healer who tried his best to treat Semkyi's condition, as did "Uncle" Chungwa, a local lama. He recited mantras and cast spells, and the rest of us could only pray to gods and supplicate spirits for intervention. The condition became worse and worse, and in the end, Semkyi passed away in her bed. By the time she died, the infection had covered her entire body, and it was no longer possible for her to eat or drink. During the course of her illness, friends and family had gathered around, everyone desperately wanting to help, but no one was able to do anything to reverse the course of the affliction. All of us, together with Semkyi herself, lost all hope for her recovery. To the very end, however, she showed no fear of death nor trepidation about what was to come afterward. She maintained her gentle expression, she continued to smile when she saw us, and, although she could no longer speak more than a few words, she continued to express her loving concern for us until her final breath. I was convinced that she maintained this peaceful and kindly attitude because her knowledge of the Dharma and the blessings of her lamas had taken root in her heart.

Regarding the implications of my grandmother's passing, this is what I came to believe: In general, there is no doubt that if one gains knowledge and practical experience in the views, meditative practices, and deeds of the Buddha Dharma, one will have peace and happiness in both this and future lives. This is clearly elucidated in the case studies and life histories of the famous adepts and lamas of the past. Even if one lacks such profound knowledge and experience, if one has sufficient faith to open oneself up to the blessings of the Dharma and the lamas, such constant faith will draw forth these blessings and empower one to face harsh realities such as terminal illness and death, just like my grandmother Semkyi, with a peaceful, content attitude free of fear and anxiety.

Just before her death, my grandmother Semkyi's nephew, an incarnate lama by the name of Tulku Drakga, had just been released from a prison camp. He arrived on a horse, I remember, and approached Semkyi as she rested on her pillow. He greeted her and asked about her condition. She said to him, "Dear Tulku, my illness is extremely painful, and my condition is beyond hope of remediation. The time has come for me to move on. Please perform now the transference of consciousness (Tib. *'pho ba*)." As she said these words, she attempted to press her palms together in the gesture of supplication but could only approximate it. Tulku Drakga immediately commenced the practice of the profound path of transference. First, he gave Semkyi a clear explanation of the process, including a full description of the stages of dying, the moment of death, and the exigencies of the postmortem state. He then began the actual process of transference, chanting in a strong, clear voice of sublime beauty. To this day, I still remember his words and the supernal sound of his voice.

Tulku Drakga was a true lama who had endured the rigors of the prison camps and came forth to extend the blessings of his kindness and wisdom to alleviate the afflictions of the people. Unfortunately, he had not escaped the tortures and beatings in the prison and eventually succumbed to their effects, dying while still a young man. This was, and still is, the fate of so many lamas and educated people in Tibet. The Chinese authorities seek out the most educated and respected people in Tibetan society, take them to prisons, and submit them to a process they call "patriotic re-education" or simply "re-education." I have seen so many Tibetans who were healthy and strong when they went into prison camps but who came back with horrific evidence of this "re-education" by the authorities. Some came out with limbs broken and twisted. Others came out blinded and deaf. Some had brain injuries that caused them to shake and go into seizures. Many others suffered from irreversible catatonia or other major psychiatric and neurological impairments.

Knowing the nature of "re-education" by the Chinese, some found unique methods to avoid it. In my monastery of Bayan, there was a lama by the name of Labrang Rilu. One day, the police came to the monastery when the monks and lamas were engaged in a prayer convocation. The police rounded up every single one and marched them in strict single file down the long road to a prison camp. Along the way, Labrang Rilu managed to slip his only remaining possession, his prayer beads, to the monk in front of him. He then left the file and sat down with his legs crossed by the side of the road. He quickly engaged in the transference procedure such that his consciousness went forth out of his body. When the soldiers came to beat him, they found only a lifeless corpse.

I do not recall seeing external signs of torture on Tulku Drakga. I remember only how he came and helped my grandmother through the process of dying and transmigration with his wise guidance, his clear and beautiful voice, and his deeply reassuring manner. As I was very young, I was kept at a distance from where Tulku Drakga was conducting the transference procedure. However, while he was engaged in that practice, I began my own efforts to help by quietly chanting the six-syllable mantra (i.e., *Oṃ Maṇi Padme Hūṃ*) and reciting some prayers I had learned. In my meditation, I generated an aspirational prayer that my grandmother would go quickly to a pure land (i.e., the transcendent realm of a buddha) and that we would meet again soon in that supernal realm.

At times, while continuing my recitation, I would reflect on the situation, and my mind would be filled with sadness that my beloved grandmother would soon be gone. Around me, my mother and her sisters were alternately crying in grief and praying in hope. The others were giving advice and reassurance, saying how grief at this time was futile and that in the face of death, only Dharma can help. Therefore, they said, it is always vital to cultivate virtue and flee from sin. Others in the house were busy discussing what to do after my grandmother passed away—how to bring the remains to the cemetery, which lamas should be asked to conduct the services, and how to accomplish the other tasks associated with the end of a life.

The following morning found my grandmother passed away, and her remains were taken to the cemetery. From that day onward, we were bereft of her loving presence. We did not know exactly where she had gone, but we knew she was no more to be found in this world.

After my grandmother was gone, I kept wondering, "Which of my family members will be next to pass away from this world?" I could not help but realize from that moment on that, like every one of us, I too would exit from this world, leaving behind every possession, every friend and relative, and everything that was familiar and valued. I too would have to go forth from this life by myself. I thought again and again of my mother's words when I inquired about death:

After death, one must embark upon a tumultuous journey through the bardo. This journey brings one back to life in either a happy or an unhappy rebirth, depending upon the balance of one's good and evil deeds in this life.

Thinking in this manner caused me to seek a full understanding of the nature of the bardo. I became more and more concerned with finding a way

3. A Virtuous Mind Augmented by Difficult Circumstances

to accomplish goodness and avoid evil, but I had no clear idea of how to proceed. These were difficult times in my country, and opportunities for education and access to teachers had been almost entirely destroyed. I was anxious about this, thinking that if I were to die today, I would go into the bardo like an arrow shot into the blackness of the midnight sky. How could I have any certainty of my path or destination? Likewise, I felt completely confused about how to actually accomplish virtue and avoid vice. In this way, I felt a bit like a blind person wandering helpless and alone in the midst of a vast, empty wilderness. These trepidations filled my mind at times. However, I was still a young child, and at other times I was diverted by childish games with my fellows. As I played and consorted with the other children, there would often arise in my mind the palpable feeling that this was all just like a dream. And so, with this complex of thoughts and feelings, the days of my childhood rapidly passed.

4

Gradually Coming Under the Influence
of Spiritual Teachers

FROM WHEN I was around twelve years old, I gradually came into contact
with the ambrosial rain of the sublime Dharma of the All-Compassionate
Teacher, the Lord Buddha, which is so rare and difficult to find in this world.
I gradually came under the influence of some kind spiritual teachers who
bestowed this precious rain upon the parched field of my mind, which was
tormented by the fever of afflictive mental states (Skt. *kleśa*).

The first of these teachers was Lama Gonpo Norbu, a devoted and assiduous practitioner of the Dharma, who was in fact a true yogin who kept his
vast and profound attainments well concealed. Lama Gonpo Norbu lived
nearby in our nomadic settlement. He had been confined for many years in
a Chinese prison camp and had only recently been released on a restrictive
parole that required frequent attendance to the dreaded Chinese "struggle
sessions." Lama Gonpo Norbu taught me the preliminaries to the practice
of the Dzogchen, including *The Words of My Perfect Teacher*[6] and many other
fundamental texts. He guided me in the preliminary practices that consist
of the accumulation of five sets of 100,000 ritual and meditative practices.[7]

Lama Gonpo Norbu had a light complexion and was a person of imposing physical stature. It seemed to me and my fellow disciples that he was a
bit taciturn, even forbidding in his demeanor. However, due to his continual
spiritual practice, his mind was always in a deep state of peace and tran-

quility, of serene and luminous awareness. Lama Gonpo Norbu was what is called a "person free of worldly occupation" (Tib. *bya btang*). This title, however, is often assumed by those who desire recognition as a person of high spiritual status but who lack the inner attainment. Lama Gonpo Norbu was one who truly merited this title, as he eschewed the comforts of worldly life, rejecting, for example, any offerings of furnishings or resources other than the most basic needs of survival. His quarters were a study in austere and minimalist living.

As the Chinese authorities had placed Lama Gonpo Norbu under close police scrutiny and restrictive parole, he had few visitors during daylight hours. During the night, however, in the absence of easy visibility, people came in large numbers to receive teachings from this illustrious lama. In particular, every night, Lama Gonpo Norbu showed his deep compassion by revealing to his nephew Thangpo and me the mysteries of the texts on the profound preliminary practices and the special techniques for accomplishing the 500,000 accumulations of preliminaries. He motivated and reinforced our learning by requiring us to pass frequent examinations and quizzes on the material. Thangpo and I were of the same age and became close friends. As such, we played together with such lack of restraint that our distracted states of mind exposed us to the danger of failing our examinations and facing the quiet but fearsome censure of our teacher.

When we did fail an examination, penalties were imposed. Sometimes, the penalty was that we would be assigned a certain number of full prostrations on the ground outside the lama's quarters. If the moon was out, we would need to do the prostrations close by the wall, so as to be in the shadows. If we were to be seen from the road, this could attract attention, and Lama Gonpo Norbu could find himself back in prison for violating the terms of his parole by teaching Buddhism. As we did our prostrations, Lama Gonpo Norbu would count each one on his prayer beads. Often, our penalty was one or two thousand prostrations. Other penalties imposed on Thangpo and me were tasks such as memorizing a number of pages from a text or presenting a detailed interpretation of the underlying meaning of a text.

When we did well on an exam or any assignment, Lama Gonpo Norbu would reward us well. Sometimes, he would regale us with marvelous accounts of historical figures or legends of Buddhism. In particular, he would tell the stories, in the most enthralling manner, of the lives of some of the more famous lamas and yogins of Tibet. He would make these illustrious practitioners of the Dharma come alive for us, as if they had come to the lama's little hut and told us their own life stories. I remember these accounts well and how at the time they inspired my faith and moved me to emulate these sublime figures of wisdom, compassion, and spiritual power.

At that time, however, I was unable to realize these aspirations in any reliable way. These aspirations and the deep faith in the Dharma that generated them were like a flash of lightning in a dark sky. It illuminated everything for a moment, but it was quickly gone and replaced by the darkness of habitual negative attitudes and untoward ways of thinking. The mind that turned away from the frivolities and vain pursuits of the world had arisen within me, but it had little strength. I continued to be seduced by the temptation of the senses and caught up in the proliferation of thoughts, desires, and emotions. Because of this, the childish games and silly activities of ordinary people still held their grip on me.

Sometime later, my father went on a journey to see Lama Gonpo Norbu. In the winter, we lived nearby him. Once the weather improved, however, we traveled with the flocks and herds in accordance with the exigencies of our nomadic lifestyle. Upon returning to our camp, my father brought me a package from the lama. It was a book, *The Words of My Perfect Teacher*, with an accompanying note that consisted of a poem written to me by the lama:

> This old man has a big wish
> That the tulku Pema Lodoe
> Take up *The Words of My Perfect Teacher*,
> Read it carefully ten times through,
> Or at the very least five complete times,
> And like pieces of gold and silver,
> Continually hold each word in his mind.[8]

At this point in time, possessing a Tibetan book was a crime in occupied Tibet. The Chinese regime had destroyed the libraries and burned all the books they could find. Even before the invasion, books were scarce, for they were all individually printed from wood blocks or handwritten. So, receiving such a book on loan was a very significant event. My father was worried that I was still a child, only around thirteen years old, and might be too young to be trusted with a book. However, his fears lessened when he saw how I treated the book. Tibetan books are loose pages. They are unbound but are wrapped in a ritual cloth (Tib. *dpe ras*). Between the lama's habit of placing the pages together in a somewhat untidy manner and their being jostled on the journey by horseback in their hiding place in my father's long coat, they arrived in some disorder. However, I quickly had all the pages arranged and stacked perfectly. My father then sewed a beautiful ritual cloth in which to wrap them.

When the poem and the book first arrived, I was overjoyed, and my sense of faith and devotion increased. In the beginning, I had some difficulty reading this large, complex book. However, each time I read it, the words and their meaning became more accessible and familiar. Soon, I had memorized the extensive table of contents, and most of the important concepts of the text were fairly clear to me. Each time I took up the book, I devoured its words like a hungry guest at a banquet. More and more, the teachings of the book, including the rare, precious nature of the fully qualified human rebirth came to occupy my thoughts and fill my mind. With an ever-growing sense of faith and devotion, I managed to read the entire text thirteen times during those three to four months.

During this initial period of studying the text, I would go to my father and share with him some of the key points, encouraging him to practice these high forms of ethics, patience, compassion, and so forth. He would nod his head appreciatively and say,

> It sounds very good to me. You are making yourself out to be a real expert on these things. However, I cannot say now whether you have it right or not. When you have met with the lama and passed his examination, then we will know for sure.

My father had in fact some understanding of the text. He had been a monk and studied it at the monastery until the Chinese destroyed his monastery and forced the surviving monks into lay activities.

When I returned the book to Lama Gonpo Norbu at the end of the three or four months, he was extremely pleased to receive it in good order, wrapped in a nice new ritual cloth, and to learn that I had indeed exerted myself beyond his expectations in reading it many times and learning many of its teachings. He explained his pleasure, by saying how he had some trepidations in lending this precious book to a child and had expected me to study it, but he had not anticipated the extent and thoroughness of my study.

This important text, *The Words of My Perfect Teacher*, was written in the early 1800's c.e. It was composed by a mighty being (Skt. *mahāsattva*) who was the emanation of three very significant individuals. His outer manifestation, visible to all, was that of the Bodhisattva Shantideva. His inner manifestation was that of the Mahasiddha Shavaripa. His secret identity was that of the lord of the world, Arya Avalokiteshvara. In fact, he was the blending of all three into one inseparable manifestation. His religious name was Orgyen Jigme Chökyi Wangpo, although he was commonly known as Dza Patrul Rinpoche (1808–87). It is this last name by which his fame has spread throughout the realms.

The Words of My Perfect Teacher is the epitome of Lord Shakyamuni Buddha's teachings. It presents and explains the path whereby an individual can, within a single short lifespan of this degenerate age, attain the peaceable kingdom of highest nirvana. It gathers into its single volume all the prerequisites and preliminaries necessary to succeed in the practice of the Great Perfection (i.e., Dzogchen [Tib. *rdzogs pa chen po*]) of the Mahayana. This sublime text is like a true panacea that cures all the miseries and diseases of the world. Within it are three divisions: the common external preliminaries, the uncommon internal preliminaries, and the instructions on the auxiliary to the Great Perfection practice known as the shortcut to the transference of consciousness. Within each of these three main divisions are detailed instructions and lucid illustrations for the many complex aspects of this system. Those who are interested will be much rewarded by looking into this text.

As for the main point of this text, and all other authentic Buddhist texts, it comes directly from the famous mandate of the Lord Buddha to "gain complete control over your own mind." Those who possess such an aspiration to gain full control over their own mind and have thereby taken up the practice of the Buddha's Way with confidence, faith, and devotion must first acquire the lineage precepts from the grace of an authentic guru. Then, they must carefully examine the deeds of excellent practitioners of the past and take up the study of the sutras and tantras without any sectarian bias. They must carefully study the activities and behaviors of the Buddha's heirs, the bodhisattvas. As for the manner of their practice, it should be free of laxity and should be respectful, continuous, and diligent, like a skillful archer whose bowstring is neither too tight nor too loose, whose aim is precise, and who draws back and releases the arrow in a smooth, well-controlled, and fully nuanced manner. When you proceed in this way, the powers and blessings of the Dharma and the guru will gradually enter into your mind, and without any doubt, the inner sun of peace and happiness will rise and fill your mind with its illumination and warmth.

4. Gradually Coming Under the Influence of Spiritual Teachers

Some people, perhaps many who are newly introduced to the Buddha's Way or those who are continually busy with the exigencies of modern life might feel discouraged. They might feel intimidated by the demands of this path or otherwise think that it is beyond their ability or strength. Such lack of confidence, however, while understandable, is not productive. Perhaps one will not be able to attain the ultimate goal in one's present life. Ultimately, however, one will indeed succeed as long as one is willing to accept two things. The first is to engage in the practice and study of the sublime Dharma to whatever extent one is able, with a pure motivation based on the sincere aspiration to fully accomplish it. The second is to act for the benefit of others with a stable mind of unwaveringly benevolent resolve. The inevitable byproduct of such altruism is that one will gain peace and happiness in this life and will plant the seeds that will ultimately ripen so that one gains perfect fruition in the future. There is no need, therefore, to be discouraged by the lack of immediate progress and attainment.

Furthermore, in the practice of the Dharma, one must always bear in mind these words of our teacher, the Lord Buddha:

Hearken, O monks and people of discernment.
Just as you would not accept something to be pure gold
Without first analyzing it by melting, cutting, or rubbing,
You must first closely examine whatever I say
And never accept it just because I said it.

A central theme and vital principle of the Buddha's teaching is that wisdom and realization never arise from naive acceptance of other peoples' words based on one's own hopes, fears, and prejudices. Rather they arise from thorough empirical analysis, careful study, and systematic examination that search for truth without preconception or bias. Understanding that arises in this way is not easily shaken. It forms the basis for a genuine faith and conviction in the Buddha's teaching. It underlies confident and appropriate action. It leads on to further and more profound examination and discovery. This is why followers of the Buddha's teachings cultivate an inquiring curiosity that leads to thorough investigation, rather than a naive acceptance that leaves questions unanswered and realization unattained.

In 1979, at the age of fifteen, I traveled with my uncle Gelek and around ten others on a pilgrimage to Je Tsongkhapa's own monastery, Kumbum Jampa Ling, and to Labrang Tashi Khyil. In Amdo alone there were several thousand monasteries. However, other than the damaged remnants of these two monasteries, all of the others were completely destroyed and removed without a trace by the Chinese invaders.

I remember how when we arrived at Labrang Tashi Khyil we paid our devotions in the main shrine rooms. When we saw a few elderly learned monks (Tib. *dge bshes*) and some other monks in religious robes engaged in some prayers and rituals, all of the pilgrims spontaneously bowed down, and could not restrain the tears that filled their eyes. Why was that? For all these years, since 1959, the Buddha's Dharma, the precious treasure that has been like a wish-fulfilling jewel to the Tibetan people for over 1400 years, has been plunged into a deep, dark hole by the brute force of the Chinese. So now, when once in a while Tibetans manage a brief glimpse of it, their inner feelings must have some outward expression.

I recall my own particular impressions on this occasion. This was the first time I had ever seen a monastery with monks wearing religious robes and engaging in their sacred activities. I was completely amazed at what I saw that day, and was filled with a particularly deep feeling of pleasure and a pervasive sense of peacefulness. Then, a very special sensation started to arise within me upon witnessing the activities in the shrines. I felt that somewhere, somehow, I too had a monastery like this with a gold ornamented roof. A vision then came, went, and came again more clearly of my own room in my monastery. I was looking out of my window. The sun rose in the morning, spreading its golden light over a vast plain of green fields ornamented by colorful wild flowers. Although this vision was like a dream, its clarity and stability suggest, I think, the presence of genuine memories from the past.

We remained at Labrang Tashi Khyil for around two weeks. It was at this time that I received my novice monk (Tib. *dge tshul*) vows from one Lharampa Geshe (a monk scholar of the highest attainment) by the name of Geshe Tsulrol. In order to receive this vow, the senior monk must subject the prospective novice to a detailed interview, in which he asks various types of questions and carefully weighs the responses. At the conclusion of the examination, he bestowed the vows. After this, he spoke to my uncle. The Geshe said:

> This young fellow has an especially sharp mind, and possesses many signs of auspicious distinction. It would therefore be wise to enter him into residence at this monastery where he may have the best opportunity to pursue his studies.

4. Gradually Coming Under the Influence of Spiritual Teachers

However, there were apparently reasons why my long-term residence at the monastery was not feasible, so I returned to my home.

For a time, from around 1979, the Chinese authorities began to be slightly less draconian in their opposition to Buddhism and Tibetan culture in Tibet. Although the occupation has remained quite harsh, this temporary easing of restrictions was welcomed by the Tibetan people like one whose death sentence has been postponed. At this time, it became possible for some Tibetans to go on pilgrimages within Tibet to the remaining centers of religious significance such as the handful of remaining monasteries and the holy city of Lhasa. To the extent permitted by the Chinese regime, and by their own impoverished condition, Tibetans also busied themselves trying to reestablish some of their local monasteries and shrines.

5

Practicing the Dharma Within
the Monastery

IN 1980, my seventeenth year, I entered into the practice of the Dharma in my home monastery, Bayan Serthang Gön Tennyi Dargye Ling, "The monastery of Bayan of the Golden Land, where the Two Teachings Spread and Flourish."[9] However, at this time Bayan Monastery actually existed in name only. As mentioned before, the Chinese regime, in its invasion and subsequent "Cultural Revolution," had destroyed virtually all of the monasteries of Tibet, including Bayan. They destroyed every trace of the shrines, assembly hall, monks' quarters, and other monastery facilities.[10] The former grand assembly hall of the monastery was now "rebuilt" only as a large cotton tent, and the huge monastic dormitories and study halls existed only as groupings of small cotton and yak hair tents. My uncle Gelek and I lived and studied together in a square cotton tent.

The older monks, after 21 years of imprisonment or internal exile, were happy to finally be allowed to gather together and practice their sacred traditions in a monastic community. Invariably, however, their pleasant conversations would become quiet and strained as their thoughts turned to memories of the former grand monasteries—the buildings desecrated and destroyed, the books burned, the sacred images smashed, and to news of which of their fellow monks had died in prison, how they were tortured, which one's were executed, and so forth.

As for the other young monks and me, we were new to the monastery and had much to learn. Lama Gonpo Norbu gave us teachings on the preliminaries practices that prepare one for the practice of Dzogchen. This included the study and practice of various "mental training" (Tib. *blo sbyong*) texts. *Gelong Jinpa Gyatso gave us teachings on the general practices of Buddhism and Buddhist monasticism including the study of the Three Sets of Vows.*[11] Further, we had the wonderful opportunity of learning from the renowned yogin and Dzogchen master Lama Rikden Zangpo. He gave us extensive teachings and training in the tradition of the sacred arts that are transmitted from generation to generation only by direct demonstration and guided practice. These included the three basic arts of the fabrication of ritual objects, playing wind instruments, and using percussion instruments. Here we learned to create the large varieties of specialized ritual cakes (Tib. *gtor ma*) and other ritual offerings, to play the wind instruments such as the Tibetan oboe *(Tib. rgya gling)*, the long horns *(Tib. dung chen)*, short horn (Tib. *rkang gling*), etc., and the percussion instruments such as the hand drum (Skt. *ḍa ma ru*), the various bronze cymbals, and the various big drums. He drilled us in the elements and requirements of the monastery's repertory of sacred rituals including deity dances, chants, melodies, and mandala forms. For example, each ritual may require a different mandala. Each mandala has hundreds of distinct elements arranged in precise grids, drawn in specific forms, and meticulously colored with dyed mineral powders. Here we were trained in the intricacies of a multitude of different rituals, each of which follow different liturgical texts, and each of which may be conducted in different ways and in alternate orders, with different emphasis and elements according to the requirements of the occasion, the deities involved, the goals to be advanced, etc. We each took copious notes in order to keep everything straight, and to be able to pass the rigorous examinations. These ancient traditions have survived and prospered over the centuries only because of careful and thorough training in each generation. Our greatest fear was to introduce a mistake or variation in the ritual that might impair its efficacy or compromise the unbroken lineage of transmission from master to disciple that brought the blessings and powers of these ancient traditions to us down through the centuries, and enabled us to transmit them to future generations. To help guard against such errors, the monastic system provides us with the monk disciplinarian (Tib. *dge skos*) who patrols the rows of monks during the practices and performances of the rituals and catches even the smallest mistake. To maintain good standing in the monastic environment, one must avoid the censure of the monk disciplinarian.

This precise and complex variety of ritual practices has been transmitted within the different monastic lineages since the time they were established by the Lord Buddha. It is the subject of thousands of liturgical texts. Unfortunately, many of these texts were lost in the invasion and subjugation of Tibet. However, the surviving masters of these traditions have gathered the surviving texts and worked together, in exile or in the few surviving monastic communities, to reconstruct the ritual practices so that they will not be lost.

As we learned and gradually became more competent in these practices, our days became filled with ritual. There were the general Buddhist rituals such as those of the summer retreat and the commemorations of the Lord Buddha's sublime life and deeds, the rituals unique to our monastery, the rituals for special days of the month and year, for the propitiation of various deities, and there were the many services on behalf of others, such as rituals for good crops, healing the sick, funeral rites, and so forth. With these many duties we were kept quite busy.

Now I was recognized as a tulku, which gave me some special status. In addition, I seemed to excel in reading and interpreting the texts, in the correct practice of the rituals, in good comportment and monastic discipline, and in intellectual challenges. Because of this I was well respected among my peers and in the monastic community in general. I remember feeling that I was the first among my fellows, and was rather handsome as well. Maybe this was just the foolishness of youthful pride. I was particularly good at the various games and mischievous activities of youth. This helped to make me popular and well liked among the other young monks. Whenever we had opportunity to play away from the supervision of the older monks, I was a leader of the games and the main troublemaker who encouraged the others in various pursuits of distraction, wildness, and foolishness. But as I wished to maintain my good reputation in the monastery, I was clever enough to show this mischievous side of my personality only out of sight of the elders, like a cat concealing her claws.

Do Khyentse Yeshe Dorje (1800–66)[12] established Bayan Monastery in the Fire Bird year (1837). In the years that followed, Wangchen Gyerab Dorje (ca. 19th century)[13], known as the Grand Khenpo of Lab or the Supreme Teacher of Lab, established the three foundations of monastic training[14] at Bayan Monastery in the year 1866. Amdo Geshe Jampel Rolpé Norbu (1888–1936) and Khewang Lozang Dongak Chökyi Gyatso (a.k.a. Nyen-gön Sungrab Tulku,

1903–57)[15], and many others came to Bayan Monastery after that, making it into a main center for the study and practice of the Lord Buddha's Dharma. In 1868, the Fifth Rabjam Rinpoche of Shechen Monastery, Nangzé Drubpay Dorje, established at Bayan Monastery the Mindröling[16] tradition of the yearly ten days intensive mantra meditation and accumulation practice known as the Tsechu Drubchen with its concluding two days of monastic sacred dances (Tib. 'chams). Then, in the year 1936, the Omniscient Ninth Panchen Lama, Thubten Chökyi Nyima, bestowed upon Bayan Monastery its official charter. From the founding master of Bayan Monastery, Do Khyentse Rinpoche, until 1959 the monastery has had a succession of twenty-five abbots and thirty-seven head lamas, each supporting and teaching a distinctive non-sectarian (Tib. ris med) approach to the Buddha's Dharma.

In the holocaust of the 1950s and the "Cultural Revolution" that followed, the invading armies destroyed Bayan Monastery so thoroughly that not even a trace of it remained.[17] It was not until around 1983 that the monastery began to emerge again on the slopes of Bayan Mountain. At first, tents were erected on the site where buildings once stood. Later the monks and lay supporters were allowed by the Chinese authorities to begin the formidable task of reconstructing the buildings of the monastery on Bayan Mountain.

In 1986 Lama Rinpoche (Khenpo Münsel) arrived and promoted the vital process of re-establishing the monastery by maintaining the ancient continuity of the lineage of vows and practices. Accordingly, he ordained novice and senior monks and re-established the monastery as a regional center of Buddhist study and practice. From there he taught Dharma to many thousands of disciples, and gave initiations such as the Amitabha initiation together with instructions and precepts for practice. It was at this time that Lama Rinpoche, having trained me extensively at his hermitage as will be described below, gave me the position of master of Bayan Monastery. It was as if he placed a golden crown upon my head, and charged me with the responsibility of directing all monastic affairs and guiding and protecting all the monks and followers of the Bayan community. This is how the honor of leading such an important and historic monastic community, with the associated heavy burden of responsibilities, came to rest upon my shoulders.

The name "Bayan Monastery" is a case where the name of the locality is applied to the monastery. Bayan Mountain is renowned as a fabulous "water mountain." Volcanoes are said to be "fire mountains." Other mountains are composed mostly of earth or metal. Bayan Mountain is known as a "water mountain" as it contains subterranean lakes, aquifers, and springs, with fabulous fish found nowhere else. The monastery built on the "lap" of the slope, on a flat area half way down from the summit, is called Bayan Monastery.

Bayan Mountain is celebrated both for its beauty and its imposing appearance. It is the highest mountain in a region of high mountains. Its peak seems to reach half way into the heavens. Some mountains are of barren rock. Others have a mantle of forest. Bayan is covered with grasses. In the spring and summer its luxuriant grasses make it seem like a divine mandala of turquoise whose blue-green radiance colors both earth and sky. In the winter it is covered with deep snows, and its sparkling white slopes and magnificent high peak make it appear just like Mt. Kailash. At the foot of Bayan Mountain, overlooked by the monastery, is the confluence of two large rivers: the long, placid Machu[18], and the sparkling, swift Gyachu.

Bayan Mountain possesses many auspicious qualities along with its legendary beauty. Its slopes are covered with rare grasses and precious herbs that are prized for their medicinal properties. The green of the mountain is variegated by the soft glitter of myriads of jewellike wildflowers around which happy butterflies ply their colors and jovial bees sing their songs, eager to taste the fine savors and imbibe the rare essences of various floral nectars. The fragrance of this mountain, with its alpine grasses, herbs, and flowers, is most particularly wondrous, as if it was specially prepared as an offering to the gods and goddesses dwelling above in the pellucid skies.

Bayan Mountain is an incomparable location for a secluded monastic retreat. By abiding in such a place, one may enjoy the company and support of propitious local divinities and ancient gods of the best character and deportment. For these reasons, this commodious and well ornamented area, filled with rare and precious attributes, is beloved by both men and gods, and has been frequented from ancient times by the foremost of scholars and the best of yogins.

Upon reaching my late teenage years, I found myself at Nyen-gön Monastery. I had gone there in the company of many of the lamas and monk-students of my Bayan Monastery in order to receive from Ven. Lama Lola Kadag (circa twentieth century) an extensive series of initiations, oral transmissions, lineage precepts, and Dharma teachings chiefly from the Longchen Nyingtik tradition. This was the first time that I had the good fortune to receive the spiritual revelations and profound instructions of the Vajra Vehicle of Secret Mantra, the teachings that mature and liberate the body, speech and mind. It was from this venerable lama, acting as chief preceptor (Tib. *mhkan po*), accompanied by the requisite number of devout monks serving in their assigned capacities, that I received my vows of full ordination (Tib. *dge slong*). As I found Lama Lola Kadag's great kindness to be beyond anything conceivable in the ordinary world, my desire was to remain with him and receive more and more of the ambrosia of his teachings. Sadly, this was not to be. Lama Lola Kadag was needed in other realms, and soon after my ordination he departed from this world.

Lama Lola Kadag was, in fact, one of the true pillars of Buddhism in the world, who held up the firmament of the Buddha's precious teachings on the broad shoulders of his vast compassion and deep wisdom. At the time of the Chinese invasion, he was among the most famous and influential Buddhist teachers in eastern Tibet. This made him a high value target for the Chinese in their continuous efforts to eliminate Tibetan culture from Tibet. He was captured early in the invasion, and taken to a prison. Somehow, he avoided the summary execution that was the fate of so many lamas and influential Tibetans at that time. He survived and was taken to some of the terrible "re-education camps". There his hands were tied behind his back and he was suspended by his arms, sometimes for several days. While he hung there in agony, the "educators" would deliver lectures on the virtues of Mao Ze-dong's "worker's paradise" and the "terrible vices" of Tibetan and Buddhist traditions. Suspending a human being in this manner tends to dislocate the shoulders fairly quickly. After some time, the main nerves in the arms are destroyed and the arms and hands become permanently disabled. Thus, the Lama Lola Kadag that I knew was powerful in spirit and intellect, but unable to use his arms. He would give initiations that required the use of sacred implements such as the bell and vajra. These would be tied to his useless hands and he would proceed with the ritual. He passed on at an early age, largely because of the damage done to him in the prison camp. This was a tremendous loss to Tibet, and to me personally.

By this time, thanks to the wisdom and kindness of my many lamas and preceptors, I had gained some ability to distinguish good from bad, and to act accordingly. I had mastered the fundamentals of our standard repertory of recitations and rituals. In this way I qualified myself to be recognized as an ordinary lama and sit alongside the other lamas and monks. I felt satisfied with my efforts and accomplishments to this point, but was not content with the path of an ordinary lama. I was honored wherever I went as a lama. People paid respect to me, gave me offerings, and requested my help with rituals and my intervention in spiritual affairs. However, I was not confident that I truly merited the honor they showed me or could meet their inner expectations. I was not confident that I could invoke for them the blessings of any respectable god or that I could frighten away or tame any competent demon. I was not even confident that I could take care of myself should I encounter the agents of Yama, lord of death, on a narrow mountain path or in a dark prison camp. I knew that I needed a true and particularly powerful spiritual teacher to guide me to a higher level of spiritual maturity. There is a saying that goes, "Although the smart and comely maiden is not content to remain single, she patiently waits for a worthy and lasting lover." Though I had learned much from many excellent lamas and had become adept in the deeds and practices of ordinary lamas, I knew that I had not grasped the profound essence of the sublime teachings. Only by reaching that essence does one gain true authenticity as a lama. And so, I remained dedicated to a patient search for a true spiritual teacher who would help me fulfill my deepest aspirations. But how could I manage to encounter such a person? How long must I wait? Where could I search? I had no answer to such questions. Therefore, I simply continued to follow the established norms and practices of a country lama's life. Together with my fellow lamas and monks, I carried on with the regular monastic duties and disciplines. I would talk for hours with other young monks and go on leisurely walks in the beautiful countryside. In this manner I passed my days and nights as if in a pleasant but rather pointless dream.

6

My First Meeting with Lama Rinpoche, the Source of My Refuge, and a Brief Account of His Peerless Deeds

I WILL now speak of my unique good fortune to meet with a peerless "wheel-protecting" lama.[19] At the age of twenty, a complex matrix of interdependent causes and conditions, fructified by my merit and wondrous good fortune, allowed me now to obtain a supreme crown ornament on top of my head: a true and authentic spiritual teacher. When your innermost being, your heart of hearts, finds an object whose value and benefit transcends anything you have known or imagined in the world, how can you describe or even name it? Therefore, to identify this lama with a mere name is difficult for me. However, as we have here no other artifice, I will tell you that he who blazed before my eyes with the glory of the Buddha's own auspicious signs from the first time I met him is known in this world as Lama Rinpoche, Khenpo Münsel (1916-93) and also by the exalted name Thubten Tsultrim Gyatso. He is the divine protector of my innermost mind who encompasses for me the hundreds of buddha lineages within his singular being. For me he is the true Vajradhara; the precious lama who showed me the three types of kindness.[20]

At this time, the fame and veneration of Lama Rinpoche had spread throughout the land. People came from near and far to sit in his presence and receive his peerless instructions on the nature and practice of the Dharma. Many people I knew aspired to establish an auspicious connection with Lama

Sogan Rinpoche's root lama, "Lama Rinpoche,"
Khenpo Münsel, Thubten Tsultrim Gyatso (1916–93)

Rinpoche, including Lama Tenchö and a number of other lamas and monks from my monastery. When I heard that they were going to see him, I sent with them many valuable and auspicious offerings together with a deity-greeting scarf (Tib. *lha reg kha btags*).[21] With these gifts, I sent a message to Lama Rinpoche requesting that he look upon me with favor and bestow upon me the divine nectar of his sublime teachings. When they returned, they brought from him an answer that provided me relief from all my trepidations, and filled me with the blissful anticipation of gaining my heart's deepest desire. Lama Rinpoche said, "Please come at your convenience. I will be glad to share with you whatever I know of the sublime Dharma." Upon hearing these words, I was like a thirsty peacock hearing the first rumble of thunder announcing the summer rains. From that moment on, my thoughts both night and day were continually fixed on the moment when I might first see the visage of the exalted Lama Rinpoche and hear the wondrous sound of his voice.

6. My First Meeting with Lama Rinpoche

In the late fall of that year, I received the news that Lama Tenchö, a senior lama of my monastery, was preparing to travel again to visit Lama Rinpoche. I immediately ws gripped by an unshakeable determination to accompany him. However, before I could go, I had to win the acquiescence and support of my parents. This did not prove to be an obstacle, as they rejoiced that I had such a rare opportunity, and with endless kindness and generosity provided me with all the requisites of the journey, including horses and all the supplies I might need.

We set off from my monastery, each of us riding one horse and leading another one carrying our tents and other supplies and luggage. In this manner we journeyed down the narrow trail. We crossed vast meadow lands where emerald grasses waved gently in the mountain breeze, and wildflowers plied their delicate fragrances and tendered their brilliant colors. From the lofty snow mountains and the high, rolling hills flowed crystal streams that descended in rapids and fell in sparkling waterfalls. We traveled through many deep canyons where we could see nothing but shadow and rock, and then up over high passes from where the entire world seemed to stretch out at our feet. In this way we traveled for three days. At noon on the fourth day, the welcome and much anticipated sight of our destination appeared. We had arrived at the site of Lama Rinpoche's hermitage at Tronggo Valley in the Wangchen Bum region of Golok.

Lama Tenchö indicated to me two yak hair tents that were set up nearby, and said, "Those are the dwellings of Lama Rinpoche and his attendants." We dismounted and slowly led our horses up to the tents. Lama Rinpoche was seated outside of his tent and looked over at us. In this manner we first met. At that moment, an indescribable sense of joy and faith arose in my heart, my entire body and mind vibrated with excitement, and unstoppable streams of tears suddenly flowed from my eyes.

We had given no announcement of our coming, so it seemed to me that Lama Rinpoche had gone to sit in that particular spot at that particular moment because he possessed some inner realization that gave him foreknowledge of our arrival. I also remember thinking that it was very auspicious that my first sighting of Lama Rinpoche's golden countenance occurred at the moment that I first arrived at his hermitage.

Lama Tenchö and I proceeded to offer Lama Rinpoche special white greeting scarves that were extremely long and of the best quality. However, before offering the scarves, we offered him our devotions by making the three full prostrations on the ground at his feet symbolizing the offering of our body, speech, and mind. Lama Rinpoche accepted these offerings and said, "I expect that this young fellow may become one of my best students." Turning to me he said, "Don't be in a hurry to return home. By remaining here for an extended period, I will be able to give you all of my teachings and precepts." Saying this, he imparted a type of initiation to me by fondly touching my head in the gesture of bestowing blessings. For several moments two sensations competed for prominence. I experienced the most sublime and inexpressible sense of joy, while at the same time my body vibrated with excitement and all the small hairs stood up in a singular sense of transcendent awe. What was this about? I believe these unique and powerful sensations were a result of my past life karmic connections and aspirational affinities with this lama, and of my deep and long cherished wish to find him once more.

Lama Rinpoche is my crown jewel of refuge. He is my supreme lama, as he showed me the three types of kindness. There is a prophecy about him by the First Do Drubchen, Jigme Trinlay Özer (1745–1821),[22] which is widely known in Tibet:

> Near the headwaters of the Machu,
> Close to the slopes of Dar Mountain,
> Drimé Özer will come again as a *nirmāṇakāya*,[23]
> A sublime being who will provide clear instructions
> Regarding the essential method of attaining inner realization.

Accordingly, there arose a divine incarnation, possessed of the marks and signs of an enlightened being, in the Male Fire Dragon Year of the Fifteenth Sexagenary Cycle (1916) in the Tibetan province of Golok, in the district of Wang-Chen, in the nomadic settlement "village" of Pönkor. This is nearby Dar mountain by the source of the Machu, which is a tall, rocky peak, covered with beautiful stones and outcroppings of various colors, surrounded by lesser peaks covered in green and blue grasses. It is like a huge turquoise mandala offering to the transcendent gods of the empyrean.

From childhood he exerted himself in study, contemplation, and practice. He entered the monastic university of Katok Dorje Den in the Tibetan province of Kham. There he pursued advanced studies in the thirteen main canonical works and the hundreds of treatises and minor works. After five years of this study and practice, he was awarded the degree of Khenpo, certifying his ability to elucidate the vast treasury of the Buddhist canon. Many students eventually attained the degree of Khenpo, the highest academic and religious degree. However, Lama Rinpoche received a special distinction. One of the most respected lamas and teachers of twentieth-century C.E. Tibet, Jamyang Khyentse Chökyi Lodrö (1893–1959), came to visit Katok Dorje Den at this time. He became acquainted with Lama Rinpoche, and at graduation presented him with a special certificate, a letter written in his own hand, saying, "Golok Münsel (Lama Rinpoche) has reached the highest pinnacle of Buddhist scholastic and spiritual achievement."

At the age of twenty-five, Lama Rinpoche traveled to the district of Jönba. There, in the village of Nyöshul, he met Khenpo Ngagchung (1879–1941), who was an emanation of Paṇḍita Vimalamitra. From him he learned the entirety of the teachings and precepts of the lineage of the Distilled Essence (Tib. *snying thig*) of the Secrets of the Clear Light—the Great Perfection of the Mahayana—the processes of the cutting through to primordial purity (Tib. *ka dag khregs chod*) and the all-conquering realization of spontaneous presence (Tib. *lhun grub thod rgal*).[24] Lama Rinpoche learned these teachings and practice from Khenpo Ngagchung in the manner of a vessel of pure water poured completely into another container of pure water. He received and integrated it completely, and cleared away every trace of doubt or uncertainty. Having in this manner received the teachings, he returned again to his native region.

In this manner Lama Rinpoche turned his back on the busy affairs and distractions of life in the monasteries and towns and set out for a solitary abode, far from the presence or sight of men. He came to a place called the White Rocks of Harchen. There he lived for the next eight and a half years. His abode was on top of a high grassy mountain, with vast, open vistas in all directions. There his only companions where the mountain birds and the alpine deer. He supported himself in the austere manner of a mountain hermit. For this entire period of over eight years, Lama Rinpoche maintained an unbroken state of one-pointed concentration on his practices, until finally there arose within him the stable and unmistakable certainty of direct experiential realization. This was the precious harvest of the sublime crops grown from the seeds acquired from his teacher, planted in his fertile mind, nurtured in marvelous solitude, and fructified by years of happy, undistracted diligence.

Lama Rinpoche took this precious harvest of realization into the innermost fortress of his mind, and from there it motivated and guided every aspect of his thoughts, words, and deeds. This was the realization of the innate perfection that pervades reality (Tib. *ka dag gnas lugs*), the profound emptiness that liberates all animate and inanimate phenomena. Armed with this invincible realization of primordial, transcendent truth, Lama Rinpoche passed his days and nights in deep meditation. His powerful realization of ultimate truth expanded and deepened and he gradually rose through the grounds and stages of perfecting the processes of cutting through to primordial purity and the all-conquering realization of spontaneous presence, passing the signposts of sublime accomplishment on the path to highest enlightenment.

One day, without warning, a group of Chinese soldiers, part of the army invading Tibet from the east, arrived at Lama Rinpoche's retreat. They took him into custody and, knowing nothing of the language of Tibet, spoke to him only in the language of cudgels, chains, and rifle butts. Lama Rinpoche was innocent of any crime known to civilized man, but was guilty of a capital crime known only to the Chinese invaders: the crime of being a faithful Buddhist in the ancient Buddhist land of Tibet. The cruelty the soldiers inflicted on Lama Rinpoche was beyond conception. It can only be described in terms of the behavior of devils of some infernal realm. They took Lama Rinpoche to the prison camp of Darlag Dzong. There, together with all the lamas, community leaders and educated citizens of the surrounding area that the soldiers could find, Lama Rinpoche was subjected to systematic degradation and regular beatings. He was sentenced to death, and forced to work day and night until either the day of his execution or the day of his death from beatings, exposure, and disease. The mode of execution was an elaborate and rather bloody public ceremony inflicted on a certain number of Tibetans every day. Lama Rinpoche recalled to me his thoughts at the time:

> Although we committed no offence to any living being, we are now imprisoned in a place of torment and pain. We await our own murder with no way to appeal or petition, no one to hear or to listen, no court of laws, no power to speak, no ability to move.

With all external sources of help and relief closed off, Lama Rinpoche looked for and found them within himself.

During the two-year period at the Darlag Dzong prison camp, Lama Rinpoche, as all inmates, was assured a violent execution, but was given no indication of the date or time of his impending slaughter. His mind retained, even under the most brutal beatings, an inner calm that never departed. Having seen the face of ultimate reality, he could not be shaken by the illusion-like exigencies of this troubled world. However, Lama Rinpoche realized that the inner science of the path of the Great Perfection was meant to be practiced in a well-controlled, isolated environment. The chaos and violence of the crowded prison contrasted starkly with the vast openness and profound peace found in the sacred space of his mountain hermitage. Moreover, the key meditative practice that must be done in the moments approaching one's death, and especially at the actual moment of death, required the full concentration of a calm, clear mind. Being beaten with clubs, degraded by tortures and so forth, as one is led to the culminating act of a bloody public execution, hardly established the favorable conditions for realizing the clear light of ultimate reality at the time of death.

This posed a problem for Lama Rinpoche. The way he described it to us, he and his fellow prisoners in this hellish death row were awaiting their end in full knowledge of its horrific details. The Chinese authorities designed the death procedure in such a manner as to keep prisoners in constant terror. On a regular schedule, a group of prisoners would be randomly selected for execution. They would be led to the killing ground in the center of the compound, with all other prisoners forced to witness the killing. As with most types of killers, the executioners might retain some human feeling. They need to perceive the victim as somehow worthy of death. It is hard to kill someone who is seen as noble, or even as fully human. So, the killer first subjects the victim to various degrading torments so as to induce a state that seems to fit the killer's preconceived notions. As the victims are led to the execution ground, they would be beaten savagely, kicked, and insulted, and made to wallow on the ground in the carnage of those who had gone before. With the victim hog-tied with hands in the back, the Chinese officer shoots a large caliber bullet into the back of the head, so that large parts of the face are blown off, and the contents of the skull are splattered widely on the ground.

Knowing that this was his imminent fate, Lama Rinpoche's mind was focused on finding a method to remain grounded in the sublime teachings that he had cultivated for so many years. Even under more normal circumstances, the process of dying cannot be expected to be easy or trouble free. So, part of the Buddhist method of transcending ordinary death is to cultivate the ability to maintain a peaceful and focused mind despite any ailments or other difficulties encountered in the actual death process. Calling these to mind, Lama Rinpoche prepared himself to face the executioner and accept whatever happened without losing his inner focus. In particular, he concentrated on the teachings of his own lama, Khenpo Ngagchung, which had introduced him to a direct realization of ultimate truth. This realization, he knew, must not be lost no matter how painful the death. Because of the power of his realization, he had confidence that he would retain it during those crucial moments. However, he must be fully prepared. With this in mind, Lama Rinpoche had secretly spoken to a relative who had been allowed a brief visit to the prison. He asked him to contact a certain friend from the monastery and request that he find a way to smuggle a certain text to him. The text was *The One Thought of Vastness—An Aspiration for the Bardo*[25] by Jigme Lingpa (1730–98). So, it happened that one day, Lama Rinpoche received a bottle of yogurt from this friend. Gifts of food were sometimes permitted at the prison. Inside the bottle, carefully sealed in a wrapper, was the text. It was of tremendous benefit, as it is the guide book by one of the greatest figures in Buddhist history to the journey through death and into the afterlife.

As the slave labor derived from the death row inmates was of some value, and as Lama Rinpoche, despite his injuries and maltreatment, remained relatively strong, he was not executed quickly. He remained under these conditions for two years. At the end of this time, the Chinese regime's policies were altered so that death sentences for some "political status" crimes, such as being a monk or lama, were commuted to life in prison. Lama Rinpoche was transferred from the death camp of Darlag Dzong to the notorious penitentiary of Trapa Trang in Ziling (Ch. *Xining*) where prisoners with life sentences were kept.

Trapa Trang penitentiary functions as a slave labor camp and a training center for the vast Chinese prison camp system where they engaged in developing and refining techniques of communist "re-education," that often amounted to beatings and torture. Lama Rinpoche's incredible inner strength allowed him to survive the torture and remain productive enough in the workshops that he remained alive, year after year, to witness the terrible crimes against humanity being committed there. His close confrontation with death at the Darlag Dzong camp, where he came to face a horrific end with inner strength and confidence, had been like a crucible of intense fire and pressure that refined his inner realizations and fused his deep wisdom and vast compassion into a powerful unity. He met every difficulty, every beating, torment, and deprivation with a peaceful attitude.

From all over Tibet, the occupation authorities sent thousands of prisoners to Trapa Trang penitentiary. Most were monks, lamas, khenpos, geshes, and any who were seen as embodying the Tibetan religious culture. They were quarantined at this penitentiary under a life sentence, while the authorities attempted to re-educate the population of Tibet to accept their new overlords and their materialistic communist Chinese culture. Of these thousands of highly educated Tibetans, holders of the treasury of Buddhist thought and practice, only a handful survived the horrors of Trapa Trang. This was not a death camp like Darlag Dzong, but there was little food, virtually no medical care, no heat in the depths of the alpine winter, nor shelter from the blazing sun of the Tibetan summer. The slave labor was brutal and endless, and the mercy of the Chinese guards was absent or inaccessible. Thousands succumbed to disease, hunger, thirst, hypothermia, overwork, sleep deprivation, beatings, and various other torments.

Lama Rinpoche, Sogan Rinpoche's root lama, in his prison camp photo

For nineteen full years Lama Rinpoche continued to live under these conditions. Never angry or depressed, he became a shining beacon of hope and strength, a source of blessing and support to all who encountered him. He quietly attracted all who sought the inner peace and active compassion that he exemplified. Whenever there was the opportunity, he taught techniques of meditation on impermanence and the *tong len* cultivation of universal compassion.[26] He gave teachings on whatever would be of the most benefit to each of his fellow prisoners. Food was scarce, and was strictly rationed. Lama Rinpoche always managed to sustain himself on just part of his ration, and gave the remainder to whomever was in the greatest need. On the feast days of the tenth and the twenty-fifth of each month, Lama Rinpoche would offer his ration in a secret extensive Tsok offering (Tib. *tshogs*) ceremony for the benefit of all beings, and then would distribute it to his fellows. In every way, on every occasion, Lama Rinpoche engaged in the deeds of the bodhisattva, and thereby transformed his environs in this inferno of communist imperialism into the paradise of the compassionate Buddha. He inspired and strengthened even the uninitiated, and trained the elite to become full embodiments of the path to enlightenment. His disciples within the prison gained many benefits for their spiritual practice and peace of mind, even as most eventually perished before leaving the prison walls. Those few who survived are counted as some of the most influential teachers and spiritual masters of recent times, such as the Drikung Kagyu Kyabje Garchen Konchok Gyaltsen, Gar Migyur Thubten Tsultrim Gyatso, Karma Kagyu Tsarchen Khyenrab Gyatso, Nangchen Sangye Tenzin (1917–78), Drukpa Kagyu scholar Nangchen Drubchok (1931–2007), Geluk Kumbum Geshe Tenpa Rabgye (1959–2015), Lab Sonam Tsemo, Alak Chukya Tsang, Geshe Tsondrü Gyaltsen of Tashi Lhunpo in Tsang, Rebkong Ngakmang Lama Jigme Özer, and Drubwang Namkha Jigme (b. 1938).

After nineteen years of imprisonment in this burning charnel ground of endless suffering, merciless torment, and death, priorities in China shifted and Lama Rinpoche and some other surviving political prisoners with life sentences were paroled. Under the conditions of his parole, Rinpoche was forced to wear the black hat of the criminal whenever he was in public, and remained under the scrutiny and supervision of the "security police" for several years.

At the end of this lengthy process, Lama Rinpoche was finally allowed to return to his hermitage in Wang Tö, in the upper region of the Wangchen Bum province of Golok. It is said that his long journey from Ziling in the north to Wang Tö in the south was like that of the mighty dragon returning to his home, his roar the first thunder of the season of the summer rains that quench the dry hills and valleys, bringing the crops that sustain the country, and the grasses and flowers that adorn the mountains. This auspicious roar of the dragon echoed the length and breadth of Tibet, calling those hungering for the long-suppressed Buddhist teachings to come and sit before this bodhisattva of Golok. They came like flocks of swans migrating in the summer to a lotus lake in the remote mountains. Now the time for the vast deeds of the bodhisattva had arrived. The people of Tibet have long struggled under the oppression of their alien overlords, who oppose the compassionate teachings of the Buddha and take what they want from any who lack the resources to oppose them. Tibetans have become like blind people longing to see the light of day shining on the faces of their loved ones. Lama Rinpoche's subtle and powerful teachings gave new eyes to the people and restored their ability to rejoice in their precious heritage.

Having confronted a brutal death with a smile on his face and calmness and love in his heart, Rinpoche had no further need for spiritual practice. But his limitless kindness caused him to turn the three sublime wheels of the Dharma for the sake of his people and for all who seek transcendent liberation. His teachings encompass the pure essence of the Buddha's teaching both in their theoretical form as sublime philosophy and their applied form as the practice of pure ethics and profound meditation. It cannot be overlooked how these bodhisattva deeds of Lama Rinpoche help to restore the fragile golden thread of the Buddha's precious teachings that had been worn so thin over the last several decades. This golden thread has sustained the people of Tibet and of the world beyond for so many centuries, but has now been almost completely severed by the continuing dark deeds of the invaders. Rinpoche's efforts that have strengthened this thread and, for the moment, made it shine its golden light for the benefit of gods and the welfare of men. With it he has drawn up out of the abyss of alien oppression countless disciples. How did Lama Rinpoche repair and strengthen this golden thread of the Dharma? He did so by combining his vast learning with the adamantine insights developed in the crucible of his powerful inner practice. The core of this thread is the essence of Dharma that we know as the Great Secret of the Dzogchen. This is formed by the subtle precepts of the incorruptible golden lineage of the Nyingtik. It is incorruptible as it is nothing less than the pure realization of the clear light of reality, the realization of which has been transmitted from enlightened master to disciple in an unbroken lineage since ancient times. As it lies at the very heart of the Lord Buddha's teaching, its presence brings about the manifestation of all the other aspects of the Dharma and makes possible the full attainment of enlightenment. It is this unique sacred thread that Lama Rinpoche so skillfully protected from destruction by the barbarous force of the invaders, and bestowed upon us and upon generations yet to come.

There is a famous prophecy that is well known in Tibet. I often heard it described and celebrated by various wise teachers, including Lama Rinpoche and my other lamas. It is from the prophecies of the famous Tertön,[27] Do Drubchen Kunzang Shenphen (1745–1821):[28]

> From the highlands will come forth the roar of a mighty lion,
> Who will cause the teachings of the Lord Buddha to flourish,
> From the lowlands will come forth a mighty peacock,
> His flapping wings will fan the dying embers of the moral doctrine,
> And cause them to blaze forth once again,
> From the midlands will come forth a glorious dragon,
> His melodious Dharma roar will echo far and wide.

The first two lines refer to His Holiness the Dalai Lama, Our Sublime Refuge and Protector, who is the political and spiritual leader of Tibet. The reference to him as a mighty lion is given because the lion is the symbol of the Tibetan nation. The roar of the lion refers to the words of His Holiness. These are the fearless words of truth and wisdom that he proclaims for the benefit of Tibet and the welfare of the world, words which reach every corner of the world, and are cherished in the hearts of people everywhere. These are the words that embody the essence of the Lord Buddha's teaching, words that set in motion the transcendent wheel of peace and happiness that frees the world from all bondage and harm.

The third, fourth and fifth lines speak of the revered teacher who saves the beings of the world in this degenerate age, His Eminence Khenchen Jigme Phuntsok (1933–2004).[29] He was born in the Year of the Bird and therefore the prophecy uses the bird symbolism. In recent times, the entirety of Tibet has been subjected to a horrendous holocaust that has nearly annihilated its singular treasure, the pristine Buddhist culture, reducing it to something resembling a pile of smoldering ashes. Faced with the annihilation of this source of all the world's welfare and happiness, Khenpo Jigme Phuntsok fanned the dying embers of the Buddha's doctrine with the mighty wings of his teaching, causing it to again blaze forth and bestow its light and warmth on Tibet and upon the entire world. He corrected errors, misconceptions, and ignorance about the Buddha's teaching, and reestablished its firm foundation of personal and social ethics, as well as the pure transmission of its scriptures, the profound teaching of its theories and its authentic practice that brings about inner realization. In these ways, he caused the teaching to again shine forth in the Land of Snow Mountains, like the rays of the sun illuminating the eastern face of the Himalaya at the dawn of a new day.

The sixth and seventh lines speak of the mighty dragon who will come as a lama who possesses the three types of kindness. This refers to my own Lama Rinpoche who was born in the year of the Dragon, 1916.[30] In general, Lama Rinpoche attracted aspiring students from near and far, teaching them by words and example how to master the sacred teachings and internal practices of the Lord Buddha's tradition, as well as its external deeds that contribute to social welfare and environmental protection. In this way he restored and nurtured the Buddhist tradition and caused it to increase throughout Tibet and beyond. If the details of his accomplishment were to be presented, they would exceed the ability of words to express or thought to encompass. In particular, Lama Rinpoche taught the essential Dzogchen teachings of the Mahayana that come forth from the very heart of Buddha Samantabhadra himself. Because of his efforts, these precious teachings spread across the snowy land of Tibet, like the sun light dispelling the darkness of night and illuminating the entire land, from the highest mountain glaciers to the deepest green valleys. Indeed, Lama Rinpoche was a true fulfillment of the prophecy of the Tertön Do Drubchen Kunzang Shenpen.

How is it that Lama Rinpoche possessed such sublime qualities? From his early years he manifested a variety of indications of high attainment. He had many mundane and transmundane visions of, and encounters with gods and lamas, yogins and adepts (Skt. *siddha*). They would appear to him in various ways, including in his dreams and meditative sessions. They would give him special teachings and precepts, answer questions and forecast future events of relevance and concern. They took Lama Rinpoche into their confidence and assisted him in his studies. In particular, he was always supported and protected by Ekajaṭi, the Guardian of the Tantras, as well as other Dzogchen Dharma protectors of the Nyingtik tradition such as Rahu and Damchen Dorje Lekpa. He was tutored by the magic wisdom body[31] of the master of enlightenment, Longchen Rabjam (1308–63). In his meditations, Lama Rinpoche met face to face with many ancient lamas and powerful gods, including the sublime master Je Tsongkhapa, who answered his questions and gave him blessings and subtle powers. His meeting with Je Tsongkhapa (1357–1419) was particularly important, as it took place in Kumbum Monastery in Amdo, site of Je Tsongkhapa's birth, shortly after Lama Rinpoche had been released from his long imprisonment by the Chinese.

As a yogin, Lama Rinpoche attained the fourth of the four levels of Dzogchen, the state of non-duality with the limitless expanse of reality. In this manner, he joined the exclusive company of the illustrious saints (Skt. *mahasiddha*) of Buddhist history. However, Lama Rinpoche always maintained his humility and simplicity, as if he was just an ordinary member of the monastic community. Although he had reached the summit of accomplishment on the path, he never failed to engage in the ordinary daily practices of meditation, prayer, and ritual. He adhered to even the smallest regulations and specifications of Buddhist morality and ethical behavior.

Lama Rinpoche was altogether free of any sectarian preferences with regard to the various schools and lineages of Buddhism. He had no interest in any of the eight worldly concerns.[32] By nature he had few desires and was always easily satisfied. His passion and delight were to accomplish things that were of benefit to others. His loving kindness to other living beings, be they powerful, ordinary, or feeble, was like a mother to her own children. To those who came to him with an interest in the sublime Dharma, he showed them the loving concern and guidance of a kind father for his only son. Although in actuality Lama Rinpoche had long since dissolved every trace of conceptuality (Skt. *vikalpa*) and delusion in the infinite sphere of suchness,[33] and had ascended to the limitless, non-dual ultimate reality of the truth body (Skt. *dharmakāya*),[34] he remained always fully observant of the law of karma, continually focusing on even the smallest details of cause and effect in his every deed, word, and thought.

Lama Rinpoche's true identity is best expressed by the words of Padmasambhava, the Lord of Oddiyana:

Although I may fully possess the sublime Dharma of the Dzogchen,
Combining perfect view with perfect action and perfect precepts,
And even though my level of realization may soar beyond the highest
    heavens,
It is my concern with the details and specifics of karma and the law of
    cause and effect that is more precise and finer than particles of
    barley dust.
I am the Guru Padmasambhava.

Likewise, Lama Rinpoche's realizations, such as his perfect cognition of transcendent reality, is beyond the limits of the vision and understanding of ordinary people. He is free of any delusion and is beyond the realm of conceptuality, having dissolved all such limitations in the expanse of ultimate reality. He abides continually in the state of *dharmakāya*, beyond all conventional thought and meditative practice. However, for the sake of us students, Lama Rinpoche always maintained the discipline of engaging in the daily practice of the Four Session Yoga. He guarded his actions in accordance to the inexorable law of karma, protecting his moral commitments as assiduously as someone protects his own eyes. Lama Rinpoche always emphasized the fact that the monastic system is the root and foundation of the Lord Buddha's teaching in the world. In accordance with his constant devotion to this principle, he bestowed the vows of novice and fully ordained Buddhist monk on disciples. Because of that, those upholding and honoring these vows have been increasing throughout Tibet.

Lama Rinpoche was a master of the Buddhist tradition in all its detail, depth, and expanse. In regard to the early transmission of the Dharma to Tibet, the Nyingma system, he understood it thoroughly. Although he maintained the appearance of a simple monk, underneath that appearance were the limitless labyrinths of Dharma treasures. In this way he was like a mushroom with a plain, smooth top and an underside of rich complexity.

Lama Rinpoche's knowledge encompassed all nine of the vehicles of the Buddha's teaching: the three outer vehicles (i.e., the shravaka, pratyekabuddha, and bodhisattva vehicles) that save living beings from the sources of great suffering; the three inner vehicles of austerities and rituals (i.e., Kriya, Ubhaya, and Yoga); and the three secret vehicles of the methods of initiation (i.e., Mahāyoga, Anuyoga, and Atiyoga).[35] With regard to the later transmissions of the Dharma, including those of the Geluk, Sakya, Kagyu, and Jonang, his deep knowledge and experience extended to all aspects of those lineages.

Whatever he received in offerings or gifts went directly for the virtuous purposes of fulfilling the needs of others, both secular and spiritual. He received a tremendous amount of offerings, but gave them all away in charity, keeping only the simple robes and eating utensils required of a Buddhist monk. I saw this many times with my own eyes, and still hear similar accounts of others who witnessed his generosity.

Lama Rinpoche had no interest in acquiring followers to serve him or in possessing a luxurious home or an impressive hermitage. His lifestyle was just like that of the great Kadampa lamas who followed Atisha (982–1054) and exemplified the sublime qualities of a true embodiment of the Lord Buddha's path. This is just a short summary of a few of Lama Rinpoche's outstanding characteristics. The full extent of his good qualities is beyond the ability of ordinary words to convey, and is beyond the ability of ordinary minds to conceive.

In summary, this is not simply some extravagant praise and adulation of a lama offered by a devoted disciple. Rather it is my own direct knowledge and experience of the blessings that I have received from him that has definitively convinced me that Lama Rinpoche is an authentic spiritual teacher who has come to protect and guide living beings of this degenerate age in accordance with the words and intent of the Lord Buddha. Moreover, these blessings of the lama are not something that can be pointed out like a distant mountain peak can be indicated with an extended finger.

How can I convey this in an accurate and effective manner? Perhaps I can only suggest its broad outlines, and trust you to find the true dimensions of its reality in your own quiet reflection and direct experience. Often that which is of the greatest value is not immediately apparent. Only with effort and the passage of time can the true be distinguished from the false, like grains of gold separated from sand and dirt. For example, when we hear that the things of this world are impermanent, this might contradict one's immediate sense impressions. However, with close observation over time, with progression of the seasons and the passing of years, we will see that indeed there is no compounded object that does not change and pass away. This teaching on impermanence gradually yields its blessings when we find that, through holding it in our mind, we eventually appreciate its truth and become free of the painful clinging to the illusion of the permanence of the things of this world. Likewise, the blessings of the teachings on compassion arise over time, when we find that in the depth of our heart there arises a virtuous state of mind that seeks to protect each and every being. For all beings over our limitless former lifetimes have been our own mother in some life, and have cared for us with unfailing love and kindness.

Further, there might arise in our minds an accurate perception of the philosophical tenets of all the different schools of Buddhism that sees them to be like so many rivers that come together to flow into one mighty ocean. With this there will arise unshakeable faith and devotion toward all the enlightened beings, without regard to lineage or school. When the truths of impermanence, universal compassion, strong faith, and true perception arise spontaneously without obstruction or limitation and are fully integrated in one's mind, one has certainly received the blessings and powers of a true and authentic teacher. These powers and blessings are not like a tangible, material thing. They are more like a supernal radiance that penetrates the darkness and dispels every fear and difficulty. This is not easy to describe, but must be self-evident when it is directly experienced.

I have no illusion that I rank in the sublime progression of enlightened masters and disciples that come down to Lama Rinpoche and his own lama. However, I am among his disciples, even if I may be the very lowest and least worthy among them. Somehow, I feel this to be a cause for some genuine pride as it leaves me in a state of grace whereby I always usually possess a happy attitude and an unburdened mind.

To have even the briefest opportunity to meet with such a sublime teacher can only be the result of an extensive store of merit accumulated over many former lifetimes. It is my fervent wish and prayer never to be separated from such a wondrous influence. I make this prayer every day, without fail, thinking always of Lama Rinpoche's limitless kindness to me.

PART TWO

7

The Good Fortune of Gradually Acquiring the Profound Precepts

AS MENTIONED above, I first met Lama Rinpoche in the company of Lama Tenchö. After staying for about a week, Lama Tenchö began his journey back to his home at Bayan. Rather than taking me with him as planned, he returned alone with a message from the great lama to my parents assuring them that he would take good care of me. Lama Rinpoche gave me a tent that would be my new residence. It was white canvas on the outside, but the inside had a colorful lining with bright floral motifs that made me feel like I was living in a celestial garden.

In the beginning I was a bit homesick. This was the first time I had lived on my own. I had always been surrounded by many people at home as we had a large family and many friends, and little privacy. Here I found myself on a remote mountain, far from any village or encampment, with only Lama Rinpoche and his attendant. At first the days seemed long, and the nights brought restless sleep as the unaccustomed isolation disturbed my sense of identity and place and left me feeling lonely. I would sit there in my bed, saying prayers to Lama Rinpoche and reciting the mantra of the Vajra Guru Padmasambhava. With the passing of days and weeks, I gradually became more comfortable and grew accustomed to my new situation.

One day, Lama Rinpoche's attendant, who I knew as Uncle Chergo, came to me with a directive from Lama Rinpoche indicating that the time for my first formal teaching had arrived. However, before I get into that, I should say a word or two about Uncle Chergo. I don't know what his proper name was, but to me he was Uncle Chergo, and he came to be my very best friend. He was beloved far and wide among the many who came to receive blessings and teachings at the feet of the great lama. Uncle Chergo was uncommonly large. He walked with a limp, slightly dragging one foot. He had a dark complexion, and his face was pocked with the scars of some old skin problems. He had come upon Lama Rinpoche soon after the lama had been released from prison. Many visitors came in those early days, and Uncle Chergo was always the first to see a need and take care of it in a natural, easy manner. Did Lama Rinpoche need some more tea? Another cushion? A scarf or a blanket? He was first to notice and to provide. His faith in Lama Rinpoche was deep and spontaneous. His kindness toward all was as free as the clouds and warm as the sun. He was an embodiment of the ideal Buddhist practitioner. If you looked into his humble living quarters, you would be surprised by the lack of amenities or possessions. This was not because of poverty, as Uncle Chergo had countless generous friends and admirers among Lama Rinpoche's legions of followers. It was rather a reflection of the purity of his mind and the singleness of his purpose. He lived only to serve the world, to serve all the beings of the world, through serving the great lama.

Uncle Chergo remained as Lama Rinpoche's attendant until the day the great lama returned to his heavenly home. At that time, he traveled back to his home village, built himself a house, and lived out his years in study and meditation. During his time with Lama Rinpoche, Uncle Chergo had built a hut that was just big enough for him to lay down with his head touching one wall, and his feet the other. When I visited him at his new house back in his village, I found that he had built it with exactly the same dimensions. A spoon, a pot, a tiny stove, and one simple monk's robe were the total of his worldly possessions. The total of his other-worldly possessions, however, was wider than the sky, and deeper than the ocean.

And so, the time came when Lama Rinpoche sent Uncle Chergo to summon me for my first formal teaching. When I entered his room, I found that several lamas from Kham, together with their attendants, were already present. The teaching was from a text by Lungtok Tenpay Nyima (1829–1901)[36] entitled *A Sage's Song of Disinterest in the Things of the World*. Its subtitle is: *Some Urgent Advice from Those Who Know Better, Inspiring Engagement in the Dharma with Definitive Statements of Harsh Reality, Accompanied by Pleasant, Humorous, and Instructive Anecdotes.*[37] Lama Rinpoche then proceeded through the text, giving us both a detailed explanation of its meaning, and in the process, giving us the spiritual transmission.[38] When the teaching and transmission had concluded, Lama Rinpoche lent the book to me. He was reciting from the text, and had come to the following verses:

When we examine the deeds and behavior of the tulkus of today,
Are they found to be covetous, greedy, arrogant, and vain?
Do they perform rituals simply to gain a good livelihood,
Going about selling their services like hawkers at the market?
Do they have no real interest in study and practice,
Never engaging the vast and profound Dharma of sutra and tantra?
Do they have nothing to offer but the mere appearance of a tulku
To those of true faith, both the living and the dead,
Who come to them with hope for refuge, guidance and protection?
How disgusted I am to see such things!

Reciting these verses, he handed me the book. Then he said to all of us, "This is not an ordinary book. Understand that it contains powerful blessings that are difficult to find in other texts."

Lama Rinpoche introduced me to the disciples, saying:

This boy is a tulku from the Akyong region of Golok, from the sunny side of the Machu. He will be staying here for an extended period of time. Today is the occasion of his first teaching from me.

Saying this, he touched my head lovingly, and I felt his deep kindness.

Later, I took the book back to my room and contemplated the significance of the teachings, and reflected on those verses he was reciting as he handed me the book. Am I such a bogus tulku? If not, how can I avoid such flaws. If so, how can I reform myself. Fortunately, the text had clear answers to these and many other questions. Uncle Chergo brought me some blank paper, and I proceeded to copy the entire text with my quill pen. From that time, I took to studying this book, reciting it over and over, contemplating the significance of each verse until I had memorized the text almost from beginning to end. The instructions and advice contained in this text have, to this day, been the focus of my personal practice and the guide for my life.

As winter approached, my father and my younger brother Guru arrived bringing me food, clothing, my own tent, and all the other supplies that they thought might be useful. They had received the message that I was not returning after the anticipated short stay with Lama Rinpoche, but was staying on as his disciple. It took them three days of travel from our home. Usually this is a journey of two days by horse, but it took three days as they brought the supplies on yaks. Having delivered these supplies, my father and brother departed for home, leaving me feeling just a bit lonely and homesick. However, I had little time to dwell on such feelings as I was too busy with my work. Lama Rinpoche had set me to accomplish again the extensive Five-Fold Preliminary Practice.[39] I had already done this under the direction of Lama Gonpo Norbu when I was younger. I suspect the quality of my earlier preliminary practice was not so good, as I had a limited understanding of what I was doing. Now I was also busy studying other topics such as presentations of philosophical tenet systems and preparing for the Hundred Days Retreat that follows the accomplishment of the Five-Fold Preliminary Practice in the Longchen Nyingtik tradition.

In this way the time passed, and the Tibetan New Year holiday approached. My mother and father arrived for a visit with my uncle Lhotsen.[40] Although there was never any difference in the kindness shown to me by my loving mother and father, it is somehow always thoughts of my mother that are foremost my memory. The depths of the loving relationship between my mother and me might be hard for some to appreciate. She was a person of vast insight and kindness. When she passed away, people came from all over the countryside to express their love and gratitude to her and send her on her way with their prayers and fervent best wishes. However, in this lifetime our karma allowed my mother and me very little time together. This is something I really regret.[41]

As the time passed with my many activities as a disciple of Lama Rinpoche, I continued to miss my mother. Without any means of communication, I did not know when I would see her again. However, I knew that at some point my parents would visit. After many months, they came. It was a warm and sunny late winter day. I was in my tent after lunch, taking a short break from my studies and practices. I was laying down, reading one of my many adventure books. Maybe it was the epic of Gesar, or perhaps the history of King Drimé Kunden. I heard the sounds of horses and human voices. This was very unusual. Lama Rinpoche, Uncle Chergo, and I lived a solitary existence in this remote mountain hermitage. The green hills and valleys, blue sky and white clouds, the occasional wild yak, the raven, and the marmot were our only companions. So, the sound of visitors roused me from my reading. I emerged from my tent and there were my dear parents, calling out, "Hello! Anybody here? We are looking for the hermitage of the famous lama!"

And so, on this occasion, I was able to meet with my mother, to see her directly in front of me. When she first came into view, my happiness was so powerful that the entire world disappeared, and I could see only her. With this immense joy came the sharp pangs of sorrow at having been parted so long. My vision was blurred with tears as I rushed heedlessly to embrace her. My mother expressed similar feelings as she held me tightly, gently sobbing.

Over the next five days, before my parents returned to their home, I was able to spend much time with mother. Lama Rinpoche instructed me to take a break from my studies and practices, and to fully enjoy the opportunity to visit with my family. My father and uncle left to visit relatives in a neighboring valley, and returned only at night. One night they stayed over, but every other day they returned and spent time with us. Otherwise, I spent all of the time with mother. We would go for walks up the ridge and across the meadows, talking of things past, of the beauties of the present moment, and of the mixed anticipation of things to come. Sometimes Uncle Chergo would accompany us, and we three would have a picnic in a scenic spot in the alpine meadow. Lama Rinpoche did not need Uncle Chergo to be constantly present. The great lama's day was as determined as the course of the sun across the heavens. Most of his time was spent in deep, solitary meditation. His needs were minimal and almost completely predictable. Uncle Chergo was free much of the day, and was always ready to make delicious meals, generously supplemented by the supplies and treats brought by my family. During meal times and tea time, mother would speak with Lama Rinpoche. They had much to talk about. My mother spoke of her life in our settlement, of the people and their good and bad fortune. She told him of the decimation of our area by the Chinese, the destruction of our schools, monasteries, and infrastructure; the slaughter of so many of our people and the suppression of our culture as it was happening during Lama Rinpoche's decades in the prison camps. She spoke in particular of her own family members who were slaughtered by the soldiers, some in front of her own eyes. He told her of some of the horrors of the camps and of the passing of all the things of the world. Together they reflected on the beauties of nature and the value of the precious teachings of Buddha that once again could occasionally be heard in remote corners of Tibet. The torments and tragedies of this world, when experienced by superior people like Lama Rinpoche and my mother, serve to increase their insight and empathy, and to increase their compassionate deeds.

At night, my mother and I would stay up late, careful not to forget things we wanted to share. The five days of their visit passed quickly. As my parents prepared to return home, they approached Lama Rinpoche and requested a special spiritual bond (Tib. *chos 'brel*).[42] On this occasion, Lama Rinpoche gave my parents some teachings that helped to put their minds at rest. In particular, he explained why it was important that I stay with him. He told them that as a tulku I should be instructed in all the lore of our sacred tradition in order to be endowed with all the tools necessary to carry out their intended function in the world. A tulku is a person who returns to the world in order to help all its living beings. To have the confidence and knowledge necessary to do that effectively requires extensive study and practice. Life back in our home settlement would not provide me with what was needed. He showed them how I had everything necessary to develop spiritually, and to stay healthy and safe. After Lama Rinpoche reassured and banished all their major concerns about my wellbeing, it was time for us to part. I took advantage of the opportunity to demonstrate to them my confidence in Lama Rinpoche's words, and to assure them that I would be comfortable and well cared for. In this manner our inevitable separation became a little more agreeable.

Much later on, my father told me how difficult this parting was for my mother; how she rode for many hours bent down by the sadness of leaving me behind. My feelings were much the same, and it was some time before the heaviness of this parting lifted from my heart. It helped me to read the many accounts of those who had preceded me, those who, with much sadness, turned their backs on home and hearth whenever their devotion to the sublime Dharma left them no other choice. It also helped that I had so much to do and was now deeply and diligently involved in accomplishing the Five-Fold Preliminary Practice and preparing for the hundred-day retreat that follows. When I finished my daily practice sessions, or had a break between sessions, I would have my study sessions with Lama Rinpoche. In these formal sessions he tutored me in a variety of general Buddhist topics such as bodhisattva mind practice (Tib. *blo sbyong*), and in many other topics such as Buddhist tenet systems, and the grounds and paths of both sutra and tantra. Lama Rinpoche supplemented these teachings with many stories and personal accounts that made them come alive and illustrated key precepts about the way to live in this world and the way to transcend it. I am sad to report, however, that the pernicious thief of forgetfulness has robbed me of many of these wonderful stories.

7. The Good Fortune of Gradually Acquiring the Profound Precepts

At this time, I was also learning the distinctive Tibetan calligraphy of the Denang area of Golok. My tutor in this was Uncle Chergo. He was an expert in this, having learned it from a teacher who held that particular lineage of calligraphy.

Most people involved in this kind of Buddhist practice are anxious to receive the actual Dzogchen teaching. I was no exception. As I was nearly finished with the task of accumulating the five sets of 100,000 preliminary practices, I was continually thinking that the time was not far off when I would finally receive the essential Dzogchen instructions and would then be able to repose in the true bliss of that exalted state. However, the actual situation was quite different, and not at all as easy as I was thinking. After the satisfactory completion of the preliminary practices, one may then qualify to receive the Dzogchen essence teachings that point out ultimate reality (Tib. *ngo shes*). If one then is able to directly cognize ultimate reality, one may then be in a position to expand that awareness (Tib. *rtsal rdzogs*). This is like how the first faint rays of sunlight over the eastern peaks slowly grow into the great, all-illuminating orb of the sun. If one can thus effectively expand that awareness, one may then be able to gain stability (Tib. *brtan pa*) in it. Until one has succeeded in all of these, there can be no slacking off of the high level of diligence in practice. This is said to be like a bowman who never loosens his bow string until all the arrows have been shot and have hit their targets.

After finishing the preliminary practices, I entered the next phase of training that precedes receiving the Dzogchen precepts. This is the hundred-day retreat. It is highly structured in that every one of the hundred days is divided into four sessions, with breaks in between. There are strict rules governing what is to be done during each session, and what is done between sessions. During the sessions one covers all of the topics of Dza Patrul Rinpoche's classic, *The Words of My Perfect Teacher.* Starting with the first topic, the rare and precious nature of the fully endowed human rebirth, and concluding with the final topic, transcendent wisdom (Skt. *prajñāpāramitā*), each of the 400 sessions of the retreat is devoted to mastering a particular topic. We use *The Words of My Perfect Teacher* as well as a commentary on its topics by Lama Rinpoche's own teacher, Khenpo Ngagchung. Each session has its preliminary preliminaries, its actual preliminaries, its main topic, and its concluding practice. The preliminary preliminaries consist of activities necessary to the effective engagement in the actual session, such as taking care of bodily functions and setting up the room. The preliminaries consist of setting the body and mind in the posture of meditation. The body is set in

Sogan Rinpoche in Golok, 1984

the sevenfold posture of Buddha Vairochana. The mind is set in the altruistic motivation of the bodhisattva. The actual session then focuses on the prescribed topic from the text. The conclusion is where the merit of the session is dedicated to the benefit and happiness of all sentient beings.

As I was engaged in this practice, a young monk arrived from a remote area called Nangchen in the southeastern part of Kham. He was sent by one of Lama Rinpoche's distinguished disciples, Garchen Rinpoche. His name is Bu Nyima, and he came to engage in the accumulation of the preliminary practices under the guidance of Lama Rinpoche. At this time, we were experiencing the intense cold of the Tibetan winter. I recall seeing Bu Nyima sitting outside hour after hour, ignoring the cold, constructing and offering his 100,000 mandalas. As spring arrived, I finished my hundred days retreat and Bu Nyima finished a section of his preliminaries. Although we were both deeply immersed in our demanding practices, we now had a little time to relax and socialize. We were able to get to know each other.

This was a very good time for me. I remember one beautiful spring day Bu Nyima and I went for a walk in the area surrounding the hermitage. The vast ranges of mountains stretched out in every direction, inhabited only by groups of grazing yaks, herds of wild goats, and flocks of birds soaring across the pellucid sky. The mountains had begun to put on their new coats of emerald grasses, and the grey overcast of winter dissolved into the endless blue of spring, ornamented by the occasional fluffy white cloud. As we returned to the area of the hermitage, we saw the unusual sight of an alpine mole making his way along the ground. Bu Nyima cried out in surprise. He had never seen such an animal. I knew what he was, and rushed over and picked him up. His skin was scaly and hard. As he flailed his arms, Bu Nyima again cried out in alarm, not knowing what to expect. I ran toward Bu Nyima, scaly mole in hand, and delighted in his further expression of dismay. He then got the joke, and we both broke into loud laughter. I put the mole into my Golok cowboy hat, and the three of us went to show off to Lama Rinpoche. "You are very lucky," he said. "If you did not hold him tightly, he would have turned around and burrowed right under your skin. He would not stop until he reached solid bone." Somewhat chastened, and with a greater level of respect for the mole, I carefully took him outside and placed him back on the ground where we had found him. For his part, he abandoned his interrupted foray above ground, and quickly disappeared back to his underground empire.

In the time that followed, I would occasionally get together with Bu Nyima or other friends, and our strict adherence to meditative routine would give way briefly to the pleasures of storytelling and laughter. But quickly we would return to the rigors of our practices, anxious to get on to the next stage. After I had finished the strict hundred-day retreat, I prepared myself for a key meeting with Lama Rinpoche. Having completed the many prerequisites for the Dzogchen, I now came into Rinpoche's retreat, offered the threefold prostrations of body, speech, and mind, and presented him with the actual substance mandala and the mental manifestation mandala.[43] I then called upon my deepest aspirations and most eloquent words to humbly but urgently request that Lama Rinpoche bestow upon me the profound and secret precepts of the Dzogchen. With much solemnity and limitless loving kindness, Lama Rinpoche put his hands upon my head and accepted my request. In this manner I had the true good fortune of receiving my first Dzogchen transmission.

In the lineage of the Dzogchen, the essential instructions have been passed down from master to disciple by word of mouth, always memorized, never committed to writing. However, every hundred years or so, Vimalamitra (eighth century), the master who originally brought the Dzogchen teachings from India to Tibet, returns in human form to clarify and amplify these essential instructions. In the nineteenth century, he was born as Khenpo Ngagchung (the teacher of Lama Rinpoche). His teacher was Lungtok Tenpay Nyima (1829–1901) a chief disciple of Dza Patrul Rinpoche. Due to the tumultuous the nature of the times, Khenpo Ngagchung decided that it was finally time to commit the essential Dzogchen teachings to writing. He gave the text he produced to his disciple Khenpo Münsel (Lama Rinpoche) as part of the complete transmission of the Dzogchen. The text was given to Lama Rinpoche only after he had memorized and mastered its entire contents by way of the traditional process of oral transmission and instruction.

The text is entitled *Notes on the Topic of Cutting Through to Primordial Purity: The Refined Essence of the River of Oral Teachings from the Mouth of Tenpay Nyima.*[44] In this text are teachings that are common to both sutra and tantra, as well as those that are exclusive to the tantras, especially to the Dzogchen. The common teachings include the analysis of the nature of the mind, the search for the hidden, innate tendencies in the structure of the mind that allow faults and afflictive conditions to arise, and the study of the mind's origin, whether it comes, goes or stays, if it has a size, shape, color, weight, or other such basic features. The uncommon teachings concern the recognition and determination of the clear light of ultimate reality that comes from meditative analysis of the true nature of the mind itself. In other words, the uncommon topic can be said to be the sudden, vivid cognition (Tib. *ngo sprod*) where the mind realizes its own nature. This is the reflexive awareness that arises from a correct understanding of the esoteric instructions of the Dzogchen. Having bestowed upon me these common and uncommon teachings as outlined in this text, Lama Rinpoche guided me through the processes of differentiation (Tib. *shan 'byed*) and resolution (Tib. *la bzla*). This is the differentiation between the fundamental concepts and the realities of the Dzogchen, such as the distinction between the mind (Tib. *sems*) and the intrinsic awareness or primordial insight-wisdom (Tib. *rig pa ye shes*); between perception, conception, and reality and the various other key aspects of Dzogchen. The resolution or determination is the process of taking these distinctions and determining the true nature of each one until all doubts have been resolved.

For a period of several months, Lama Rinpoche instructed me every day. He covered all of these topics of Dzogchen, including the underlying philosophical view, the meditation practices, the associated activities and requisite behaviors, and the aims and goals. Though these teachings were organized in a systematic, scholarly manner, they were in fact the revelation of his inner realization. The kindness of Lama Rinpoche in giving me these teachings is inconceivable. Even if I could cover the entire surface of the world with gold, and give it all to him, it could not entirely repay the kindness he showed me by bestowing these teachings.

Having finished the preliminary practices according to the ancient tradition, each of Lama Rinpoche's disciples would be led individually through the Dzogchen instructions in a similar manner. The nature of this process required that it be given separately to each disciple. Lama Rinpoche would devote several months to transmit these priceless Dzogchen teachings to each disciple. Each must be introduced to the ultimate nature of his mind by way of the direct pointing-out instructions of the Lama, according to individual needs and proclivities.

As was the case with all of Lama Rinpoche's disciples who had reached this stage of receiving the essential Dzogchen transmissions and teachings, I now ventured forth from the hermitage. In accord with the ancient tradition, I went out each day to engage in solitary meditation in special places that possessed the most propitious qualities. Such a place must be isolated and free from the distractions of the ordinary world. It should have an extensive, unobstructed view of a far horizon, such as a hut on the side of a mountain, or on a high outcropping deep in the alpine forest, or a rock cave high above a valley. So each day, after an early breakfast, I went out from Lama Rinpoche's hermitage to such a place to engage in the meditation practices. In this way the knowledge and insights I gained from Lama Rinpoche's teachings were slowly transformed into my own inner knowledge and personal experience. Each evening I would return for dinner and then rest in my own quarters. If the weather was particularly inclement, I would carry on with my meditation sessions without leaving the hermitage.

One day, Lama Rinpoche came to my tent after lunch, at a time when we are usually resting. I heard the sound of his big bamboo walking stick, and got up to receive him. Placing his hand upon my head, he spoke to me, "My child, today there has come to me a precious Dharma treasure (Tib. *gter ma*).[45] He said, "I want you to listen and transcribe it exactly as I speak it to you." Together we walked over to his hermitage and sat down. "Very well then, let us begin." he said:

> But I was just joking about the Dharma treasure thing. The truth is that today I have decided to compose a commentary on *An Aspiration for the Bardo*. As I have told you in the past, when I was in the prison camp, I derived

tremendous blessings and benefits from studying and meditating on these very teachings. Death is something that will come to each one of us. The only question is when it will come. When it does come, no one else can provide us with help or protection. The only thing that can provide refuge and protection in the face of death is the Dharma that we have internalized in our own mind. In the Dzogchen, there are two systems of practice either of which will readily overcome the obstacles posed by death. By following the path of cutting through to primordial purity, the entire body, down to the atomic level, dissolves into the very nature of the mind itself, leaving at death no corpse, just the hair and nails.[46] By means of only following the profound practice of the all-conquering realization of spontaneous presence, one accomplishes the rainbow body of the transference at the time of death.[47] However, these are things that can be done only by the most fortunate, energetic and diligent among the elite practitioners of these esoteric arts. For most people, in this degenerate age of short lives and many types of adversity, such accomplishment is indeed difficult. For this reason, I am thinking that it might be a good idea to compose an explication of the four states of existence[48] to bring clarity to the minds of those who seek success in their spiritual practices at the time of death.

Lama Rinpoche proceeded to compose a commentary on Jigme Lingpa's *The One Thought of Vastness—An Aspiration for the Bardo.* The title of his text is *Elucidating the Secret Path of the Clear Light: a Commentary on the General Meaning of Jigme Lingpa's Aspiration for the Bardo.* In the year after my handwritten edition was completed,[49] I often asked Lama Rinpoche for clarifications on specific statements. As I made notes on these, I asked him to compose a secondary commentary elucidating the meaning of the original text. He usually answered that the text was already clear as written. However, Tenzin Zangpo, the head abbot of Tarthang Monastery of the Palyul lineage, soon arrived to request further teachings and explanations. Lama Rinpoche then agreed to provide the two of us with the more extensive explanation. Again, I transcribed and published these teachings. The result is a text entitled *A Bright Lamp: A Word by Word Commentary on The Aspiration for the Bardo.* This text is extant today.[50]

It was around this time that disciples and seekers of sacred knowledge began to arrive vat Lama Rinpoche's compound from throughout the land. This was the period of the early and mid 1980s when the ravages of the "Cultural Revolution" had receded to the point where Buddhist teaching and practice

7. The Good Fortune of Gradually Acquiring the Profound Precepts

Sogan Rinpoche meditating at Lama Rinpoche's place
in Golok, 1986

was no longer criminalized and persecuted in some of the more remote regions of eastern Tibet. Large gatherings were then, and still are, prohibited.
However, small groups listening to or practicing Buddhist teachings were
often not disrupted by the police or soldiers. In particular, a rebirth (the
speech emanation) of Lama Rinpoche's own teacher, Khenpo Ngagchung[51]
had been found. He was born in the Nyöshul region of Kham, and is known
by the name of Tulku Nyima Gyaltsen (b. 1942). He now came to receive the
instructions on his own teachings, that he had imparted to Lama Rinpoche
in his last life, but now required a thorough review, having lost memory of
many details in the process of his recent death and rebirth. Now he required
the review of his former teachings as well as the spiritual transmission of
the powers and blessings of the lineage that he had given to Lama Rinpoche
in his last life, and now must receive himself. This is the nature of the transmission of the lineage—each generation of teachers must transmit it to each
generation of disciples so that the lineage remains unbroken.

Tulku Nyima Gyaltsen arrived in a humble state, having given up all worldly possessions and interests in order to pursue the profound Dharma. His only

possessions were the ragged robes of the itinerate monk that he wore with great dignity. Lama Rinpoche therefore asked me to provide him quarters in my own cloth tent. Together, the two of us received a large number of lengthy and detailed teachings and precepts on the sutras and the tantras. These included the entire body of teachings on the Dzogchen from the collected works of the Great Abbot, Lord of Speech (i.e., Khenpo Ngagchung), and many other teachings such as Jigme Lingpa's *Peerless Wisdom*[52] and its commentarial traditions, which provide a detailed presentation of the Dzogchen practice of the all-conquering realization of spontaneous presence. I expended much effort in my meditative sessions on the related practices such as the practice of separating the three doors in samsara and nirvana (Tib. *sgo gsum 'khor 'das ru shan*) that entails deep meditation which connects the meditator with the experiences, the states of body, speech, and mind, and the perceptions of living beings in each of the six realms of existence. Further, I received extensive teachings from Tulku Nyima Gyaltsen on such teachings and practices as the winds and channels (Tib. *rtsa rlung*) of the Longchen Nyingtik together with their physical yogas (Tib. *'phrul 'khor*).

Throughout the year, from season to season, day after day, Lama Rinpoche maintained a regular schedule. Rising early in the morning, he would take his tea and breakfast, walk around for a breath of fresh air, and then return to his small quarters at the hermitage, close the door, and enter his deep states of meditation, not to be disturbed by men, gods, or demons. He seldom departed from this routine. However, one day, Lama Rinpoche, instead of returning to his quarters, said to me and Uncle Chergo, "This morning we should travel across Tronggo Valley and take a look at the mountains on the other side." Tronggo Valley is the site of Lama Rinpoche's hermitage, and we had little occasion to go up the ridge and see the vista on the other side. So, we walked over to our lone neighbor, Kunzang, who lived with his family further down the valley. Kunzang loaned us his good blue-gray horse. Lama Rinpoche mounted the horse. I took the lead, holding the reins, and Uncle Chergo brought up the rear. As Lama Rinpoche was nearly 80 years old, a good horse was indispensable on such a journey. He took off his long coat, and used the sleeves to tie it around his waist. He held his walking stick across his knees in the manner of a fine gentleman of leisure. Uncle Chergo and I, however, were a bit anxious and constantly vigilant lest our elderly teacher lose his grip and become unbalanced in the saddle. In this way the three of us, revered master and devoted attendants, finally reached the summit of the ridge. Looking out over the vast expanse before us, we saw a sky that was unusually clear and bright, without a single cloud to vitiate its turquoise perfection. On this late spring day, the warmth of the late spring was moderated by the stirrings of a gentle, cool breeze fragrant with the rare essences of the wildflowers and the fine savors of the herbs of the alpine meadow. Arriving at the moment of the full blossoming of springtime, when the goddess of the earth appears as a beautiful maiden in the glory of her charming and fertile youth, we found endless seas of emerald grasses from which emerged occasional islands of shrubberies with their malachite leaves. Everywhere flowers were bursting into blossom. Violets called to us with their deep purples and lavenders, while the alpine poppies plied their golds, and the mountain daisies hawked their blues, reds, and silvers.

The height of our position on the ridge, and the clarity of the air allowed us to see the glories of the land far off into the distance, where the horizon shimmered like a mirage and the mountain peaks danced in grand procession, row after row, on to infinity. Up in the sky, a gigantic Tibetan eagle soared above the valley in huge circles, and another was floating almost motionless far above a nearby mountain top. Off in the distance one or two other huge eagles circled and soared across their vast empyrean realm. Down on the ground we could see small clans of crows and ravens competing in their blackness, confidently proclaiming the truth of their "caws" and asserting the importance of their "craaaks." The world we experienced at that moment was marvelously free and limitlessly grand. It rose above and seemed to completely transcend the busy intrigues, narrow paths, and endless strife of ordinary societies.

Lama Rinpoche descended from the blue horse. Proceeding stick in hand, he walked briefly around this high outpost carefully choosing a spot to sit down. He sat solidly on the ground with his back perfectly straight and his hands in the posture of reposing in the nature of the mind (Tib. *sems nyid ngal gso*)—legs crossed, arms straight forward, elbows slightly bent, hands on knees, fingers straight forward). His eyes looked upward into the sky, as he said, "Yah, Yah! Now, we shall meditate on the Great Perfection." With that he settled into a deep meditative state. The two of us were caught up in the power of his meditative radiance. It was the rarest of moments, most vividly clear, but totally indescribable. With our flesh trembling and small hairs standing on end, we lowered ourselves on the spot where we were standing and instantly assumed the meditative posture.

As it is said in the Dzogchen tradition:

Even though you may have a moment of realization of the supreme
    ultimate (the nature of your own mind),
If you do not protect, sustain, and nurture it with mindfulness,
You will be carried away by the powerful enemy: conceptuality,[53]
Like a small child in the middle of a tumultuous battlefield.

This was all fairly new to me. I had no real experience in the type of sustained effort needed to become stabilized in this wondrous state of pure awareness. I had only occasionally experienced brief tastes of this powerful state, like a bird who drinks some water, quickly dipping his beak, and just as quickly raising his head up to the sky to swallow and ingest before going down again for another tiny sip. Nevertheless, it seems that by the power of Lama Rinpoche's profound blessings bestowed in this place of awesome natural beauty, I entered into a sublime meditation truly beyond any words or description. It was like suddenly opening my eyes and awaking in a new and glorious dimension, a reality beyond anything I had seen or even imagined before. Certainly, it cannot be described with the terms and concepts of the shadowy world of conceptual limitations, dualistic thought, and senseless prattle.

That evening, when we returned to the hermitage, Lama Rinpoche said to me:

Dear child, what did you think of the place we went today? The place for the practice of Dzogchen meditation should be like that. It should be a high overlook from where you can gaze out over a vast expanse of natural wonder. Later on, when you have gained experience in the meditation and it has become more spontaneous, integrated and internalized, it will not be necessary to seek out such an ideal spot.

Lama Rinpoche then turned to a related issue:

These days there is much talk that Dzogchen philosophy is very wonderful. It is said that it provides a quick, easy, and powerful way to attain an exalted state of power and perfection. Who would not want that? So, people reach for it like a small child reaches for a shiny object on a high shelf far beyond his grasp. Therefore, it is said, "Dzogchen is far beyond the grasp of those / Whose minds are absorbed in the meditations of fools."

7. The Good Fortune of Gradually Acquiring the Profound Precepts

My child, there are two somewhat rare types of individuals who can actually succeed in the practice of Dzogchen. The first possesses strong analytical skills whereby the necessary knowledge of Dzogchen and its contemplative insight are developed. The second is one who possesses particularly powerful faith and diligence toward the Dzogchen and the lama. From where does such strong faith and diligence arise? It comes from a past life wherein a significant store of merit has been amassed, and a large amount of defilement has been eliminated. Both of these types of individuals must also have what is called the "three bases of authenticity" (Tib. *tshad ldan gsum*): "The blessings and powers of an authentic lama / The faith and devotion of an authentic disciple / The precepts of an authentic lineage."

When these three bases of authenticity come together in an individual who, as I said, possesses either profound knowledge and insight or extensive merit and purification, they function as the immediate cause for the innermost blessings and powers of the lineage of actuality (Tib. *don brgyud*)[54] to be transferred to that individual's mental continuum. In this manner you must understand that the Dzogchen is not something to be easily taught or easily accomplished without significant preparation, effort, and these other requisite causes and conditions.

"Furthermore," Lama Rinpoche continued:

There are some who speak of the Dzogchen in a specious manner, saying, "Dzogchen is without meditation." Indeed, Dzogchen is free of any meditation that is mentally or intellectually contrived. It is without meditation that is a deliberate, goal-oriented fixation on an object. However, Dzogchen maintains the essential continuum of its practice.[55] Therefore, Guru Rinpoche says: "This yoga is not "meditation," it is habituation. / When this habituation is fully consummated, / That is the highest meditation." Accordingly, until one has become in this way fully and completely habituated, it is vital to get rid of any thing or situation that could be a distraction, and then focus completely on this meditation.

I am explaining all this to you now because you have a role in my efforts to maintain and extend our lineage. After you have received all of my instructions and precepts, you must not allow anyone else to have power over you, or lead you around like an ox with a ring in his nose. Make no mistake! You must continually strive until you have completed this process. The sun of experience, realization, and blessings will gradually dawn within you. Do not be impatient or expect immediate results. Do you understand?

Lama Rinpoche gave me many other teachings as well as precepts for effective practice. He spoke to me of the future, giving me personal instructions that were like prophecies. In every way he treated me with deep affection and loving kindness. I was thereby continually filled with profound joy and happiness, and experienced feelings of a powerful, gentle grace and inner certainty. To this day, the clear image of Lama Rinpoche often arises in my mind. I see him vividly, seated there, stroking his long beard and smiling with infinite kindness as he bestows these precious, transformational teachings upon me. The deep feelings of grace that come to me at these moments are difficult to describe.

When I look back at times like this, I reflect on how I was like a person who, tormented by sickness and infirmity, had the good fortune to find a generous, kind, and extremely skillful physician. Lama Rinpoche continually cleared away my confusion about the proper integration of meditative experience and realization.[56] He provided me with the specific instruction needed to free me from the bonds of lethargy, drowsiness, and other obstacles to meditative progress.

How wonderful that I had the fortune to be with him at that place and time. In this cosmos of endless cycles of birth and death, how very difficult it is to find such a rare and precious opportunity. From the perspective of gaining more insight over the years that have passed since that time, I am certain that I would have progressed much more had I more fully realized the unique value of that opportunity with this sublime teacher. Unfortunately, I was in the grasp of the illusion of permanence, always expecting things to remain the same. I was too much deceived by the false appearances of this world and by visions of the five types of worldly desirables.[57] Especially, I was caught up in the role of being known as a tulku and thereby came too much under the influence of the eight worldly concerns. Because of these factors, I was unable to take full advantage of that wondrous opportunity, and must now live with bitter regret.

After many years at Tronggo, Lama Rinpoche packed up his few possessions and moved to a place near Dorje Phak Jinmo. There he established his new hermitage on an auspicious site overlooking a river and a vast expanse of alpine wetlands. Now there came from every part of Tibet, from Amdo, U-Tsang, and Kham, legions of new disciples, like constellations of stars appearing in the clear evening sky. There were beginners, scholars, yogins, and noted tulkus. Lama Rinpoche instructed each one according to his individual needs, abilities, and dispositions. He taught us the words of the supreme teacher of gods and men, the Lord Buddha Shakyamuni, conveying the texts of the sutras, and explaining the essence of the Buddha's path. He taught us the shastras, the canonical commentaries on the Buddha's teachings by luminaries of the Land of the Noble Ones (India) such as the two mighty charioteers of the Mahayana (Nāgārjuna and Asaṅga). He taught us the wondrous canonical works of the most illustrious teachers of Tibet such as the three sublime manifestations of Mañjushri—Sakya Pandita Kunga Gyaltsen (1182-1251), Longchen Rabjam (1308-1364), and Je Tsongkhapa Lozang Drakpa (1357-1419). In particular, he transmitted and explained the works of Jamgön Ju Mipham Gyatso (1846-1912) such as the pure precepts and instructions that Mipham gave to his disciple, who was Lama Rinpoche's own teacher Khenpo Ngagchung. He bestowed the initiations that bring maturity, the precepts that bring liberation, and the oral transmissions that establish the disciple with the sacred lineage and help the lineage to increase and prosper. He also taught aspects of the tantras that make it possible for a fortunate disciple to attain the state of Buddha Vajradhara within the space of a single lifetime. In all these ways, Lama Rinpoche turned the wheel of the precious Dharma of the Lord Buddha, causing it to spread, to flourish, and to continue abiding in this world despite any efforts to destroy it.

As for Lama Rinpoche's own teaching style, it reflected his sense of responsibility as one who has an opportunity to pass the authentic treasure of the Dzogchen to future generations. To do this effectively, he carefully evaluated each disciple to determine the appropriate method of instruction. His disciples then fell into three broad categories, each requiring a different didactic approach: 1) those who have just enough knowledge and ability to begin Dzogchen practice on their own; 2) those who have already gained experience in Dzogchen; and 3) those who are capable of explaining and transmitting Dzogchen lineage to others.

In regard to this, Lama Rinpoche always said:

There are two main requirements that are needed before the precious jewel of the Dzogchen precepts may be bestowed upon a disciple. First, the teacher must have certain knowledge of the disposition of the potential disciple's mind. Second, the teacher must obtain permission to teach Dzogchen from the tutelary deities (i.e., *yidams*) and the lamas. On the other hand, if the teacher gives these instructions to others based on an interest in thereby obtaining influence or wealth, or if he imparts them to anyone who is not well versed and sufficiently practiced in the common path,[58] he will face dreadful punishment by the dākinīs,[59] the proprietors of the Dzogchen. In addition, anyone who publicly purveys these secret precepts of Dzogchen is guilty of a serious spiritual crime, and will not be able to escape from its dire consequences, that will bring about the destruction of both himself and those who listen to him.

Fortunately, Lama Rinpoche possessed the consummate wisdom that perfectly understood the nature, disposition, and potential of each disciple and, without doubt, hesitation, or error, lovingly bestowed upon them precisely the precepts, guidance, and inspiration that allowed them to gain realization and transmit it to future generations.

In this manner, Lama Rinpoche traversed the entirety of the Dzogchen path of clear light and thereby arrived at the summit of sublime attainment. This entailed his completion of the *four stages of perception*,[60] whereby he entered into the infinite expanse of the primordial foundation. From the viewpoint of the ordinary person who is perpetually caught up in superficial appearances, Lama Rinpoche was just a humble monk engaged in the practice of the Dharma, intent on progressing step by step through the stages and along the paths taught by the Lord Buddha. However, although he was always a perfect monk, a compassionate bodhisattva, and a consummate Dzogchen practitioner, in reality Lama Rinpoche was a true embodiment of the perfect realization and perfect activity of all the enlightened ones.

Lama Rinpoche often said this to us disciples:

My Dzogchen lineage must be transmitted for the sake of future generations. However, when I look to find suitable disciples to teach this precious lineage, I must determine first whether a prospective disciple has the necessary karmic connections to the lineage and has the adequate motivations and aspirations to be a true and successful disciple. Not only that, but the transmission of this Dzogchen lineage absolutely requires that the disciple has the full permission of his own root lama and of the tutelary deities (i.e., *yidams*), heroines (Skt. *ḍākinī*), and divine protectors of this lineage. You cannot determine this merely with your intellect, but must have some profound insight from visionary experiences with yidams, heroines, and Dharma protectors and be guided by that to determine the suitability of teaching any potential disciple. Make careful note of this vital principle. If you do otherwise, if you teach Dzogchen to someone for some valuable consideration such as money, property, or influence, or teach it to anyone who has not completed the required preliminary practices of Dzogchen's ordinary, common path, then there will ensue very bad consequences. The Dzogchen yidams, especially Ekajaṭī, and the heroes (Skt. ḍāka) and heroines, will punish you severely, and obtaining good fortune in future lives will be very problematic. As for your unqualified disciples, they will get no benefit from these teachings, and will become lost and frustrated. Therefore, teaching the Dzogchen to those who are not fully ready and prepared will cause both the teacher and those who are taught to experience all manner of problems, both large and small. Recognize this dangerous situation and avoid it well. Remember these verses that I have repeated many times, "The sign of the degeneration of the Ati [Dzogchen] teachings, / Is when Dzogchen is advertised along the highways, / And taught to everyone at the crossroads." As the ominous signs and symptoms of this age of degenerations are all around us, we must be extremely careful about the proper transmission of this most valuable and secret teaching.

I believe that Lama Rinpoche possessed the pure vision of high wisdom that allowed him to know even the most hidden aspects of a person's character and abilities. He recognized the dangers of inappropriate teaching and transmitting the secrets of the Dzogchen. He therefore gave these precepts of caution only to those of his disciples who might be in a position to transmit the Dzogchen to their own disciples in the future.

Lama Rinpoche kept me close to him for a little over five years, putting me through the lengthy practices of the traditional preliminary practices. It was only after that extensive and demanding process that he found me qualified and properly prepared to begin learning the special teachings of his own unique Dzogchen lineage. It was here that I began my practice of the two primary esoteric techniques of the Dzogchen, the original purity of secret transcendence (Tib. *ka dag khregs chod*) and spontaneously arising penetrating vision (Tib. *lhun grub thod rgal*). Lama Rinpoche gave me the precepts of these two techniques together with their various auxiliary teachings. During these five years, he also taught me the *Seven Treasure Texts* of Longchen Rabjam, various books on the topic of the three sets of vows (i.e., individual liberation, bodhisattva, and tantra), texts on the analysis of Buddhist and non-Buddhist systems of philosophical tenets, and the *Five Books of Maitreya* (i.e., *Abhisamayālaṃkāra, Mahāyānasūtrālaṃkāra, Madhyāntavibhāga, Dharma-dharmatā-vibhāga,* and *Uttaratantra-śāstra*). He also bestowed upon me many oral transmissions and initiations to ripen and illuminate my mind, as well as innumerable special teachings such as *Mañjushri's Net of Illusion.* I catalogued in my journal all of these teachings given me by Lama Rinpoche.

I remember the bright summer morning when Lama Rinpoche announced that it was time for me to travel. "In the time you have been here," he said:

> You have received all the teachings, practices, and precepts that I possess. With these you have made progress on the path of spiritual maturation that leads to liberation. You are presently endowed with both youth and vigor, as well as with a clear mind and a fairly sharp intellect. It would be good if you pursue further training under the tutelage of the great Khenpo Jigme Phuntsok for a while. From the point of view of his success in the vital work of preserving Tibetan culture in Tibet and helping the precious Buddhist tradition to rise out of the ashes of the invasion and destruction of Tibet, there is no person currently residing in Tibet who rivals Khenpo Jigme Phuntsok.

Having said this, Lama Rinpoche gave me detailed advice regarding the arrangements and preparations for the journey, and specific directions on how to travel and exactly what to do once I reached Khenpo Jigme Phuntsok's vast monastery in the Serta region of Kham. The monastery is known as Larung Gar and its full name is Serjong Ngarik Nangten Lobling (Tib. *gser ljongs lnga rig nang bstan slob gling*). He asked a young lama by the name of Tengpo to help me on the journey. At that time Tengpo was a simple monk of Tarthang, a large monastery in Golok. Recently I heard that he has become one of the main teachers at that monastery. Lama Rinpoche wrote and sealed a letter of introduction for me to give to Khenpo Jigme Phuntsok (1933–2004). Then he gave us horses and all the supplies that we needed for the journey, as well as the three traditional gifts to be given to a Buddhist teacher upon requesting teachings—an image of the Lord Buddha, a stupa, and a sacred Dharma text.

Upon arriving at Larung Gar and being ushered into the venerable presence of Khenpo Jigme Phuntsok, I presented him with the three gifts and the letter of introduction. After he read the letter, he looked upon me with a very special kindness and concern. I figure Lama Rinpoche must have said some especially nice things about me, as Khenpo Jigme Phuntsok treated me with much love and kindness despite how busy he was with all of his extensive responsibilities. He and Lama Rinpoche were brother disciples of our patriarch, Khenpo Ngagchung.

Khenpo Jigme Phuntsok (1933–2004) was the rebirth (Tib. *tulku*) of Tertön Lerab Lingpa (1856–1926) who was very influential because of his many excellent disciples and his many precious treasure texts. At the time I visited, Khenpo Jigme Phuntsok was preparing to give a rare cycle of teachings called *The Compendium of All Instructions* by Lerab Lingpa,[61] contained in a series of over 20 volumes, which also includes Tertön Lerab Lingpa's treasure texts and other teachings, as well as extensive tantric initiations of his lineage. I had not planned to stay for a long time at Larung Gar, but just to meet Khenpo Jigme Phuntsok and then return. Lama Rinpoche had said that I should travel here and have an audience with Khenpo Jigme Phuntsok, and that if I felt some good connection with him, I might stay for a while and receive some teachings. As it happened, I arrived just before this major teaching cycle, and Khenpo Jigme Phuntsok suggested that it would be a good idea for me to remain and receive all of these special teachings and initiations. I was happy to have this opportunity, so I sent Tengpo back to give Lama Rinpoche the message that I felt an auspicious connection with Khenpo Jigme Phuntsok, and would be staying for this entire teaching cycle and would then return.

Khenpo Jigme Phuntsok asked two of his senior disciples to arrange a place for me in their compound. One was Khenpo Rangdrol (b. 1975), the head of Yarlung Monastery. The other was a lama who we knew as Uncle Jungnay. Khenpo Jigme Phuntsok himself provided for all my other needs, including food and incidentals. For the next two months, we received the introductory teachings from Khenpo Jigme Phuntsok. These consisted of his reading and explaining Je Tsongkhapa's *Great Exposition on the Path to Enlightenment*,[62] the grand compendium of Buddhist theory and practice for the three levels of practitioners. For the next two months he bestowed on his vast assembly of disciples all of the initiations of Tertön Lerab Lingpa's *The Compendium of All Instructions* together with extensive commentary and auxiliary teachings. Following that, Khenpo Jigwang of Nupzor Monastery, Khenpo Jigme Phuntsok's home monastery, gave us the oral transmission on the entirety of Tertön Lerab Lingpa's collected works. In this manner Khenpo Jigme Phuntsok bestowed upon me the greatest of all gifts, the gift of the Dharma. In addition, he took care of all of my needs during those wonderful months at Larung Gar. It was, however, the limitless kindness of Lama Rinpoche that made all this possible for me.

There were between six and seven thousand monks, nuns, and laypeople from all over Tibet and beyond, who attended this grand convocation. As it was coming to a close, Khenpo Jigme Phuntsok commissioned all of us to take copies of a proclamation he had made and distribute it in our home localities. In it he gave detailed advice of how to rebuild our local Buddhist monastic and lay communities and rectify any errors in our personal practice and our community organizations in order to restore Buddhist culture and traditions in Tibet. The proclamation was written by Khenpo Jigme Phuntsok in red ink, and was organized into three main themes:

1. The root and foundation of the Lord Buddha's Dharma is pure ethics.
2. The essence of the Dharma is found in its two aspects: the verbal Dharma taught by the Buddha and elucidated by his authentic followers; and the living Dharma that is the realization of the verbal Dharma in the deeds, words, and minds of practitioners.
3. The fruit of the Dharma is the accomplishment of the ultimate benefit of oneself and others.

This proclamation was distributed to all who attended this convocation, However, the tulkus were given special responsibility. We are considered leaders in our various regions and communities, and to have the most influence among the general population and the monastic community. Khenpo Jigme Phuntsok took me aside and said that I was one of very few tulkus in my homeland region of Akyong Bum and the nearby areas along the Machu, and therefore it was important for me to travel around these areas to distribute his proclamation, giving explanations of its contents as needed.

After leaving Larung Gar, I made arrangements to carry out that commission. After completing that task, my plan was to visit Lama Rinpoche, then go to see my parents, and then return to Larung Gar and accept Khenpo Jigme Phuntsok's invitation to continue my studies and practices under his guidance. However, like so many other plans in this dreamlike world, these plans did not all work out. I was unable to return to see Khenpo Jigme Phuntsok again, as I was obliged to travel to Awo Sera Monastery for my enthronement, and then go to Bayan Monastery to assume responsibility for its leadership. These sorts of administrative functions led to many other entanglements in worldly activities, as the political situation in occupied Tibet made it impossible to freely pursue my spiritual path. The loss of my opportunity to return to Larung Gar filled me with sadness.

This loss of freedom to pursue my studies is related to the general situation in the country. Tibet cannot be compared to any country where freedom, democracy, and self-determination prevail. Under the Chinese regime, Tibet is like a person who has been afflicted by a serious disease that causes much pain, injury, and depletion of strength and vitality to the point where death is all but certain. Indeed, the destruction of Tibetan culture has always been, and continues to be the goal of the Chinese regime's policy. However, there have been deliberate inconsistencies in the application of their policies. While engaging in large-scale efforts to expropriate Tibet's natural resources and displace the Tibetan people and their culture with massive population transfers of Han Chinese into Tibet, there have been occasional attempts to mollify international opposition to such imperialism and cultural genocide. Therefore, the Chinese regime has shifting policies in regard to expressions of Tibetan culture. Monasteries are torn down and monks killed, but then they are allowed to partially rebuild. However, only a skeleton crew of monks is allowed to reside in the large monasteries where once thousands of monks practiced their ancient spiritual traditions. Tibetan temples and shrines are rebuilt from the ashes left by the invasion, but their use is so restrictive that they function effectively only for the Chinese regime's propaganda purposes. Grand monasteries still standing become Tibetan theme parks for Chinese and foreign tourists. Indeed, Tibetans refer to these superficial "improvements" in the Tibetan situation as being like obtaining permission to build "a sand castle on a frozen lake" (Tib. 'khyag rom steng du mkhar las byed pa). In Tibet, we build our monasteries to last 10,000 years. But now the Chinese regime, as it were, forces us to build our monasteries and cultural centers out of sand or upon the thin ice of a frozen lake. The structures may appear attractive to tourists, but they have little utility. If you actually try to use them, they will collapse on your head. How many tens of thousands of Tibetans were imprisoned, tortured, and killed for no crime other than living as an ordinary Buddhist monk or nun—a virtuous friend to all living beings?

This continues to be the dire situation in Tibet where I was born and raised. However, my personal situation was not one of great misery. Thanks to the internal powers and blessings of my teacher, I was largely sheltered from external threats and was given the means to avoid any substantial inner conflict. Indeed, these were the very best days of my present life up to this point. How could that be? There are several good reasons for my happy state of mind. Both of my parents who brought me into this world remained at that time alive and well, so I was confident that I could go and see their smiling faces. At that time, I continually imbibed the elixir of the sublime Dharma as I sat in the presence of Lama Rinpoche, a precious spiritual teacher whose words bestowed the essential instructions on the path that leads to the state of changeless happiness. With much pleasure I shared my days, my thoughts, and my studies with spiritual brothers and sisters, my religious companions, whose friendship is deep and constant, and whose loyalty in this life and in lives to come is beyond any doubt or question. We are like the wick and the flame of a candle, our functions and our destinies intertwined and inseparable.

At that point in my life, the heavy duties of a tulku responsible for two monasteries had yet to settle on my young shoulders. I was endowed with the vigor and beauty of youth. How happy were those days, almost too happy to imagine. Now, reflecting on those wonderful times, I feel a little like a person suddenly awakened from a blissful dream and faced with the exigencies of mundane affairs. Since that time, I have wandered alone in exile, blown like a solitary feather in a strong wind. I have been seized and propelled by the implacable force of my own karma of former lives. I have been displaced in accordance with the all-pervasive reality of impermanence whereby all birth ends in death, all gathering ends in dispersal, all meetings end in parting, all building ends in collapse. I find myself a lone wanderer in strange and foreign lands, as the sun of my present life moves inexorably toward the horizon of mortality. Certainly, this all seems rather depressing. However, such circumstances never seem to disturb the basic tranquility of my mind. I always experience the palpable presence of Lama Rinpoche as if he is actually residing upon the crown of my head. As long as I maintain a clear awareness of him, the wellspring of my mental serenity, my inner sense of peace and happiness is never disturbed by the pleasures or pains, the good or the bad, the lucky or unlucky things and events encountered in my life and travels. Because of this, I am able to live in such a manner that I never give up my efforts to benefit others in both small and extensive ways.

8

Enthronement on the Monastic Seat
of My Former Lives

AS MENTIONED before, a number of monasteries in our part of the country were claiming me as the rebirth of their own leader. Each advanced offers and proposals to recruit me for their monastery, supported by detailed narrations of the wonders I was thought to have performed in their region in my former life as well as evidence offered to establish my identity as the rebirth of their former lama. The issue hung in the balance for quite a while. The final decision would be made only upon the arrival of an authoritative document of investiture that established my identity beyond any doubt. When it arrived, it would prove me to be the sixth birth of Sogan Rinpoche of Welshül.[63] On the basis of this document, I was to be enthroned as the head of Awo Sera Monastery, the monastic abode of my last birth. Before this occurred, from around the time of my fifteenth year, I had been pursued continually by representatives of the monastic leadership counsels of both Bayan Monastery (Bayan Serthang Gön Tennyi Dargye Ling)[64] and Awo Sera Monastery. The monks of Bayan Monastery were convinced that I was a tulku; that is, the rebirth of an important and powerful lama. However, they had no idea which important and powerful lama. Therefore, they used my own name and called me "Tulku Pema Lodoe." The monks at Awo Sera were convinced that I was the rebirth of Sogan Rinpoche, the founder and head of their monastery. Until the document arrived my teachers and Uncle Gelek refused to commit to any offer despite the many requests.

The time finally came as I was living in my quarters at Lama Rinpoche's hermitage. One day there arrived an official notification of my identity as Sogan Rinpoche from the hand of His Sublime Holiness, the All-Knowing Fourteenth Dalai Lama of Tibet. With his supreme "eye" of wisdom that is the non-dual realization of the limitless sphere of truth, His Holiness identified me by my place of birth, my childhood name, and various other unique and unmistakable attributes. His Holiness in this manner placed upon my head the crown of an influential tulku, and granted me the rebirth name of Sonam Dawé Wangpo. As there was no longer any room for doubt, my teachers and family now accepted the entreaty of Awo Sera Monastery. That venerable institution now busied itself with the elaborate preparations to welcome me as their spiritual teacher and install me on the lion throne of their grand temple on the dates and times they had determined to be most auspicious.

My designation as the rebirth of Sogan Rinpoche did not contradict the position of Bayan Monastery. They had not identified me as the rebirth of any particular individual, but had only insisted that I was the rebirth of an illustrious lama. The recognition by His Holiness now confirmed their original assertion, and they were all the more anxious to have me seated on their monastic throne. This would complicate matters a little, but not necessarily in a bad way.

The first birth as Sogan Rinpoche was known as Bumshul Lama Sonam (1687–1747). His personal name was Sonam, and he was the chief lama of the Bumshul region. He was born in the twelfth Tibetan calendar cycle.[65] His father was Bumshul Lama Namgyal. From early childhood he manifested the characteristics of a bodhisattva, always finding ways to protect others from harm and save living beings from danger. He joined with the upright Jigme Gawé Lodrö and the dauntless Awo Lama Lozang Özer on an epic quest culminating with their entrance into Palyul Monastery. There he studied the vast canon of the Buddha's word, the sutras and the shastras, as well as the extensive esoteric teachings of the famous masters such as Namchö Migyur Dorje (1645–67), Rigzin Karma Chakmé(1613–78), and Terchen Ratna Lingpa (1403–79). At length, after years of study, contemplation, and meditation on these profound teachings, he attained mastery of them and was presented by Tulku Karma Chöphel with the precious lineage hat of the beloved founder of the Palyul lineage, Rigzin Kunzang Sherab (1636-98). In this manner he was acknowledged to be the master of all the Palyul traditions, and was charged with the responsibility of safeguarding the Palyul heritage. Tulku Karma Chöphel prophesied that the Sogan Rinpoche would cause the Palyul heritage to spread and flourish. In accordance with this prophesy, the First Sogan Rinpoche now proceeded back to the region of Sera where he was given land and funding for the establishment of a new monastery by the ruler of that region, Khashul Gyagar Tashi. This began the glorious story of how the Awo Sera Monastery came to extend the Dharma for the benefit of so many in this region and beyond.

The second Sogan Rinpoche birth was Pema Thongdröl Ling (18th–19th century). He was born in Ling Lhawa Tsang. He possessed many unique marks and signs of high yogic attainment. Despite that, he gave up that body at a young and early age, without having entered a monastery.

Jigme Trinlay Pelzang was the third birth of Sogan Rinpoche. He was born in the Wood Dragon year of the 13th Tibetan calendar cycle (1784). His father was Sangshül Rinpoche. From his early years he progressed rapidly in his spiritual attainments and eventually attained the high stages of the path, becoming one of the most famous yogins of his time. As master of Awo Sera Monastery, he protected and increased all the good activities and traditions of his two previous births. Accomplishing extensive deeds for the benefit of the Dharma and of living beings, Jigme Trinlay Pelzang lived to an advanced age.

The fourth Sogan Rinpoche was Natsok Rangdröl. He was born in 1869, the Earth Serpent year of the fifteenth Tibetan calendar cycle, as the son of Prince Sonam Dorje, the ruler of Welshül. He was guided in his studies by the most respected teachers of the time such as Tulku Drimé Özer (also known as Rigzin Sang-ngak Lingpa, 1881-1924) and Terchen Dudjom Lingpa (Pema Ledrel Tsel). He distinguished himself in the attainment of high status both as a scholar and a practitioner. He established at Awo Sera Monastery a retreat center whose main focus was the practice of Terchen Dudjom Lingpa's profound treasure text *Buddhahood Without Meditation*. Urged by gods and lamas, Natsok Rangdröl moved the monastery to Nyilung Chutri Laka.[66] He built an entirely new structure and invited a new compliment of divine images to reside there. In his own realm of Welshül/Serta, and in many adjacent kingdoms, Natsok Rangdröl established the ten virtues[67] as the custom, and in many ways, as the law of the land. He became the personal lama of the powerful King of Derge in Kham.

At the urging of his advisors, both human and divine, Natsok Rangdröl accepted the dākinī and highly accomplished tantric adept Dekyong

Wangmo (1892–1940) as his "secret friend." They joined forces and were thereby able to extend to all directions the teachings and virtuous work of their two illustrious lamas.[68] This venerable master of the sublime teachings and practices, Dekyong Wangmo, is known also by another name: Sera Khandro. This is because after becoming the consort, or "secret friend" of Natsok Rangdröl, she remained at Awo Sera for many years teaching and revealing treasure texts to a growing circle of disciples. For more on Sera Khandro, refer to her autobiography.[69] There are also biographies of Natsok Rangdröl that detail some of his many accomplishments and deeds, such as the time when the powerful Muslim warlord Ma Bufang (1903–75) massed his hordes of well-armed soldiers on the borders of Serta in preparation for his long-planned invasion. Natsok Rangdröl proceeded to the sacred mountain of Drongri Mukpo[70] in the valley of Serta. There he accomplished the esoteric Vajrakila rite of expulsion which caused Ma Bufang to flee for his life, never to approach Serta again.

The Fifth Sogan Rinpoche had a dual manifestation. The first was known as Choktrul Pedé. He was born as the son of Tsedor, the governor of the region of Detse Dralag. He was recognized as Sogan Rinpoche by a number of local divinities and distinguished lamas including Jamyang Khyentse Chökyi Lodrö. He was then enthroned on his monastic seat at Awo Sera, and charged with the leadership and guidance of the monastery. However, he did not remain for many years on his monastic seat. The Chinese regime under Mao Zedong was now in control of China, and began to turn its attention to expanding its territory by invading the lands beyond its borders. Serta and Detse Dralag are in the eastern part of Tibet, and came under pressure first. Choktrul Pedé therefore gave up the safety of the monastery and the monastic robes. He learned the arts of war and rode his war horse into the teeth of the invading Red army. There are many tales of his heroism and his superb martial arts. He was a man of impressive stature and famous for his handsome face and his ability to inspire faith and confidence even in the darkest hours. He had many outstanding military successes against the invader. Some say he gave up his life in his quest to protect the monasteries and the people. Others say he joined the Chushi Gangdruk (Tibetan Defence Forces) and continued the heroic struggle across Tibet into the next decade (the 1960s).

The second of the two Fifth Sogan Rinpoches was known as Choktrul Thubga. He was born as the son of the Tertön Kunzang Nyima, also known as Nüden Dorje. As a small child he recounted fine details of his former life in a manner that filled the eyes of witnesses with tears, and their hearts with faith and joy. Choktrul Thubga developed into an inspiring young lama and continued to increase faith, devotion, and sacred knowledge in an increasing circle of followers. To this day his miraculous activities continue to be told by those who knew him well such as the Ven. Gyaltrul Rinpoche (b. 1925) who now lives in America.[71] Unfortunately the occupation forces arrested Choktrul Thubga, took him to a death camp for Tibetan lamas and community leaders and soon put an end to his life.

In summary, the first five Sogan Rinpoches accomplished many important activities that had a profound impact on the people and institutions of their times. Because of this, there is much written about their lives and activities by various authors. A search for and study of such texts would undoubtedly find a multitude of material. As for me, the Sixth Sogan Rinpoche, known as Pema Lodoe and as Sonam Dawé Wangpo, I have already outlined the story of my early years, and need not repeat them here.

As mentioned above, the First Sogan Rinpoche, Bumshul Lama Sonam, founded Awo Sera Monastery, known officially as Sera Thekchen Chokor Ling (i.e., the Abode of the Mahayana Dharmacakra at Sera). He established the monastery in the Sera district of Serta in the year 1736. After this, the Second and Third Sogan Rinpoches continued to develop the monastery in that place. However, sometime after the Fourth Sogan Rinpoche, Natsok Rangdröl, had taken charge of the monastery, his gods and lamas informed him that conditions would be improved by changing the location of the monastery. He therefore moved the monastery out of the Sera district and reestablished it in the Trötri district in the valley of the River Nyi. Although no longer in Sera, the monastery retained that name. The monastery is popularly referred to as Awo Sera. Awo is the name of the nomadic clan that is centered in the area around Sera.

The time came when I was asked to take my place on the throne of Awo Sera Monastery. News of this spread throughout the land. The people of my Bayan monastery and its surrounding communities were of a mixed state of mind. They rejoiced in the honor of having one of their own recognized as the master of another important monastery, but worried that this would reduce their access to their spiritual leader. When the time of the enthronement approached, I set off on the long journey to Awo Sera in the company of a crowd of friends, relatives, and well-wishers. They accompanied me for the first stage of the journey, but took their leave and headed back to Bayan in time to avoid the difficulties of spending the night in the open.

The autumn had come to the high mountains of Southern Golok. Cold winds chased up and down the valleys and around the peaks, scattering the clouds until the bright stars winked brilliantly against the velvety blackness of the sky. The configuration of the planets among the constellations portended a safe and successful journey. My father, my brother Guru, and several other relatives and close friends including Lama Chönam (b. 1964) accompanied me. Of the ten of us, some were monks, others laypeople, each had a strong sense of purpose and an important role to play. We each rode a horse, and everyone except me was leading a second or even third horse carrying our tents and supplies. Together we formed what is called a "lama troop" (Tib. *sgar gzhis*)—a traveling lama and his entourage recognized and welcomed wherever they go in Tibet. A lama troop distinguishes itself from a military troop or other group of travelers by certain features recognizable from a distance. These include the lama's special hat, the maroon robes, colorful tents ornamented by auspicious signs, and distinctive bells worn by the horses. In these ways, the people of the countryside know in advance that they are not encountering armed soldiers or random visitors from the world of ordinary men, and they can take the opportunity to prepare a suitable welcome for followers of the Lord Buddha from whom they can receive blessings and spiritual direction.

From my birthplace in the Sunnyside district of the Akyong province of Golok to Awo Sera Monastery there was no direct road. We crossed the mountains and valleys following old horse trails so that we could arrive at our destination in a little over five days. On the way there, as well as on our return journey, we made a brief stop at the hermitage of Lama Rinpoche to pay our respects and to receive his benedictions and advice.

We arrived at a place that is one and a half days' journey from Awo Sera Monastery called Swan's Pass Plateau above the valley of the River Nyi. There I received the first of a series of formal welcomes from the monks and lay supporters of the monastery. The location, date and approximate time of these welcoming ceremonies had been set in advance when I met with representatives of the monastery. On this early morning occasion, as a bright autumn sun shone on this wide expanse of long grasses and flowering herbs, the welcoming committee of about thirty people approached with their flowing white greeting scarves and colorful festival costumes. The monks, followed by the lay patrons, expressed joyful appreciation for my arrival and offered fine food, fruits, and drinks to my entourage and me, including the horses. After some ceremony and talk, we proceeded on

8. Enthronement on the Monastic Seat of My Former Lives

Awo Sera Monastery at the time of his enthronement as the Sixth Sogan Rinpoche in 1985. Left to right, Tulku Rinchen Trengwa; Sogan Rinpoche; the Tertön Sera Yangtrul Rinpoche; Yarlung Tenpé Nyima (1865–1926); and Sera Jigga Tulku

the way, each with a new horse, and me on an especially grand and handsome stallion.

We rode together all day, and as the sun approached the far western ridge of mountains, we arrived at a broad expanse known as the Plain of Good Fortune. Brightly colored tents with auspicious symbols and lucky signs dotted the plain. A mass of at least five hundred people had traveled here to set up an elegant welcoming celebration. This was the second of the series of formal welcomes. Here there were troops of musicians, dancers, and singers offering me the best of our traditional performing arts. Tent after tent welcomed me with fragrant teas and lovely comestibles that vied for attention with their delicious aromas, fancy settings, and gorgeous arrangements. The officials, monastic and lay, as well as the ordinary people greeted me with eyes filled with tears of happiness to see their beloved lama returned from his journey through the realms of the dead, once again in possession of a robust human form and ready to continue blessing them with the wisdom and kindness of the Enlightened One.

This was only the preliminary to the large welcoming ceremony. After spending the night in the hospitality tents on the Plain of Good Fortune, we arose early in the morning. As the first light of the sun spread down the valley and across the River Nyi, we could see in the distance, at the lower end of the valley, a sea of people gathered in honor of my arrival, waving their colorful banners and raising their proud flags. This would be the third of the formal welcome ceremonies. As we continued down the valley, we were joined on either side by legions of Tibetan men mounted on horses ornamented by brocades with polished brass trappings. They were in battalion formation for formal review, dressed in all the finery of the old Tibetan army, with welcoming white greeting scarves streaming from their rifles and ornamenting their swords. As we passed they offered their ceremonial military salutations, and joined our party on both sides as a huge honor guard.

As we approached the lower end of the valley, we looked up to see some of the buildings of Awo Sera Monastery sitting grandly on the slopes of the mountain. Suddenly the morning sun rose over the eastern mountains and illuminated the Monastery in golden glory. The white walls of the buildings with ornaments of gold crowning their roofs, and structures that appeared to be ancient ruins all welcomed us with supernal brilliance as the sound of the deep monastic drums, long mountain horns, and echoing conch shells blended with the roar of the crowds chanting mantras and calling out auspicious greetings. The lamas and monks stood respectfully in order of rank and seniority, each wearing his ceremonial robes and monastic hat indicating his position and affiliation. Local officials lined up with governors and mayors in the first rank and lower level functionaries massed in the rows behind. Also present were a number of Chinese officials and other agents of the Chinese regime from Dartsedo and Serta Dzong (the district centers for the occupation forces). They were easily identified by the drabness of their clothing and the dourness of their demeanor. Their presence was the only dark cloud on this otherwise perfectly radiant and auspicious day, and was a sign that underneath the superficial "religious freedom" was an abyss of alien control. I wondered why the Chinese regime, with absolute authoritarian control of the country, is allowing this putative renaissance of Tibetan culture in this locality? In what ways will they be exploiting it for their own ends?

However, as I now looked about, I saw thousands of ordinary Tibetans gathered from nearby and far off. Fathers and mothers led their children and guided their elderly parents. Dogs barked happily and clouds of incense filled the sky. In particular, smoke offerings arose from every rise and hilltop as far as the eye could see, fed by devotees offering the grains, succulent sweetmeats, and alcoholic beverages to produce the most auspicious smoke. The people gathered on the pathways and stood respectfully in long lines that crossed the plain. Each wore their finest festival costumes and most precious jewelry. As I passed by, everyone, young and old, bowed down to me and lifted their greeting scarves, their turquoises, their coral and silver ornaments, their guns, knives and swords as faith offerings and tokens of their deep devotion. In this manner I was welcomed as if by ten thousand heroine goddesses and battalions of fearsome warrior gods (Tib. *dgra lha*).

The weather was perfect; not hot and not cool. The sky was clear, with just a few puffy white clouds to make the blue sky seem even bluer. The bright sunlight made everything radiantly clear and made the colors come alive. I recall my feelings at this time. I am just a child of poor nomadic family who was now being placed on a high throne of leadership and influence, beloved by the masses and respected by the leaders of monasteries, militias, and governments. Yet my feeling this day was not one of pride, surprise, or awe. This all appeared to me like one more episode in a continuing dream. However, I was intensely aware and involved in everything around me. It was a clear vision of a dreamlike world in which I played a part, but was never deceived into believing it to be inherently real. I felt a little like one of those white puffy clouds that ornamented the blue sky—passing through this world, seeing it all very clearly, but always moving on without attachment to anything.

The fourth in the series of formal welcomes was the official one. We finally reached the precincts of the monastery after greeting and bestowing benedictions on various individuals and groups. I was invited into the grand front entrance of the monastery, and ushered into the central temple. There I was requested to ascend to the high throne in front of the main altar. The monastic community arranged itself in front of me, standing up respectfully for the entire duration of the ceremony. To the accompaniment of Tibetan oboes, silvery vajra bells, brass cymbals and giant drums, the assembly made their formal offerings and extended greetings filled with warmth and aspiration. In the center of the first rank of lamas was the beloved master Sera

Yangtrul Rinpoche (circa twentieth century). His personal name is Tsultrim Gyatso and he is also known by his tertön name, Sang-ngak Drodul Lingpa. He was flanked by other senior lamas of Awo Sera as well as distinguished lamas from monasteries in the surrounding regions. Many other venerable lamas and cave-dwelling yogins had joined thousands of ordinary monks to participate in this grand enthronement ceremony of the return of their beloved teacher, the Fifth Sogan Rinpoche, who, as noted above, had valiantly given his life in the struggle against the alien invader.

The enthronement ceremony was the culmination of a year of planning and preparation, and many years of anticipation. It included the usual rites of enthronement and special rites exclusive to Awo Sera Monastery such as the ritual cleansing of the magic mirror (Tib. *me long*). Sera Yangtrul Rinpoche[72] himself conducted these rites. He stood before me in all his magnificence, with his long flowing beard, his high ornamented lineage crown, his broad, radiant face, and of course, his wonderful penetrating eyes that gave him a personal power and charisma that no one, having experienced it, would ever forget. When he used the mirror in the ritual cleansing procedure, although not a drop of the consecrated fluid physically touched my body, it seemed as if he was immersing me deep in the all-purifying waters of Vajrasattva.

As I sat on the monastic throne that day, I was offered the devotions of the monks and lamas of the monasteries and of the people who inhabit our high and beautiful land. Along with their devotions there settled upon my shoulders an uncomfortably large share of responsibility for their welfare in this world and in the world to come. This was made clear explicitly by the words of their prayers in the enthronement rituals, and implicitly by the aspirations of their hearts reflected continually in their eyes and in their every act of service or devotion.

At the end of the enthronement ritual I was invited to take rest in my private monastic quarters on the topmost floor above the temple. However, the monastic ceremonies continued in the main temple below and throughout the monastery grounds, while on the broad plain below the monastery the festivities of the huge gathering continued far into the night.

Early the following morning the leaders of the monastic community, led by the monastery provost and Sera Yangtrul Rinpoche, together with the most important officials and leaders of the secular community, arrived outside of my apartments playing royal oboes and burning precious incense made from the finest herbs and rare elements refined from the earth. This was the invitation to ascend the monastic throne for the final part of the enthronement process. We formed a procession with the provost leading the way. He held the burning bunches of precious incense waving them to one side in order to attract the gods and benign spirits of heaven and earth, and waving them the other way to frighten the demons and repel the evil spirits. Entering the main temple, I saw that it was packed tightly with the highest-ranking monks, lamas, and officials. I proceeded to take my seat on the throne, and immediately the chief monastic official, the monastery's provost (Tib. *dge skos*), came forward to officiate in the ceremony. It was conducted in accordance with the ancient rites of the Buddhist order and the laws, customs, and proprietary rituals of Awo Sera Monastery. He spoke in a deep, resonant voice, amplified by a microphone and large speakers arranged so everyone could hear, whether in the monastery or in the gathering below. He explained how the five aspects of perfection[73] had come together for this auspicious occasion. He recited the history of the monastery and gave an account of the lives and deeds of each of the former lives of the Sogan Rinpoche.

The provost then presided over the offering phase of the ceremony where a large number of the distinguished lamas, monks and layperson came forward to present me with gifts. The gifts represented faith offerings accumulated by various groups in Awo Sera Monastery, other monasteries, and in the lay community. They were given in anticipation of the return and enthronement of Sogan Rinpoche. For the ceremony, a person was chosen by each group to represent them in presenting their gift. As each person presented an offering, the provost would describe it to the assembly. In this way I was offered many fine examples of the traditional offerings to the Buddhist teacher given in anticipation of receiving teachings. These include jeweled mandalas of gold, silver or bronze, many sacred images of the Buddha, various precious and rare texts of the Dharma, and a large number of golden stupas, both large and small. Sera Yangtrul Rinpoche presented me with the first and most valuable set of these traditional offerings to the teacher. The provost then directed everyone else, in order of rank and seniority, to come up one by one with their offerings. Senior monastic officials of Awo Sera offered me various tokens of my office, and special objects from the hands of the Sogan Rinpoche in the past lives. Others presented treasures manifesting aspects of the Buddha's body, speech, and mind; ritual items such as vajras, bells, and hand drums; a variety of traveling accoutrements such as tents, horse trappings, travel beds, and other large items too large to bring into the temple including horses and sheep. I was presented with objects of sacred as well as material value including quantities of gold, silver, and other valuable commodities. The quantity and quality of all these offerings was dazzling. At the conclusion of the offering ceremony, the provost again spoke. He said that as spokesman for the assembly and all the donors, he requested that in response to all of these offerings and prayers, I was to ascend to the throne of Sogan Rinpoche and continue the work of my former births.

Immediately after this ceremony, I was asked to take my seat on a second throne that had been set up outside, in the courtyard right in front of the main entrance. The outer gates were thrown open, and the masses of the faithful were invited in to present their greeting scarves and whatever else they had to offer, to receive my blessings, and in this way to establish a direct spiritual connection with the new manifestation of the Sogan Rinpoche. Thousands filed up to me in an orderly but seemingly endless queue. Each received the traditional hand blessing (Tib. *phyag dbang*) wherein I placed my hands upon their heads and extended the inestimable blessings of the Lord Buddha that were passed down to me through my spiritual lineage. At the end of this very lengthy blessing ceremony, the massed disciples chanted as if with one voice: "Precious lama! We beseech you to assume the position of spiritual teacher at this monastery!"

Sogan Rinpoche (center) with monks at Bayan Monastery—1985

However, once all the ceremonies had been concluded, the time came for my companions from Bayan Monastery to come forward and present their concerns. They explained that I had already been installed at Bayan Monastery and had accepted the role of serving as its leader and teacher, with all the duties and responsibilities of a presiding lama. Once such installation has taken place, the duties and responsibilities must be carried out. The monastic council of Awo Sera argued in the same manner that I had now been duly enthroned as the master of Awo Sera Monastery, with all of the considerable obligations and responsibilities of that position. There followed much earnest debate between the two sides, with no agreement on the issue.

I was indeed installed as the leader of Bayan Monastery, but there had never been an actual enthronement ceremony. Lama Rinpoche had come to Bayan Monastery and had asked me to accept the teaching throne as the leader and teacher of the monastery. I had accepted this position, and had been sitting upon its throne and giving teachings. The lamas of Bayan Monastery, both junior and senior, were students of Lama Rinpoche. Most had been the members of Bayan's monastic council who had recognized me as a tulku and had been insisting that I become their leader. So, the issue was not an easy one to settle. I was suddenly in a difficult position, with the weight of many responsibilities and the hopes and aspirations of so many people resting on my shoulders. But I actually had limited powers and very little experience.

Reflecting on the situation, I realized that the tremendous reception that greeted me at Awo Sera Monastery, the adulation of masses of Tibetans, the honors showered upon me by lamas and powerful secular leaders, and the attention of Chinese officials who came from Dartsedo and other remote locations, all arose from a confluence of many causes and conditions. In particular, at the time of my enthronement at Awo Sera Monastery in 1985, the iron grip of the Chinese regime, that had all but squeezed the life out of Tibetan culture, was occasionally letting up on its death grip when it served the occupiers' purposes. After over three decades of unrelenting oppression and misery in Tibet, the regime was now finding it useful to allow some appearance of religious freedom in the more remote areas of Tibet such as Golok and Serta. Indeed, I was one of the first major tulkus to be openly recognized and enthroned in this way since the cataclysmic invasion.

My reception at Awo Sera Monastery reflected the powerful and long suppressed hopes of the Tibetan people for the freedom to live as Tibetans in their own land and practice their ancient religious culture. In addition, the

Fourth Sogan Rinpoche, Natsok Rangdröl was the ruler and virtual king of this country of Welshül/Serta, and, as the spiritual master of the King of Derge, his power and authority extended throughout much of Eastern Tibet. His rebirth, the Fifth Sogan Rinpoche Choktrul Pema Dorje, was the son of the ruler of the region. As mentioned above, he left the throne of Awo Sera Monastery at the start of the invasion in the early 1950s and fought the invading hordes heroically from one end of Tibet to the other. So, the enthronement of the Sixth Sogan Rinpoche represented many things beyond any special abilities I might or might not personally possess.

As I mentioned before, my very first sight of Awo Sera Monastery as I approached on the occasion of my enthronement included beautiful, shining monastery buildings, and also what appeared to be ancient ruins. I soon learned that things were not as they appeared. Awo Sera Monastery had once been one of the major monasteries in Eastern Tibet. We had around 500 monks at the time of the invasion in the 1950s. The Chinese invaders killed, arrested, or scattered all the monks, looted all the valuables, and destroyed all the buildings. The "ancient ruins" were glorious temples and monastic halls smashed to their foundations only twenty-five or so years earlier. The beautiful buildings of Awo Sera Monastery that greeted me in the morning sun on my arrival had been rebuilt slowly by the people of the land only since 1982, when the Chinese regime decided that a show of religious freedom might be advantageous to them in their efforts to be better accepted by the rest of the world. In the months before my arrival, the local people and monastic authorities made extensive efforts to make everything glorious for the big occasion of the enthronement.

When time permitted, the elders of the monastery took me on a long walk around the extensive monastery grounds. They told me of their sufferings under the occupation, of the destruction of the monastery buildings, and the recent license to partially rebuild them. As we walked up above the new construction, they took me over to some particular ruins. "This was your house," they said, "the *labrang* (i.e., the monastic compound of a head lama) of your predecessors." Apparently, this was the first target of the invaders. As I looked at it, the lessons on the transitory nature of all composite phenomena suddenly became a strong personal experience. We continued on. The ruins of the famous Awo Sera *shedra* (i.e., college of Buddhist arts and sciences) still had the foundations so that we could discern the outlines and floor plans. The *drubdra* (i.e., meditation retreat center) was more damaged and at first appeared to be nothing but a field of scattered rocks. However, close examination revealed again the outlines of this extensive facility.

As I continued on the walk with the elders, we reflected on the history of Awo Sera Monastery. It has always, since the founding by the First Sogan Rinpoche, been known as one of the greatest centers of the non-sectarian study and practice of Buddhism. This means that the focus is always on the essential teachings of the Lord Buddha Shakyamuni, without preference for any of the particular lineages of masters who elucidate it. The various lineages, such as the Geluk, Nyingma, Sakya, Kagyu, and Jonang, all have their revered geniuses who wrote profound works of commentary and explanation of the Lord Buddha's word. Sogan Rinpoche, in all his lives, has taken full advantage of every lineage's principle works, using them to polish the facets of the sublime jewel of the Buddha's Dharma as it was passed on to each generation. Of course, there are practices such as guru yoga, where the focus is on a specific lineage of transmission. For this we use the Palyul lineage of the Nyingma.

For a week or so after the enthronement I stayed at Awo Sera Monastery and remained extremely busy. Every day many hundreds of people, filled with faith and devotion, young and old, male and female, stood in long lines and waited patiently for the opportunity to meet the new Sogan Rinpoche, to be touched by his hand, to receive his blessing, and to establish a spiritual connection with him. Then there were the many daily meetings with dignitaries, officials, and delegations. I had little rest. Then there were the special friends and many disciples of the Fifth Sogan Rinpoche, and even a few disciples of the Fourth. Some came with laughter and rejoicing. Most came with eyes filled with tears. They all came with stories—stories of my former lives and activities by those who witnessed them; stories of the monastery, the people, the lamas, the mystic saints and yogins, and intriguing accounts of the present situation and the possibilities and probabilities for the future. I was fascinated with all of this, and wanted only to hear more and more. Sadly, I did not have much time to spend with these wonderful people, and by now most have passed on.

The faith and devotion of so many of these people was unfathomably deep. Some people's faith is like a puddle on the road after a brief rain; it is easily disturbed and quickly dries up. But many who came to see me during my time at Awo Sera Monastery had faith like a vast lake of vast depth—profound, clear, and serene. Some were young, some old, but all had eyes filled with sincerity, aspiration, and tears with which they again and again begged me to remain in this place as their lama and mentor, to guide them out of

Dreams and Truths from the Ocean of Mind

Sogan Rinpoche's brother Guru, Sogan Rinpoche, and Namté
in Golok—1986

the intractable problems of this life and establish the foundation for a better world beyond. Unfortunately, I have not been able to fulfill their hopes and aspirations. As you will see, the powerful winds of inexorable forces and contrary conditions drove me far away from that beautiful land.

Welshul (Serta) is also known as Serthar. It is located in one of the two principal parts of Tibet. The western part is known as U-Tsang. It has four divisions (Tib. *ru bzhi*): 1) the valley of the Kyichu River; 2) Lhokha; 3) Tsang; and 4) the valley of the Nang. The eastern part of Tibet is known as Mey (Tib. *smad*) consisting of the upper province of Amdo and the lower province of Kham. Kham is divided into six regions which are called the six elevated districts (Tib. *sgang drug*). These are 1) Kyara Ghang; 2) Rab Ghang; 3) Pobor Ghang; 4) Markham Ghang; 5) Tsha Ghang; and 6) Zalmo Ghang. Welshul (Serta) is a division of Zalmo Ghang. Zalmo Ghang is a large and diverse area with many rivers. One of its main rivers is the Nyi. Welshul is located in the long valley of the Nyi, which is known for the beauty of its high alpine meadows and its lush, green hillsides. Many powerful gods and important divinities make their homes in the valley of the Nyi, and receive regular offerings and adulation from the human inhabitants of the region. Chief among these gods is Drongri Mukpo, the resident deity of the high mountain known also by the name Drongri Mukpo.The people of this entire area of Welshul (Serta) are known for the depth of their devotion to the way of the Buddha, and for the purity of their Tibetan culture. Some other regions in Tibet have a tendency to mix influences of different cultures in with their Tibetan Buddhist culture.

Their deep devotion to the way of the Buddha largely frees the people of Welshul from the problems and limitations of sectarianism. As they focus sincerely on learning and practicing the doctrine of the Lord Buddha, they tend to favor the non-sectarian approach that gratefully accepts any bona fide Buddhist teachings, regardless of the lineage or sectarian affiliation of the teacher who presents them. Indeed, many of the influential teachers of the non-sectarian movement come from this area. There were more than thirty major monasteries in Welshul that included both academic colleges for the study of the Buddhist canon, and meditation centers where students and disciples conducted extended meditation retreats. Among these are some of the most important non-sectarian monasteries, including Awo Sera.

There are both farming communities and nomadic herders in Welshül, but the nomads seem to outnumber the farmers. However, some people, especially the elders, stick by the old saying that "Welshul has 10,000 nomads living in black yak hair tents and 10,000 farmers living in houses with wooden doors." It is hard to say. We Tibetans never intrude on people to make an accurate census, and the census by the occupation forces tends to be transparent, self-serving propaganda devoid of much in the way of validity.

In the old Tibetan system, before the occupation, I heard that Welshul was organized into eighteen cantons. Each canton had twenty-five boroughs, and each borough had thirty constituencies. Each of these units had its own leader, and each leader answered to the leader of the next higher unit such that the leaders of each constituency reported to the leader of the borough, and each borough leader reported to the head of the canton, and each canton leader answered to the ruler or head administrator of Welshül.

Thinking back to the time when I was first recognized as a tulku, I recall having little anticipation of all of the complications involved in accepting such a high status in my society. Perhaps I had some intuitive sense of what it would be like. My childhood friends, fellow devotees of our local lamas, would tease me. "Oh, we are so impressed!" they would say:

> You are now an illustrious tulku. Abandoning us lower life forms, you will rise to a monastic throne of opulence and privilege at the head of the grand monastery. No more simple monks' food for you! You will now find only the finest of victuals on your plate, and the loveliest of libations in your cup. You will now be worshiped by both men and gods, who will compete for your favor with gifts of magnificence and will serve you as devoted servants and groveling toadies. Such wonders as these and much more will give you a life of continuous glory. How lucky you are! How immense is your store of merit!

Knowing that they were exaggerating a bit for good effect, I would tease them in return:

> Oh, it is you guys who are truly favored by fortune! Never will you have to sit at the head of the monastic hall, surrounded by the strict and austere elders who think you are something special, and who will not tolerate even the slightest lapse in demeanor or protocol. Never will you have the burden being seen as the ultimate source of wisdom, validation, reassurance and consolation by every villager, farmer or nomad in the country who has a worry or experiences a loss. No, you guys have no such onerous burdens. You are as free as the mice of the fields, wandering this way and that according to your own whim, sporting in the long grasses of the valleys and playing among the colorful flowers of the fields. Indeed, you have the joys and pleasures of your childhood to enjoy without restriction or restraint. How lucky you are! How vast is your store of merit!

We would joke in this way, but there was truth on both sides. I did get the nice food and the favors of many, but the price was daunting. How many times I sat there at the head of the monastic hall, fearing to fidget on my high throne although hour crawled slowly after wearisome hour. How I envied at those times the ordinary young monks of my same age, who would swarm this way and that around their seats, poke and chase one another for fun, doodle at their desks, and play in the courtyard during breaks and recesses like any child filled with energy and blessed by freedom. Some would sneak into Darlag Dzong, the nearby town, for entertainment and diversion,

8. Enthronement on the Monastic Seat of My Former Lives

Sogan Rinpoche's nomadic life in Golok—1988

knowing that getting caught would bring nothing but a wag of the finger or a light slap on the wrist from the elders. But should I take even ten steps in the direction of the town, it would be a huge scandal not soon to be forgotten.

In concluding this chapter, it may be noted that in Tibet there are different protocols for determining that a particular child is the bona fide rebirth of a particular lama, as each rebirth situation is somewhat unique. However, according to Tibetan religious standards and cultural tradition, both wise lamas and insightful gods must be consulted to certify the identification.[74] Once the identification has been confirmed in this way, there is a traditional protocol for the child's upbringing and education. As soon as possible after the identification and certification, the young tulku is placed under the care of a spiritual teacher called the "comprehensive tutor" (Tib. *yongs 'dzin*). This tutor is charged with total responsibility for the caretaking, upbringing, academic education, and spiritual guidance of the young tulku. Central to the tutor's task is to transfer to the tulku all the verbal and conceptual knowledge of the former lama that might have been forgotten in the death and rebirth process. He must provide the conditions and training necessary for the tulku to internalize this vast knowledge through analytical study and to fully integrate it through spiritual practices and advanced meditations. Once this process has been satisfactorily completed, the tulku is installed as the head teacher and executive leader of the monastic community and the spiritual guide of the surrounding lay community.

As for my own situation, I experienced this process at a time in history when my beloved homeland is being crushed under the ruthless oppression of the Chinese regime. The traditional religious and cultural practices of our ancient faith have been outlawed and criminalized. They are seen as a threat to the total control and domination of the Chinese Communist Party. However, there is a deeper reality that cannot be destroyed by guns and tortures. Those who are totally immersed in nihilistic thoughts and materialistic activities can never approach the realm of truth.

My predecessors' careers proceeded in an environment of openness and freedom. Their communities rejoiced and celebrated every time they appeared in public, and openly supported every aspect of their progress. Unlike that, my recognition and training had to be carried out under the baleful eye of the occupation. Much secrecy was needed to avoid detection by the agents of the regime. Anything done openly, like my enthronement at Awo Sera Monastery, required advance permission by the Chinese overlords, who allowed it to take place only when they believed they could use it to their advantage. This will become clear as I proceed with my account.

As tragic as the external situation has been, the underlying reality of spiritual truth is not changed. Although I did not receive the benefits of a free society and the open public support enjoyed in my former lives, my internal processes proceeded according to precedent. Due to whatever small merits, I may have accumulated over many eons of death and rebirth, in this life I have been able to be connected with many illustrious beings who are in fact the regents and embodiments of the transcendent Lord Buddha himself. In this manner I have had the good fortune to imbibe teachings and personal precepts that are like the supreme elixir of life that cures all illness and restores vitality to the dead.

9

Blown by the Strong Winds of Circumstance to Remote Mountain Retreats

THE STAGE was now set for me to proceed as the leader of the two monasteries. This seemed at first to be a huge responsibility. It entailed much hard work and diligence that I willingly accepted. However, it soon became clear that I would never possess the real power and authority needed to function as a proper monastic leader, to advance the Dharma and benefit the people. The occupation forces kept all the real power to themselves. The monasteries exist now only at the pleasure of the regime. They allow only an amount of superficial, make-believe autonomy and the freedom to do trivial things. They use the monastic communities for their own purposes of propaganda and social control. As the "master" of the monastery, I was reduced to being just a tool of this rapacious occupation.

My personal desire continued as before. Deep down I wished for nothing more or less than to follow the precepts of Lama Rinpoche that I had studied and practiced over the years when good fortune allowed me sit in his sanctified presence. After some time in this role as putative monastic leader, I found out how very little real authority I had. In place of even one measure of real power, I had a thousand measures of trivial duties. My days and nights were a busy, endless succession of activities and responsibilities that together signified nothing. I was in danger of participating in a phony, sham system that carried out the wishes of the oppressor rather than the advancement of the Buddhist traditions of Tibet and the welfare of its people.

The year of the Fire Dragon (1988) arrived, and with it came the cyclic obstacles of my twenty-fifth year.[75] And so, late in the winter of that year, I made a trip to visit Lama Rinpoche and seek his counsel. "Venerable Lama Rinpoche," I said:

Somehow you looked upon this miserable pile of flesh and bones, and found an inner essence of value and potential. You cared for it and nurtured it with your boundless compassion and your endless wisdom. You opened my eyes to see and distinguish between what must be done and what must be avoided. You bestowed upon me the precepts of the profound view. You taught me both the ways of the world, and the ways of the transcendent. In every way, you treated me like a wise, loving father treats his only son. In a thousand eons I will never be able to return even a small part of the limitless kindness you have shown to me. And now, in this and in all my lives to come I have no other source of refuge or trusted guidance than you. Therefore, please continue to hold me in the embrace of your beneficent regard and guide me closely until the moment when I finally cross the threshold of supreme buddhahood.

I continued:

"As is clearly understood in the clear mirror of your oceanic mind, the situation in which I now find myself requires me to compromise my aspirations, to put on the clothing and face of a true lama, knowing it to be but a false appearance to deceive others. I find myself immersed in the eight worldly concerns, and engaged in endless trivial activities that could exhaust all the time and energy that remain to me in this life. My deep desire is to return to your blessed presence and continue to receive your direct guidance and support in my diligent and single pointed efforts to put your profound precepts into practice. However, I find myself, despite my desires and wishes, to be struggling under the burden of these trivial and exhausting duties and responsibilities imposed upon me by others, and controlled by the enemy of the Dharma and our people. I find that I have come to an impasse and see nothing but obstacles to further spiritual progress if I continue in this manner. Therefore, I believe it would be better if I now go forth for a while, leave behind my home areas, and find a distant, isolated place where I can engage in solitary practice and perhaps accomplish a share of what you have taught me. Please give me your advice in this matter.

Lama Rinpoche smiled in his special way with a smile that filled the entire area with light and my heart with his warmth and confidence. "My dearest son," he said, "it would be best if you do this very thing." He then placed his saintly hands upon my head in an empowering benediction filled with endless good will. Looking into my eyes, he began a short dissertation on the fine points, the practices and protocols, of the solitary mountain retreat. I had engaged in many extended retreats at Lama Rinpoche's hermitage, with his direct guidance and support. But never had I done a retreat by myself in a remote, isolated place. The practical instructions and advice that he now imparted to me would be indispensable to the success of my solitary retreat. I remember him reassuring me, when the topic of obtaining food and such arose, "Do not worry," he said. "In the entire history of Buddhist meditators, since the time of our Teacher Shakyamuni, there is not one single account of a person starving to death when on a solitary meditation retreat."

Lama Rinpoche was concerned about me, as he said that I was a young tulku, fairly presentable in appearance, but with little experience in the ordinary world. He had always advised me and my fellow disciples to cleave to virtuous religious friends. This was certainly an occasion when a good companion could be useful.

Lama Rinpoche had another close disciple who had recently come for advice and blessing. He was the renowned Khenchen Tenzin Zangpo, senior abbot (Tib. *mkhan chen*) of Tarthang Monastery, a branch of Palyul Monastery.[76] He had also, for reasons not dissimilar to my own, decided that he would leave his busy, pressured life as head of a huge monastery and quietly go off on an extended retreat. He had just received Lama Rinpoche's blessings for this endeavor. Therefore, I approached him and suggested that we travel together. He seemed very pleased with this idea. Khenchen was over 60 years old, with many experiences, both good and bad. It was clear that we could be of mutual benefit. What better friend for my journey than this excellent lama. When Lama Rinpoche heard that we were traveling together, he seemed very pleased.

Going on such a retreat required secrecy. For people who are the active leaders of monasteries, every movement they make is scrutinized. The

Chinese overlords are concerned with anything public that might have some impact on their social control, and they are always looking to make use of monastic leaders, especially tulkus like me, for their own purposes. However, they have little interest in the daily activities, the rituals, and meditations of everyday monastic life. They keep strict control over the numbers of monks allowed to reside in any monastery such that a monastery of ten thousand monks under the Chinese has only a few hundred. However, they are not concerned if a monk, even a tulku, goes off to live in an isolated retreat unless they have some specific need for his services. On the other hand, the monks at the monastery would be greatly concerned to see their leader and teacher go away for any extended period. The need for secrecy therefore imposed itself on Khenchen Tenzin Zangpo and me. The fewer people who knew that we were leaving, the fewer obstacles we would face. Although our plans were now set for going away together, we did not set the date for our departure. We both had much to deal with, and of course we would need to determine the most auspicious date for undertaking such a significant journey.

About this time, there was an important event at the Getse Drala Monastery. Khenchen Ngagi Wangpo's rebirth, Sangye Tsering,[77] was to give the initiation of the *Treasury of Precious Termas*.[78] I arranged to travel to and attend this event together with Lama Rinpoche and his entourage. Over a month into this lengthy initiation process, I received some tragic news from my hometown, informing me that my sister had died. It did not report which sister. However, when I finally reached home I learned that it was my beloved younger sister, Phuntsok Dolma. At the age of 18, she had suddenly died. With this tragic news, and with my profound regret over not being able to receive the entire initiation, I took my leave of Lama Rinpoche and began the journey to my family home.

Of all my siblings, four brothers and three sisters, I was closest to Phuntsok Dolma. Although we did not live that many years under the same roof, we had a strong connection and always rejoiced in each other's company. Now suddenly my wonderful sister had departed this world on the treacherous path of the bardo (the intermediate state between death and rebirth). The pain of my grief was immediate and profound. There is a Tibetan proverb that says:

In the time it takes for a person with a serious illness to succumb,
It is possible that one hundred apparently healthy people will die.

My sister's situation illustrates this saying. At the age of 18 she was the very picture of vibrant, youthful beauty and robust health, filled with charm and endowed with many talents. She loved everyone and was loved by all who met her. Now suddenly she departed on an unknown path to another life. Where and when we will meet again is beyond my ability to calculate. In the words of lamas of the past: "Our families are transitory, like the birds in a treetop nest."

Individuals are joined together into a family by the forces of their own karma. In this life my karma brought to me one person, my little sister Phuntsok Dolma, who became as close and as dear to me as my own beating heart. Then, without warning, the implacable Yama Raja, Lord of Death, suddenly came and carried her off.

Among us, the surviving family members, who would be next? Despite her advanced age and infirmity, my grandmother was still with us. She would be next. My beautiful mother, our constant source of strength and comfort, would follow despite her relative youth. Who would be next? Who among our family members would be gone when next I returned home? Perhaps, with my journeys on perilous mountain paths, I would be next. Now my decision to go off to a distant, unknown place and engage in assiduous meditation practice matured into an urgent resolve. My beloved sister in this manner gave me the precious gift of a profound appreciation of the transitory nature of this life, and thus she defeated the mortal enemy of my spiritual progress: procrastination. Engagement in serious meditation practice can never take place where there is complacent attachment to the endless preoccupations of worldly life. With this new understanding of the instability and impermanence of the world, my attachment to it declined. The world in which we live now appeared all the more like the insubstantial appearances in a dream.

Phuntsok Dolma had many positive influences on me. She loved animals, both big and small. She could not tolerate the oppression of any animal, and gradually formed a resolve not to eat their flesh. It is not easy to be a vegetarian in our high and remote land. We have few dietary options, and it seems like we must choose between eating alpine grasses or the flesh of animals that eat alpine grasses. However, those with strong determination and effort can find ways to create adequate diets that excludes the flesh of living beings. Phuntsok Dolma came to me many times saying, "You and I should become vegetarians. With our combined efforts, we can make it work." I admired her compassion for animals and wanted to support her aims. Again and again I would say:

Phuntsok Dolma at age sixteen in 1986

Yes. Let's be vegetarians. We can find a good way to arrange it. I will find enough vegetarian foods as soon as I have the time. However, these days I am always too busy to locate what we can eat. Next time I come home I will bring the foods we need.

I would have done that, but the king of death, Yama Raja, dispatched his agents to fetch my dear sister before I could manage to deliver the necessary grains and vegetables.

After Phuntsok Dolma departed, I resolved to become a vegetarian as soon as possible and to dedicate to her the merit arising from my efforts to protect animals. It took a little time and a lot of dietary experimentation to find a way to abandon all meat eating. I did it gradually, but always with the vow in my heart to become a pure vegetarian. To this day I am grateful to Phuntsok Dolma for inspiring this complete change in my diet and for clearing away many tendencies toward procrastination. In this manner I continue to receive benefits from her and continue to send her the dedicated merits of the good works that she inspired, so that she receives some real benefit in whatever life she is now experiencing.

As a memorial to my little sister Phuntsok Dolma I composed on this occasion a wistful song of fond remembrance:

> In the beginning, at the time of her birth,
> My mother and father were full of joy,
> Our family's happiness and rejoicing,
> Rivaled the gods of the empyrean.

> Later, I met with a true lama,
> Devoted myself in body, speech, and mind,
> Learned from him the profound secrets of the Dharma,
> Shared it with little sister and practiced it together.

> In the end, my little sister, a delicate flower,
> Was crushed by the hailstorm of impermanence,
> And I am left like a young honey bee,
> Suffering the illness of a terrible misery.

> O implacable agents of Yama,
> The merciless lord of death,
> You have absconded with my dear little sister,
> To what unknown place have you taken her?

> She had no physical ailments,
> Nor mental difficulties,
> She was always healthy and happy,
> Why then did you carry her off to your realm of dark shadows?

> O dear little sister, mirror of my soul,
> You are transiting through the bardo with no guide or protector,
> Do not give in to fear or despair, there is no need to worry,
> Take heart and listen well to the words of your big brother.

Dreams and Truths from the Ocean of Mind

Long have you heard accounts of the terrors of the bardo,
Now you are experiencing them all right in front of you,
Don't be deceived by these appearances!
Know these to be only the projections of your own hopes and fears.

Free yourself now from all concern with what you left behind,
Do not cling to thoughts of mother, father, family, and friends,
You know the inexorable truth of impermanence,
Do not let your mind be troubled.

Though you see menacing apparitions and hear their horrific screams,
Do not fear them, though they threaten you with terrible violence,
Pay no attention to them!
They are just the nightmarish workings of your own mind.

Instead, focus on the precepts and teachings of your lamas,
Do not follow the white lights of fear nor the red lights of desire,
No matter how deep the precipices that open up in front of you, do not
    worry, do not fear, do not panic,
Think instead of the wonders that await you in the pure land.

Pay close attention to these words of your brother's song,
Let not your mind wander,
Let faith and confidence grow strong in your heart,
Help and support will quickly arrive.

O ye Gods! Gods of truth, gods of compassion,
Protectors of all beings, large and small,
O my kind and generous root lama,
Please guide my dear little sister to the pure land of bliss!

O Avalokita, Holder of the Lotus, exalted god of enlightenment,
Perfect form of the compassion of all buddhas,
With the resonant sounds of the six-syllable mantra,
Guide my little sister on the wondrous path to bliss.

Mañjushri, Hero of Enlightenment, supreme holder of the wisdom
    of all buddhas,

Who protects and guides all beings with your limitless wisdom,
Clear away the darkness, dispel the frightful apparitions,
And guide my dear sister on the path to perfect bliss.

O Vajrapani, wrathful holder of the secret treasures of the
    Buddha's mind,
Clear away all obstacles, impediments, and difficulties from the path,
So that my dear little sister proceeds directly,
To the attainment of ultimate bliss.

O all you Buddhas of the ten directions of the universe,
O sublime Dharma in all your forms and aspects,
O Sangha of enlightened followers of the lord buddhas,
Please guide my little sister on the true path to bliss.

O my dear little sister, from now on, in this human life,
You and I will not be meeting together in our familiar places,
However, I pray we will have a happy reunion in the future,
As we gather together in the Land of Bliss before the throne of Amitābha.

The days after Phuntsok Dolma's death passed with ceremonies and prayers by monks and lamas and tearful visits by friends and extended family. Finally, the forty-ninth day arrived, and the ceremony of final departure[79] took place. After all the monks, lamas, friends, and relatives left the house, only the immediate family remained. The house was so quiet. Now the reality of our dear Phuntsok Dolma's departure weighed upon us maybe a little more like a dense and dark cloud, rather than the sharp pain and agony that had afflicted us for most of the last seven weeks. The house was so quiet. Occasional sobs from one or another of us could still be heard.

One evening after the final ceremony we were all sitting around after dinner: my grandmother Dzamlo, weighed down by her eighty some years, my kindly father and my loving mother, and the others of our immediate family, all survivors of the passing of my little sister. They looked to me now, in the wake of this tragic loss, for some consolation, some way to understand it, to deal with it, and to go on with our lives. So I read to them a text by Dza Patrul Rinpoche entitled *The Tale of a Youth Who Learns Wisdom*, which teaches, in the form of a charming story, the truth of the transitory nature of the world.[80] I then explained other helpful concepts of the Dharma including the concept of the four endings.[81] Following their interest, and adjusting to their needs and states of mind, I found much in the sacred lessons I had learned that brought them a measure of comfort and strength. Then, I added to the words of condolence and instruction certain subtle hints or suggestions that I myself might not be around so much longer, not because of obstacles like the death of my dear sister, but because of the need to relocate in order to continue my spiritual training. The hints were couched in ambiguous language because a direct statement such as "Now I am now going to leave this land and move far away" would be certain to arouse alarm and opposition among my family members, friends, and monasteries. They would never agree to it. On the other hand, if I would just pick up and secretly abscond with not the slightest indication or suggestion, that would be unseemly.

And so, the very next morning I arose early and packed my bag. I did not pack much, just a little bag as would be expected for a short trip. I carefully folded some nice paper around a lock of my late sister's hair and placed it carefully in my bag. Then I departed, saying only that I was going to my Bayan Monastery. While it was true that I was going to Bayan Monastery, the implication that I would stay there was completely false. It was clear that they had little or no idea of the plan that I was now putting into action.

However, as I sat there on my horse, ready to depart, my mother rushed out. Grabbing my horse's reins, she looked up at me with a smiling face, but with pleading look in her eyes, "Dear son, do not be gone long. Please come home soon." She repeated these words several times, making sure that I understood that they were not merely pleasant words of parting, but a sincere and even urgent request. I felt bad before she did this, what with my subterfuge about just going to the monastery at Bayan, and of course with the continuing burden of my sister's death still weighing so heavily on my mother. But now her plea for my swift return brought up waves of strong emotions, none of them pleasant.

As I left our house and rode off on the first stage of my odyssey, my mother's face, her smile, the look in her eyes, and the pleading in her voice echoed over and over in my ears and resonated deep within my heart, a siren song calling me back to the comforts of home, family and all that was dear and familiar. And then there was the guilt. My second mother, who raised me from the moment of my birth alongside of my mother, and with no less caring and fondness, was my dear grandmother, Dzamlo. She was pressed low by the weight of her many years, and if I carried through with the plan to complete a major solitary retreat, there was little chance that I would see her again.

But the real guilt that now caused me to nearly turn around and abandon my quest came from thoughts of the burden of sadness in store for my family when they realized that the purpose of my trip was a long solitary retreat far, far away, and that my return was uncertain and would doubtlessly be at least several years in the future.

On the other hand, I had made a commitment with Lama Rinpoche to go on this retreat. I had now heard the news that Khenpo Tenzin Zangpo had just departed on the trail from his monastery. If I was to have such a rare and exemplary companion as him on my journey to the west, there was no time to waste. I would have to hurry to arrive at the appointed time and place that Khenpo and I had agreed upon.

Another consideration, of course, was the purpose for which I was going forth. If I am able to reach my destination, I reckoned, and if I am able to complete the practices of this solitary retreat in accordance with the Buddhist way, there is no question that significant benefit will come from it. This benefit will most probably reach a multitude of living beings both near and far off as well as have a very positive influence on me. With all of this in mind, I hitched up my resolve, abandoned all thoughts of breaking my commitment, and urged my horse forward on the long trail to the west.

Along the way, I made a quick stop at Bayan Monastery. I paid my respects and offered my salutations to the Lord Buddha and the many attendant deities residing there. I prayed before them for help, support, and protection in my attempts to accomplish my virtuous aims and fulfill my wholesome aspirations. Speaking quietly to my closest Dharma friends and associates, I gave some covert indications that my present journey was not the usual one of shuttling between my monasteries, Lama Rinpoche's hermitage, and my family home. These covert indications were things like the way I looked at a person or spoke as I said "goodbye." In some cases, in a moment of apparent levity, I would say something like, "this time my little trip will indeed be a great odyssey." My intent was that the indication would not be enough to arouse suspicion, and certainly would not be sufficient to inform, but that when the person later learned that I was far away on an extended retreat, he would think, "Oh! That's what he meant by that odd glance, expression, or joke. I should have known." Of all the people that received these hidden clues, only my father took it seriously and had a good sense that my journey would be quite extended.

Saying nothing would have been disingenuous. Telling a lie would be a violation of my basic obligations as a Buddhist. However, I could not speak the full truth, or even give a clear hint that I am on a long journey to obtain the secrets of the Buddha available only to those whose practice is undistracted, assiduous, and protracted. If I would do so, it would give rise to innumerable obstacles and problems that would hold me back and put an end to my quest.

As the eldest son in my family, and as head of two monasteries, my private and official duties were without end. Shuttling back and forth, I would accomplish much trivial activity, but would have virtually no chance to accomplish the meditations and activate the treasures of the Dharma bequeathed to me by Lama Rinpoche. In my role as a lama, I would remain an empty vessel senselessly trying to fill other empty vessels. To help others, I knew I must go far away, to an isolated and sacred place of meditation and endeavor to fill my emptiness with the sublime nectar of accomplishment. Only then could I find ways to guide and liberate living beings.

As I mounted my horse and took the first steps down the trail from the monastery, I saw my good Dharma friend Lopel walking toward the trail from the monastery's mountain spring. He was carrying on his shoulders a beam with a large vessel filled to the top with drinking water on each side. Knowing something of how to read signs and portents, this sight filled me with a sense of pleasure and relief. At key times, like the moment of setting out on a long journey, the signs that appear have profound meaning and can say much about the success or failure of an endeavor if one is able to read them. Had I seen Lopel or anyone else at this moment carrying an empty vessel, it would have cast doubt on the entire project. Reading signs and portents like this is tricky. One cannot be too literal or too interpretive. There is a strong element of intuition and subtle connectedness with one's physical and spiritual environment that is needed. If one has such skills, the reading of signs and portents can sometimes be remarkably accurate.

Now, like a wild animal who has just managed to escape from a snare or trap, I absconded with all possible haste. I crossed the Machu at the base of Bayan Mountain and entered the town of Darlag Dzong where I could seek transportation to the west. But it was not to be so simple. My dear father had indeed seen through my covert indications. He had read the signs and was convinced that I was going somewhere, somehow, that was not on the usual agenda. After I had taken leave of our family home, my father's suspicions had congealed into conviction. He saddled his horse and followed me, a few hours behind. When he arrived at Bayan Monastery, he was told of my brief, cryptic visit. Now he sounded the alarm. Everyone now set out to find me, not knowing exactly what my plans were but fairly certain that it could indicate an extended and unwanted separation. Monks and friends of the monastery spread out through the town searching for me everywhere and informing every one of the need to find me.

Snow began to fall, at first just a little. It gradually turned into a major storm. I took shelter in the home of one of my local friends. As luck would have it, two of the monks from my monastery were also staying there. They were surprised to see me and dismayed when they learned that I was leaving the area on an extended trip. With eyes filled with tears, they were at a loss to know what to do. They desperately wanted me to stay at the monastery but would never disobey a direct request from me. I told them that I needed their help. I explained exactly why I was going forth on my journey, how it could benefit many beings, how unfortunate it would be if I was turned back, and how my virtuous aims could not be fulfilled in the pressured situation in which I had been placed.

So, I posted them at the door of the house, tears and all, with instructions to turn away any inquiries about the location of Sogan Rinpoche. Their loyalty to me overcame their desire for me to stay and their commitment to speaking only the truth. They turned away inquiries, denied any knowledge of my whereabouts, and gave me the time I needed to go forth on the journey.

On the morning of my third day in town, I finally found a large truck hauling cargo to the west. It was on this truck that I finally broke the powerful bonds of attachment that had kept me close to my homeland for so long and prevented me from going off alone to the distant, isolated place where my purpose could be fulfilled.

This journey to the west, of course, was not a sudden decision; it was long planned and carefully calculated. However, there is a crucial distinction between the mental processes of deciding and planning and the physical process of actually getting up and doing what needs to be done to carry out that decision and accomplish the plans. Without the decision and plans, there is no accomplishment of the goal. But without getting up and doing what needs to be done, the best decisions and plans come to nothing. Lama Rinpoche would always tell us:

> There is no satisfaction in just possessing food: you have to eat it. There is no point in just possessing clothes: you have to wear them. Likewise, there is no fulfillment in just obtaining the profound precepts of the Dzogchen: you have to put them into practice.

"Therefore," he said:

> If you are able to take up the single-minded, one-pointed practice of these precepts in an isolated place, you will make daily progress if you are the best type of practitioner; monthly progress if you are a middling practitioner; and yearly progress if you are the lesser type of practitioner.

He also advised that although progress and improvement always comes when one makes proper effort, little or no progress occurs with inconsistent on-and-off practice. That is like a small bird drinking from a puddle, taking a drop of water in her beak, raising up her head, drinking, then going back to the puddle. "Don't be like the little bird," he taught, "but go into your meditation and drink deeply and continually from the sublime Dzogchen precepts until you have taken them all in and fully integrated them in direct experience and profound realization."

Lama Rinpoche also said:

> Having been introduced to the direct experience and profound realization of the nature of your mind, you must then develop and expand that experiential realization in protracted meditation. If you do not do that, you will never be able to fully integrate and internalize your realization, and therefore you will be unable to put an end to the states of confusion that are the very root of samsara. So long as that fundamental ignorance remains, attachment, aversion, and delusion will continually arise and frustrate you, and the precious opportunity you have obtained in this life as a fully qualified human[82] will be lost. If this happens you will have made a vanity of all your innate gifts and assiduous efforts.

Lama Rinpoche continually bestowed this kind of precept for practice upon me and all of his spiritual children, showing us with love, generosity, and precision the best way to follow our own individual paths to the ultimate goal. However, I bitterly regretted the fact that I had become a slave to so many petty duties, meaningless responsibilities, and senseless distractions. Because of that, the good results and substantial achievements that arise from putting all of Lama Rinpoche's profound precepts into practice remained like a flower garden in the sky: a mere daydream with no roots or benefits on earth. It was this bitter regret that now sealed my decision to cut all attachments and proceed apace on my journey.

9. Blown by the Strong Winds of Circumstance

Sogan Rinpoche traveling in Golok with his favorite horse—1988

Up to this point in my life, wherever I traveled it was always with the planning, support, and usually the company of relatives, friends, teachers, patrons, attendants, or other companions. Now I went forth on my own, following an unfamiliar path through a strange land to an unknown destination. A peculiar sensibility imposed itself on my mind. It was the interplay of this sense of strangeness with a sense of sublime adventure. I was now on a journey in the footsteps of a hundred generations of Buddhist yogins who took to heart the perfect example of the Lord Buddha himself, abandoning home and comfort in order to pursue the transcendent with single pointed devotion. It was a daunting task, but to have succeeded in actually taking it up was a wonderful thing. I was filled with a deep sense of happiness.

As I continued down the long road, a song arose in my heart. It was a song of aspiration and dedication. As I walked on in the direction of the setting sun, I sang this song:[83]

> Little sister, ever a piece of my innermost heart,
> Little sister, gone off all alone on a journey through the bardo,
> Little sister, I too have now gone off alone,
> To a golden place of sublime isolation.

The two of us, loving brother and little sister,
Though in this life we meet no more,
But in our future lives, I pray,
We will always find each other along the path of the bodhisattvas.

Although we never had the slightest desire
To separate from our dear homeland, parents, siblings, and friends,
However, devoted to the accomplishment of the pure divine Dharma,
Staying together has just not been possible.

So now, from this moment on,
I go forth, without benefit of friend or companion,
Knowing that the Lama, the Three Sublime Jewels,
And the guardians of the Dharma,
Will always be our refuge and protectors: on this we may always rely.

I recorded this poem, together with other thoughts, impressions, and re-cords in the little journal I always kept nearby. This journal allowed me to keep track of my comings and goings and the people I met on the way. It was valuable for recording my inner thoughts and poetic compositions, especial-ly during my extended retreats as described below. The journal was written on pieces of paper and small notebooks organized into a growing volume that I was able to keep with me during my travels and still possess today.

After three days I reached Nangchen County in Kham. Soon I arrived at the gates of a big monastery of the Drikung Kagyu lineage known as Jang-chub Chöling, the monastery of Garchen Rinpoche, the monk who was my fellow disciple at Lama Rinpoche's hermitage as related above. This was the appointed place and time set for joining up with my traveling companion, Khenpo Tenzin Zangpo.

10

My Journey to the West—
Lhasa and Beyond

NOW I joined with Khenpo Tenzin Zangpo. Here at this monastery we met with some of Lama Rinpoche's main disciples, such as Garchen Rinpoche, as well as many other people of my home area who were also Lama Rinpoche's disciples and devotees. Many had come to Lama Rinpoche after my years with him, and even if we had not met before, they knew of me and were eager to help. When they learned that Khenpo Tenzin Zangpo and I were headed west to the Lhasa area to enter an extended retreat, they quickly produced every requisite for our journey as well as our retreats, including food, money, and everything we could possibly use. We had both left our home monasteries without advertising our intentions by packing our bags for a long trip. Therefore, we gratefully accepted all that was offered, at least up to our capacity to carry them.

At this point we were joined by a number of our friends and patrons. They saw this as a good opportunity to make a pilgrimage to Lhasa. Traveling with a venerated senior lama like Khenpo Tenzin Zangpo and a well-known tulku such as me is a real advantage for a devout pilgrim, as the faithful open their doors wherever we go and greet us with warm and generous hospitality.

We took the southern route to the west, which goes through Lho-rong and approaches Lhasa from the southeast province of Kongpo. As we approached the outer perimeter of the greater Lhasa area, we reached the ancient fort of Taktse Dzong (Fort Tiger Peak). There we encounter a large roadblock. Chinese soldiers were massed with their guns, trucks, and tanks. They told us that entry into Lhasa was forbidden for an indefinite period of time. They did not tell us any reason for the blockade, and we had no way of knowing. However, the reason later became clear. This was early October of 1989. In far off Norway, His Holiness the Fourteenth Dalai Lama of Tibet was soon to be celebrated as the recipient of Nobel Peace Prize.

Lhasa is a special place. It is the historical capital city of Tibet. It was the center of both Buddhist culture and the Tibetan government. It was the royal seat of each of the successive Dharma kings of Tibet. In the seventh century, in the year 637, the Dharma King Songtsen Gampo (circa 617–650) first built the Tsuklag Khang, the Temple of Magical Emanations of Rasa. It was filled completely with sacred embodiments of the body, speech, and omniscient mind of the Lord Buddha that bestow liberation upon seeing. These include the two principal objects of worship, the Jowo Rinpoche and the Sublime Avalokiteshvara, brought respectively from China and Nepal for the glorification of Buddhism in the Land of Snows.[84]

The Mighty Orgyenpa (i.e., Padmasambhava) prophesied that a wondrous temple of the Enlightened One would rise upon the top of Red Mountain. When the time of the prophecy had come, a magical abode of gods was built upon that mountain. It is called the Potala. Within it the Lord of Limitless Compassion, Avalokiteshvara, has repeatedly taken humanlike forms, and as King Songtsen Gampo and the Dalai Lamas he has unified sacred and secular authority and guided the affairs of Tibet.

Although archeologists trace a unique Tibetan culture on the vast Tibetan plateau back at least thirty-five thousand years, written history goes back only about 2,000 years. Under the Dharma Kings of ancient times, all the way through to the early years of His Holiness the Fourteenth Dalai Lama, Tibet was a place of peace and prosperity. It was a country whose natural boundaries of high mountain ranges prevented foreign armies from invading and allowed the continuous sovereignty of a peaceful, deeply religious people. Never, until the last half of the twentieth century, did a foreign army ever occupy Tibet, nor did a foreign ruler ever impose his will. The center of Tibet's culture, religion, and sovereign power was Lhasa. Lhasa has always been the crown jewel of this land of snowy peaks and verdant valleys. It was always famed as the wondrous, perfect "heavenly realm of Lhasa", and was commonly referred to by expressions such as the "Second Heavenly Realm".

Sadly, things have changed. All of these ancient glories of Lhasa, all of its subtle powers and sublime features, are no more. They have been taken away, leaving no more of a trace than the fond memories of its past glories. Lhasa, the unique capital of the unique country of Tibet, the center of its singular culture of deep faith in the Buddhist values of limitless kindness, compassion, and wisdom, has had its ancient Buddhist culture cut out and cauterized by the merciless fires of foreign military oppression. Now crushed under the heavy boot of the Chinese regime, there is no freedom. The treasure of the Tibetan people, the sublime jewel that they ever hold in the depth of their hearts, is their beloved leader and protector, who has been exiled to distant lands by the cruel force of alien invasion. With no connection with, knowledge of, nor interest in the people, culture, and natural environment of Tibet, the forces of the Chinese regime have destroyed our cultural artifacts, burned our libraries, prohibited Tibetan education, and have manufactured a fraudulent history of our country to serve their imperialistic ends. Such a history is unrecognizable to those who are informed about the historical record. For those with no knowledge of history, it creates a harmful and deceitful impression about Tibet and its place in the world.

Walking the streets of Lhasa, the tragedy unfolds. The people fearfully go on their miserable rounds under the harsh and arrogant gaze of the soldiers and police who roam the city with their guns and clubs, ever looking for the upraised head to knock down. Wherever you go, you see that the natural smiles, the songs and prayers, the peace and the happiness of the Tibetan people have been taken from their hearts and minds and replaced with fear and foreboding arising from arbitrary controls, harsh and random sanctions, and the universal denial of their history, their identity, and their dignity.

During the several days we spent in Lhasa, we visited famous places of pilgrimage there, such as the Potala, as well as Drepung, Sera, and Ganden monasteries, to make offerings and prayers. Then we went to the Central Cathedral where we celebrated an extensive Tsok offering for the benefit of the Buddhist teachings and people of Tibet. We did this in front of the huge golden image of Guru Padmasambhava in his form as the Glorious Subjugator of Appearance and Existence (Tib. *snang srid zil gnon).* This marvelous image of the Guru resided in the Jokhang due to the skillful efforts of Amdo Lungtok that arose from the intensity of his commitment to the flourishing of the Buddhist teachings and the welfare of all beings.[85] After the ceremony, our friends from the Lhasa area returned to their homes, and I proceeded, together with Khen Rinpoche and his niece, a Buddhist nun by the name of

Akyi. We traveled to the south toward the sacred places of the Yarlung Valley in order to find a location where we could establish our meditative retreats.

My venerable companion in retreat was Khen Rinpoche, Tenzin Zangpo (1937–93). He was also known to only a few by his secret name, Jigme Trinlay. He was an influential writer whose Dharma books possess much power. That name was given to him when he was confirmed to be the rebirth of the sacred activities (Tib. *'phrin las*) of Rigzin Jigme Lingpa (1729–1798). His rebirth was the fulfillment of an old prophecy. However, most people did not know him as Khen Rinpoche, Tenzin Zangpo, or Jigme Trinlay. They knew him as Gergen Zang (Revered Teacher). Even far away from his monastery of Palyul, he was always recognized as Palyul Gergen Zang. He was venerated as a living treasure by the monastics and lay people of Eastern Tibet. Among Lama Rinpoche's students, he was recognized as one of the greatest. Khen Rinpoche was one of the principal leaders, scholars, and tulkus of Tarthang Monastery.[86] It is difficult to encompass the high stature of Khen Rinpoche in a few words. He was one of the illustrious beings in Tibet. He was universally recognized as being in that very small number of lamas who had fully mastered the Three Codes—the external code of the *Vinaya* (i.e., the code of monastic discipline, laws, and customs of behavior and training), the inner code of the bodhisattva, and the secret code of the tantras, including the ultimate secrets of the Dzogchen. I was continually rejoicing in my good fortune to have the opportunity to engage in a profound and extensive retreat in the company of such a wonderful human being. It could only be the result of some merit that I had acquired in a former life.

Khen Rinpoche had suffered terribly under the Chinese authorities. As one of the most respected and influential leaders in the Tibetan community, he was a prime target after the invasion. He was taken to one of the many "educational work centers" where they somehow hoped to break him and convert him into a follower of their materialist creed. As he was not sufficiently compliant with this plan, he was subjected to constant beatings. He now suffered the lingering results of multiple broken bones that had not been properly set; his body was covered with deep scars; and he had lost all his toes from being deprived of clothing and shoes and forced to stay for days outside on the hard ice. He had internal injuries that left him with chronic disabilities that greatly compromised his health. Our retreat was often interrupted by an urgent need to take Khen Rinpoche into a settlement where he could receive some medical treatment.

Had this precious jewel of sacred knowledge and accomplishment lived a normal lifespan, he would have been able to do so very much to restore the teaching and practice of the Buddha Dharma in Tibet that had suffered such extensive destruction under the invader. Unfortunately, this troubled world lacked the merit for such a fortunate outcome. And so, after completing the retreat, Khen Rinpoche returned to his monastery for just a year or two before his saintly but much tormented human body ceased to function, and he proceeded to leave this world in favor of a seat of honor in the transcendent sphere of supernal peace.

11

Accomplishing a Meditative Retreat in Sacred Places Such as Tsering Jong

ON THE auspicious twenty-eighth day of the eleventh month of the Earth Snake Year on the Tibetan calendar (December 25, 1989), I arrived at the first of the sacred sites in Central Tibet with which I formed a strong spiritual connection. This is a place known as Tsering Jong ("Longevity Valley").[87] Its formal name is The Realm of the Supreme Vehicle Lotus of Clear Light.[88] It is in an area known to those who follow the practices of the *Great Secret*[89] as the Forest of the Trees of Enlightenment.[90] It is renowned among yogins as a perfect place for liberation into the body of light. This area is in the Chonggye region of the Yarlung Valley, in the district of Lokha. Within Chonggye, it is a little way south of the necropolis of Yarlung where the mummified earthly remains and relics of the Dharma King, Songtsen Gampo, are ensconced. Proceeding south from the necropolis, we traveled up the Donkar Valley until we saw some ancient ruins, some newer ruins from the Chinese "Cultural Revolution", and some recent structures made of local materials—rocks, mud, and straw. This is the hermitage of Tsering Jong.

Tsering Jong hermitage is built next to the site of the retreat center built in the eighteenth century by Rigzin Jigme Lingpa, the sublime teacher and writer who was a manifestation of Avalokiteshvara, who brings comfort and repose to the minds of all beings.[91] It was from this place that the Rigzin Jigme Lingpa filled the length and breadth of Tibet with the mighty lion's roar of his incomparable teachings on Dzogchen and other Mahayana teachings and practices. After he left, his embalmed remains were enshrined there in a temple that became the center of an important meditation retreat. However, around 1959 it was looted and reduced to rubble by the Chinese forces. When we arrived there, we found some twenty Buddhist nuns working to reestablish the meditation retreat center. They had managed the construction of several small buildings and were able to offer us simple accommodations. Once they learned who we were and why we had come, they were very hospitable and helped to arrange for our basic needs for our extended retreat there. I was provided with a small but very adequate room, ideal for my purposes. Khen Rinpoche was given a similar room at the other end of the compound, and his niece was offered neighboring accommodations so that she could look after him.

Khen Rinpoche, having extensive experience in this type of long retreat, laid out the parameters. We would conduct our retreats separately in our respective areas. We would set the boundaries of our retreat areas and remain oath-bound to stay within those areas for the entire retreat, with the sole exception of the second day of the (Tibetan) month. Only on that day could we go out of our retreat area. Only on that day could we speak, meet with, or interact with any person. These oath-bound restrictions established the boundaries and parameters that made this into a proper retreat. They were like iron walls that could not be penetrated for any purpose. Sickness, even the onset of mortal illness, would not be sufficient reason to violate the set boundaries of the retreat.

At the retreat, Khen Rinpoche and I had to post notices before we began our meditations in order to ward off well-meaning but unwanted guests, while attracting certain beneficial attention. At the outer door of our respective quarters, we posted signs that read as follows:

ADVISORY TO THE PEOPLE

The humble resident of this house is in a restricted retreat. Until the retreat has been completed, this resident has taken a sacred vow not to speak, greet, or otherwise interact with any person with the sole exception of the second day of each month. We trust that you understand the importance of observing this protocol and that you will not place any obstacles in the way of its full and proper observance.

ADVISORY TO THE GODS

To the Lamas, the Three Jewels, and all Dharma Guardians, including Eka-jaṭī, Tsering Ma and her Four Sisters, Tsangpa, Rahu, Damchen Dorje Lek-pa, and the goddess Remati: I, though a lowly and rather inferior being, have come to this place in order to progress to supreme enlightenment. If I encounter any outer or inner obstacle along the way, please do your best to help me overcome it.

When my time at Tsering Jong was completed, I took these notices with me to my other retreats in Tibet. When I fled to India, the Land of the Noble Ones, I took these notices with me and used them for my retreats in Dharamsala.

In the beginning days of my retreat I felt a bit oppressed by the restrictions. I had never done such a thing before and had various fears and discomforts: How can I manage without my customary accommodations and friends? What if I get sick? What if I die? I realized quickly that the physical constraints and the mental challenges must be faced directly. I would just have to deal with them as they arise. With this attitude, I gradually became accustomed to the situation. The long days of initial discomfort and worry soon gave way to short days of full engagement in the essential work of the retreat. In the beginning, the monthly "free" day, with the opportunity for leaving my little area and actually seeing and talking to Khen Rinpoche and others, seemed always far off, eagerly anticipated and quickly passed. Gradually I stopped looking forward to it, and when it came I was anxious to return to my seat of meditation as soon as possible.

This process brought with it an internal change of attitude toward the retreat. In the beginning it was a heavy challenge. Then there arose within me some realization of my good fortune to be in this ideal place, with an ideal companion, and to be in possession of the most ideal precepts and teachings upon which to meditate. This realization grew within me. It was not an intellectual proposition but a powerful feeling that from that point on never abandoned me. It filled my days with energy and a serene sense of happiness.

My retreat room was on the side of the mountain, just steps from the main temple. The room was small. The little door was on the north side. There was only one tiny window. It was on the east side. The window allowed in a little light, but nothing much could be seen through it. However, this window functioned as my only gauge of time. By the angle of the light I could judge the time of day. Although this was not very precise and needed ongoing recalibration with the procession of the seasons, it served my limited need for chronometric technology. I had a small private courtyard outside my door. It was walled on all sides, so all that could be seen was the sky above and a little of the mountain top. At the far side of the courtyard was the hole that served as my toilet. I could go out to the courtyard but no further except for the one day per month. My meditations were conducted mostly in the courtyard. After a number of months, I noticed that my hands had turned somewhat dark from the sun. A mirror would have probably confirmed that my face was likewise darkened.

My meals consisted of *tsampa* (i.e., toasted barley flour) and bread-like objects contrived with water and flour on my small "stove." The stove was an iron can, about the size and shape of a small waste basket. It had two large holes at the base, on either side, that allowed for air and for the insertion of wood. A pot could be placed on top for boiling water and cooking. The stove was light and easily moved as needed. The tsampa and flour were the only provisions I had brought. The nuns provided me with water and wood. They would refill them from the other side of the wall, pushing them through a hole provided for this purpose. There was never any interaction or communication between us.

The room and courtyard were built above an apartment that was occupied by a small family. The grandmother, Kyizom, was about sixty-five. Sometimes extra food or drink would appear in the hole at the base of my courtyard wall. A container of milk, a cup of tea, some warm biscuits or other food would appear. I accepted it without knowing its origin. On one monthly excursion out of my quarters, I encountered Kyizom and ascertained that she was my benefactor. She asked if she could bring me hot tea each morning. I asked her if she recited the mani (i.e., the six-syllable mantra of Avalokita: Oṃ Maṇi Padme Hūṃ). She said that she was so busy with the house and her children and grandchildren that it was difficult to find time for such spiritual pursuits. I told her that I would gratefully accept the offer of morning tea, but only if she would take up the practice of reciting the mani. From then on, I always had tea in the morning and could occasionally hear her recitation of the mantra. She would occasionally leave me other treats from her kitchen.

When I left this retreat some two years later, Kyizom tearfully said her goodbyes. I assured her that I would keep in touch. However, shortly after this she had to leave the retreat compound. The nuns had announced their support of His Holiness the Dalai Lama and of a free Tibet, and were all taken off for "re-education" in the prison camp. Nearly twenty years passed before I was able to hear any news of Kyizom. In 2009 I was in Colorado and chanced to hear of a Tibetan family from Tsering Jong. When I heard that name, I hastened to look them up. There was a woman of about thirty years who said that she remembered me. She had been a young nun at the monastery, about eight or nine years old at the time. She knew Kyizom and her family. Through her I was able to reunite with Kyizom on the phone, and to send her greetings and gifts. I arranged for my brother Guru to travel to her house and take her on a pilgrimage to Lhasa. She had always wanted to go there but was too busy in her earlier years and now, at the age of 85, too infirm. On the phone, she said that she wished to go but could not walk more than a few steps. I had Guru buy her a wheelchair. He took her and the wheelchair in his car and drove her to Lhasa. There they were able to worship in the sacred places of the holy city.

When we enter an extended retreat like this, we make sure that we have sufficient *tsampa*, but otherwise do not provide ourselves with any variety of comestible provisions. We do not eat after the noon meal. Limiting intake to two such simple meals per day leads to a gradual loss of excess weight or to what some might characterize as a state of near emaciation. In addition, we have nothing to support much in the way of personal hygiene, grooming, or physical exercise; the hair on our head and face, as well as our nails, grow without restriction. Altogether, we come out looking rather frightful.

As the door of my retreat house was on the north side, not much light found its way inside through this door. Some morning light came in through the small window. There was no such thing as electrical service in this region, and one little candle needed to last many months, and so it would be used only on exceptional occasions. Therefore, the light inside was usually rather murky. In the winter, the cold was fierce and penetrating. There was no source of heat in the room, and the fuel for the little stove was adequate only for heating the cooking pot. However, I had a thick maroon monk's cape (Tib. *thul ba*) of alpine sheep's wool. This served me well as clothing, blanket, and cushion. With the dimness of the light inside and the fact that there was little to choose between the cold outside the room and the cold inside, I spent most of my days and nights outside in my little courtyard.

In the beginning, the nights were a bit uncomfortable. In the room there was little in the way of furnishings. Other than the tin can stove and pot, the only other concession to human habitation was a wooden slab, about the size of a small door. It was raised off the floor on blocks, and was covered by a Tibetan rug. This was meant to serve as a bed. Using the monk's cape as a blanket, I could get a little sleep. However, I soon found that my meditation sessions were proceeding to the point where I was entering into states of clarity and tranquility, however briefly. With practice, these states lasted longer and longer. I would arise from them with a serene mind and an invigorated body. While meditating, I kept my back straight and my breathing deep and regular so that all the systems of the body and mind were in harmony and the need for sleep was greatly diminished. After a while I rarely visited the wooden slab except for meal time. The power of the meditation in this way continued to increase.

My main daily recitation was the *Noble Samantabhadra Prayer* (*Āryabhadracārya-praṇidhana-rājā*). I would recite it several times between meditation sessions. In the morning, before beginning the day's meditation sessions, I would recite from the *Nyingtik Preliminary* text[92] of the First Do Drubchen, Jigme Trinlay Özer, with special emphasis on the guru yoga section. I also would recite a guru yoga practice composed by Lama Rinpoche himself.[93] However, this extended retreat did not emphasize recitations or rites. These helped motivate, support, and intellectually frame the main meditation, but the retreat focused on a non-conceptual, non-dual meditation rather than the conceptual tasks of practicing virtue and accumulating merit that are embodied in the recitations. In the main meditation, I worked on the process of relaxing into the calm and clear nature of my own mind. Lama Rinpoche had introduced me to this pure, uncontrived nature. However, I was at this point only a beginner. In the Dzogchen tradition, it is taught that a beginner in this meditation must practice many short meditations rather than trying too hard to remain in the non-dual meditative state for a long time. That helps keep up the quality of the meditative focus. Gradually, with experience, the length of the meditative session can be extended.

However, for us ordinary human beings, all sorts of random thoughts and concerns can disturb the meditative process. Strange thoughts can arise. For example, I remember sitting there soon after the start of the retreat. I had traveled across Tibet seeking an ideal place for a solitary, isolated retreat. Now I was there, all alone, cut off from all types of customary interaction. I thought:

If I die now, no one will know, no one will help. After a number of days, perhaps people in the other areas of the monastery will be notified of my demise only when the foul odors of putrefaction defile the otherwise pristine mountain air.

That was not of much comfort. But I was committed and fully determined to continue the retreat process at any cost. It was not easy. In those early days of the retreat I was mostly able to practice meditation effectively. However, on occasions I really was afraid, sometimes terrified. I felt so alone with no communication or contact, good or bad, with any other living being for an entire month. I was still a young person, barely past my teenage years, and accustomed to being surrounded by friends, teachers, and family. So I called out to my only remaining source of refuge and comfort, my objects of faith. I called out to my lama, to the Buddha, Dharma, and Sangha, and to my guardian deities. "Please," I would say, "I need a little help here." Then I would look at my situation and ask myself:

> Why am I bothering these venerable beings? Am I really in some bad situation that requires outside intervention? Are my living accommodations really that bad? Or is it just a case of a lack of motivation or inadequate preparatory training?

Such reflection would restore my awareness of the true privilege of the present opportunity and with it my confidence and a sense of comfort. Soon all the worries and troubled thoughts evaporated in the warm sunlight of deep meditative states.

The overcoming of the initial discomfort was instructive. What really destroyed those inner demons of doubt and fear was the power of the meditation itself. If I did not have that, I would not have been able to manage. The power of the meditation issued from the glimpse of direct knowledge of the ultimate object of meditation. That is, under the guidance of Lama Rinpoche, replete with his blessings, I had some profound meditative experiences that I knew could be limitlessly expanded in further meditation. That is what drove me to this retreat, and what sustained and empowered me.

I despair for those who would enter such a solitary retreat without this type of preliminary experience. When faced with the existential loneliness of the personal self in the vast isolation of an authentic meditation retreat, where will they turn? Without a grounding in the experience of the ultimate reality of the mind, one remains always reliant on others and must avoid such complete isolation. The successful meditator on a long retreat must have a strong grasp of the ultimate object of the meditation and then proceed to expand that grasp into deeper and deeper levels of realization. This does not happen in a day or two. For the mind to truly change it is said that one must practice in this way for months, even years. At length the flash of insight becomes clear vision, and the clear vision finally becomes one's ordinary reality. Only then are the deep shadows of false views and dualistic perceptions completely dispelled.

For a long time, as mentioned above, I had maintained a daily journal. Now, in the moments between meditative sessions, I continued to record the particular events, thoughts, and impressions I encountered in the retreat. I did not make a point of making an entry every day, especially as the meditations became more profound and I had insufficient leisure, or no adequate words, to record the day's events. Nevertheless, most days found me writing an entry in the journal. Typically, it would be one four-line quatrain (Skt. *śloka*). Each line, in accord with the Sanskrit and Tibetan literary convention, contains the same number of syllables, usually nine syllables. Each quatrain expresses a complete idea and references something in that day's thoughts, insights, feelings, or concerns. It was not directly related to the quatrain of the former day or the next day. This gives the collection of quatrains a somewhat random feel. They began on the first day of the retreat, which was the second day of the twelfth Tibetan month of the Earth Snake Year.[94] The first day's entry is:

Hey Pema! You wandering vagabond,
Terrified by death, you fled to the mountains,
Here you have all the requisites to accomplish the sublime Dharma.
Now you must focus on the essential meaning continuously and without
    distraction.

Here then is a selection of my verses reflecting some of my thoughts as the retreat proceeded:

O Lama, the Three Supreme Ones, and the guardians, consider this:
This low-born vagabond, here on the side of this remote mountain,
Please see to it that obstacles do not arise to my accomplishment of this
    task in accordance with the Dharma.
And allow me the spiritual power to attain the sublime goal that I seek.

Though I sit here on this blissful bed like Amitābha on his throne of
     supernal bliss,
And stabilize my mind on the essential unwavering object,
The maiden of my customary dualistic thought smiles seductively,
And I am helplessly drawn into the dark cave of the five desires.[95]

Here in Tsering Jong, the Valley of Long Life, is found an ideal place for
     spiritual attainment,
Unknown here previously in this life is this vagabond ascetic from Amdo,
Saying that he wishes to cut the bonds of attachment to this life, he has
     entered this retreat and sealed the door,
Who knows what will transpire at the end of his life? Only the lama knows.

Here in this glorious sacred place, in the midst of a high valley forest,
Is one who imbibes with pleasure the glorious precepts of the lama.
He is a joyful vagabond, his mind filled with happiness and free of care.
Who is this person who has left behind all the busyness and strife of the
     world, and now abides in spiritual retreat?

In former times, the exalted patriarch Khyentse Özer[96]
Journeyed to this place, lived here and set in motion the Dharma wheel.
Here he accomplished mighty deeds, including mastering the
Great Secret and attaining liberation in a body of light.[97]
Thinking of this, I realized how incredibly fortunate I am to be here.

Now, however, times have changed in this alpine valley, as it is filled with
     country folk toiling at their agrarian tasks,
Always preoccupied with their worldly pursuits and their games of
     chance.
Thinking of this, waves of sadness wash over me,
And streams of tears flow down from my eyes.

O, Padma Mati,[98]do not wallow in your grief!
All these things are transitory,
Therefore, focus your efforts on quickly accomplishing your task!

Here the fields are filled with wondrous grains that I have not seen
     before.[99]

11. Accomplishing a Meditative Retreat in Sacred Places

Every day they grow higher and stronger as they approach maturity.
I hold in my heart the fervent wish and prayer that in the same way
My own crop of good qualities, my experience and realization, will grow
    and mature.

Oh you poor beggar, desiring always to attain the ways of the sublime,
    heavenly Dharma,
You cherish hopes of perceiving the pure essence of truth,[100]
But have not even managed to cultivate true compassion in your heart.[101]
Your exalted Dharma friends would be ashamed of you.

A small bird yet to fully develop the powers of an accurate view of reality
May desire to traverse the vast space of profound emptiness where there
    is nothing to which he can cling,
But if he stretches out his little wings of limited faith and weak devotion
    in an attempt to fly,
He will just be carried off by the powerful winds of the afflictive mental
    states.

Some time ago, my peerless lama, with his profound kindness, introduced
    me to ultimate reality.
Still, I have thus far been unable to fully grasp and integrate what he has
    shown me;
The bright sun of realization has thereby been obscured by the dark
    clouds of the afflictions (kleśas)!
Oh Lama, come now and bestow the gifts of your powers and blessings on
    one who has lost touch with the essential point of your words.

The tendencies and propensities left by long term habituation to un-
    wholesome ways of thinking are like the coils of a paper scroll:
Although straightened out by new experiences, they can easily revert to
    the old crooked ways when circumstances change.
Erroneous ways of seeing the world cannot be rectified in a short time.
Therefore, Mr. Padma, resolve firmly to meditate for a long time!

As the months proceed and gobble up the year,
The days proceed and devour the month.
The life of a human likewise does not last long,

Soon we shall run headlong into the presence of Yama.

To you, o lama, wisdom holder of the three types of lineage,
This mendicant calls out from the depths of his heart:
Send the radiant light of your powers and blessings
Into the expanse that lies within the center of his heart.

The stygian darkness of this vagabond's mind was momentarily dispelled
By the brilliant lightning flash of the true meaning of renunciation,
    bodhicitta, and the Dzogchen view.
Once that light becomes steady and unremitting,
I will take up the path of liberation and follow it to the end.

Although I keep the constituent collection of elements and aggregates
    that constitute this illusory body
Upright and alert all the time,
The senseless ramblings of my trivial thoughts
Wander aimlessly in the endless fields of the six senses.

Hello there, you solitary meditator, newly arrived in this land.
You sit there, mouth slightly open,[102] spine straight as an arrow,
But keep an eye on your mental posture—is it slouching? Is it distracted?
Is your tendency to cling to a "self" getting weaker or stronger?[103]

O lama who sits here in the guise of practitioner of the Dharma,
With a vow to shun all communication with others,
Where do you get your tea, your water, your firewood? Is it not from these
    other people?
Is this perhaps an onerous imposition on the kindness of these nuns?

O you loathsome wandering vagabond, displaying yourself as some kind
    of a Dharma practitioner,
But not even reciting a single mantra of Tara,[104]
What will you do when the sneak thieves of sickness and death,
Carry away your precious and hard-won human body?

Thinking of yourself as one attending to transcendent wisdom
    (*prajñā pāramitā*),[105]

11. Accomplishing a Meditative Retreat in Sacred Places

You, old fellow with the beard, abandoned your homeland to
    come here.
So what are you doing here, living like a cow in a darkened barn?
Should you not be thinking of ways to benefit living beings, your
    dear mothers of former lives?[106]

Having prepared yourself to abide in solitary retreat in sacred places
    such as Tsari,[107]
You planned to be like a veteran monk, happily embracing austerities
    and hardships such as heat and cold.
So now, if you fail to gain vivid realizations of the profound thought
    and action of the Victorious Buddha,
Then what indeed is the point?

In this area, where the hats, the clothes, and the dialects are different
    from those of my home region,
I have gone into a retreat cut off from the noise and commotion of
    ordinary existence.
If my mind now strays to the endless distractions and confusion of
    the world outside,
I will feel shamed by those whose minds are truly exalted.

O bearded one, are you now like a mountain goat?
Wandering over the high hills and valleys,
Like a Himalayan deer or a Tibetan gazelle?[108]
Don't be like that. Instead, follow the lifestyles of the heroes of the
    past who attained the bodhisattva stages.

Ha, ha, Padma Mati, you itinerate wanderer,
Don't make yourself miserable or forlorn,
But rather gain mastery of the uncreated AH (ཨ),[109]
And you will be singing an eternal song of pure delight!

This precious human life, this ideal spiritual companion (Khenpo),
Are very rare and hard to find, like a seat under the sublime
    bodhi tree.
They have now come together in this isolated mountain retreat by
    the power of my deep aspirations in the past,

Keeping this always in mind, now raise up the glorious banner of spiritual
    victory and accomplish the goals of this and future lives for me and for
    all other beings!

O Padma Mati, wandering mendicant as a practitioner of the Dharma,
If you really desire to follow the path of the Dharma,
Then realize all composite things to be transitory, turn to renunciation,
    and generate the bodhicitta;[110]
These three must precede all other forms and practices of the Dharma.

Listen, young Padma Mati,
Pursue your Dharma practice with unfaltering diligence and enthusiasm;
Then it will gradually improve and increase, like the waxing moon,
And the day will come when it reaches its perfect fullness in complete
    realization and attainment.

This precious human life endowed with the leisure and opportunity
    to accomplish the Dharma that is so very difficult to obtain,
Now half of it is used up, and you have nothing to show for it.
Here you finally have everything you could possibly need.
Think about this, and make urgent and assiduous effort in the
    Dharma.
O bearded one, do you understand?

From beginningless time up to the present moment,
You have constantly wandered in this endless cycle of birth and death,
At this point, whether you accomplish good or evil is entirely in your
    own hand.
As this is the actual situation now, consider it carefully, wrap your mind
    around it, and do the right thing!

Powerful, unruly winds have risen up,
And blown the dusty soil and dry leaves in all directions.[111]
Like that, when the unruly karmic winds of the lord of death
Blow your subtle consciousness here and there, what will you do?

Alas! Your mind is long steeped in afflictive mental states
But has very little practice or experience with their antidotes.[112]

11. Accomplishing a Meditative Retreat in Sacred Places

Considering that, Mr. Padma, do not think you can accomplish the
(Dzogchen) practices quickly,
But steel yourself to cultivate them for a very long time.

By means of the inconceivable kindness of your protector, your
sublime lama,
You have arrived, for a time, at this solitary mountain retreat.
You now have a real opportunity to accomplish genuine Dharma.
Think about this, and rejoice from the bottom of your heart!

You have, this once, managed to obtain this rare and precious
human life endowed with the leisure and opportunity to engage
the Dharma.
If you do not now seize the essence of this sublime Dharma,
Then you are just like the foolish beggar who managed to find his way
to a desert island covered in jewels and gold,
But failed to seize any, and returned home empty handed.

The impermanence of the outer world is shown by the constant change
and instability of all material elements;
The impermanence of the inner world is shown by the constant change
and instability of all living beings in such things as their states of
happiness and misery.
The impermanence of the world is also shown by such things as the
constant change and instability of all impressions, perceptions, and
conceptions that arise in the mind.
Think about this, and you will see how all the world is your venerable
teacher who shows you the transitory nature of all things.

In the cosmic canopy of the sky goddess of the infinite expanse of the
heavenly highway (the sky),
The mighty water-holding lord whose radiance dispels the gloom of
darkness (the moon),
Was suddenly obscured by a cloud of poisonous breath from the mouth
of the villainous Rahu (the lunar eclipse).
At that time the breath from deep inside my body rushed out my mouth,
and I entered into a stable state of Dzogchen perception and remained
there throughout the night.[113]

On this night one year earlier there had also been a lunar eclipse,
My dear young sister Phuntsok Dolma came with me to visit
    Lama Rinpoche.
Thinking of this, (and how she was now gone), a deep sadness arose.

The opulent water mountain of Bayan [114] is one of the beautiful jewels
    of this golden land.
On its slopes my dear brothers (the monks of the monastery) exert
    themselves in the study and practice of the divine Dharma.
My parents, whose love and kindness is deeper than the ocean, and
    all my other dear relatives and friends,
How are they doing? Are they as beautiful, as healthy, as happy as
    before? Such questions often come to me.

The karma of the past and temporal circumstances are like winds that
    blow us here and there.
The karma of the past is what brought me together with my dear parents
    and all my relatives and friends;'
The karma of the past is also the power that caused us to now be so
    far apart.
The karma of the past, however, may be what will bring us back
    together.

Kye! The years—how quickly they pass!
Kye-hoo! Now another one has come and gone!
A tsi! How much time remains for this life?
O-o! The time of death is unknown![115]

Dza! Yama, Lord of death arrives!
Hum! He intones the ominous syllables Hum! Phat!
Bam! My precious body, now an inert mass of filth, is cast away!
Ho! He leads me away! What now?[116]

When the mind is distracted by the appearances and exigencies of
    this world,
It has no interest in the world to come.
Meanwhile the days of this life fly by like an arrow.
Who knows if you will still be alive later this evening? [117]

11. Accomplishing a Meditative Retreat in Sacred Places

The happy festival that is summertime
Is overthrown by the frosts and chill winds of autumn.
Pleasures and happiness turn sour and become miserable;
Contemplating this truth, we realize how all things are transitory.

The fierce cold of winter
Is vanquished by the warm, dusty winds of spring.
Thus difficulties and obstacles are also transitory things;
Is this truth not also clearly manifest to us all?

O Pema Lodoe![118] The white lotus of your precious life endowed with
    leisure and opportunity is so very fragile!
When it will fall down and turn to dust you cannot know,
Your beard is big, but alas, your intellect is small.
Why waste your time pursuing fame and high status?

O Sherab Gyatso![119] Place the innermost nature of your original
    mind
In the vast expansiveness like endless space!
Then with no need for tedious practices and rituals,
You will soon obtain the precious oceanic jewel.[120]

O Khyider![121] Don't be like an old dog coveting a bone!
You have detached yourself from the busyness and noise of the
    market place.
Now, like a powerful young lion, sharp of tooth and claw,
Leap across the crags and chasms to your ideal mountain retreat.

I have made my procedures very strict, and now my retreat gets better
    and better,
My happy state of mind is now continuous and uninterrupted.
But every day some people are leaving food and offerings by my door,
Fearing the ripening of the karma of these gifts, I have left a note asking
    them to give no more.[122]

If my strength of heart to take up the burden of helping all beings
    increases and flourishes,
I will fulfill my profound wish to bring to the state of perfect liberation

All sentient beings, each of whom has been my own kind mother in a
   past life;
But if I am indeed nothing but a poor beggar, then all of this is nothing
   but an idle wish.

However, His Sublime Holiness, Tenzin Gyatso, the Lord Protector of Tibet,
Has specified me in a prophecy that rose from his unerring wisdom and
   perfect insight,
He has set upon me the immutable seal of authenticity (as a tulku).
If this is valid, then indeed there is hope that a propitious time of true
   benefit to all beings, my old mothers, is at hand.

If indeed I am the rebirth of a venerable Lama as revealed in the
   prophetic words of His Holiness,
Then I must possess some qualities and attributes that distinguish me
   from ordinary people.
Therefore, even though my mind is not yet fully developed, and even
   if I am the least among those possessing the form of a tulku,
I should not be totally unable to effect some real benefit to other
   living beings.

Bad companions, nefarious associates, and mischievous assistants lead
   my mind toward what is wrong and unseemly.
The hopes and aspirations of the living and the dead cannot be fulfilled
   by one who cannot find his own path.[123]
Dharma teachings and initiations by one who has no realization or
   experience in them must be abandoned.
May I reject these kinds of things completely, and spend my life instead
   in the sublime isolation of a retreat like this!

Above me there is no superior to whom I must show respect and
   deference,
Beneath me there are no subordinates or students to whom I must
   provide care and guidance,
Here in this isolated retreat I have only the camaraderie of one virtuous
   companion who upholds the ways of Dharma;
May I now repay the kindness of my sublime teacher by accomplishing
   his teachings!

11. Accomplishing a Meditative Retreat in Sacred Places

A natural mountain cave, not a dwelling built by human effort,
Nettles, edible weeds, roots, and berries, not foods of sin such as meat
and alcohol,
Rags and discarded clothing, whatever is easily found to provide the
necessities of life;
May I go about the world always adhering to this type of yogic lifestyle!

Body in the state of non-discrimination, experiencing comfort and
discomfort as the same,
Speech in the continuous recitation of the sound of profound
emptiness[124],free of the sounds of attachment and discord,[125]
Mind, free of error or distraction, in the ultimate unity of awareness
and emptiness that is the dharmakāya,
May my yoga always be like this—like endless space without any point
of preoccupation![126]

Externally, may I realize all things to lack true existence,
Internally, may I eliminate all modes of erroneous thought by non-grasping,
Secretly, may I abide in the blissful state of mind that unites the
meditative and post-meditative states in perfect union;
By means of the mode of apprehension of the ineffable dharmakāya!

Friends and relatives may increase attachment and resentment in
this life,[127]
Faith offerings of food or drink and valuables given in exchange for
prayers and rituals may propel one to hell in the next life,[128]
Casting them all aside like so much useless spittle,
May I always follow in the footsteps of the venerable masters of
the Kadampa![129]

In regard to the past, there is no need to worry over the decline of
the monastic seat of my former lives (Awo Sera Monastery),
In regard to the future, there is no need to think up plans or make
preparations,
In regard to the present, there is no need to make diligent efforts at
worldly activities that accomplish nothing;
May I always go about in this world without attachment, as free as
the wind!

Rejecting the illusory wealth of the world as trifling and insignificant,

May I make my way in the world as a purveyor of the incorruptible seven
treasures of the Noble Ones,[130]

And may there thus be the good fortune that the fructifying rain of the
profound and extensive Dharma falls down

Upon the fertile fields of the minds of living beings who have been bereft
of the wealth of the sublime Dharma!

In a peaceful abode undisturbed by any noise, deep within a thick forest,

In an opulent mansion consisting of a wide, flat rock in a small cave, just
big enough for one person,

In a place of profound bliss under the cooling rays of the moon of good
fortune,

There may I pass my days doing nothing but cultivating the ability to
bring true benefit to others!

May the perverse way of thinking that cherishes the "self" be
immediately rectified,

Right here within this aggregate of true misery, this body that is a
receptacle of filth and impurity!

May I then soar across the sky on the wings of the non-mistaken view of
reality,

And develop the special skills to cross over the abyss of subject-object
duality!

Without the need of struggling to eliminate all types of dualistic thoughts
and concepts (Skt. *vikalpa*),

Without the need of debates, that just increase doubts and hesitations
about what is and what is not,

May the doors of the treasury of the profound wisdom that arises from
meditation spontaneously spring open,

May the eloquent teachings of the Dharma joyfully flow out without limit
or obstruction!

Perched upon a lofty stone redoubt, high above the cliffs of a jagged
mountain peak overlooking the vast expanses far below,

Feasting on the flesh and drinking the blood of freedom from the mental
afflictions that arise from dualistic perception,

11. Accomplishing a Meditative Retreat in Sacred Places

Soaring high above on the wings of meditation and seeing everything
    near and far off with the eyes of penetrating vision (Tib. *thod rgal*),[131]
May the two of us Himalayan condors, the bird and the man, aid each
    other in our lofty exertions!

On the high slopes of the majestic mountain—the sublime Mt. Kailash,
The fearless snow lion's mighty roar can scare the life force away from
    the multitudes of animals of inferior view,
Likewise the intrepid roar of the sovereign Mahayana view completely
    vanquishes all other viewpoints,
May the splendid snow lion and I range over these mountains together!

In the dense forest where multitudes of blue-green leaves cloak the
    mighty limb and ornament the graceful branch,
May the cuckoo bird, the queen of springtime, and I go together,
Singing sweet songs of sublime experience and profound realization,
That arise unhindered from the direct perception of the ultimate truth
    revealed in the natural order of all things!

On the slopes of a mighty mountain whose radiance is like sapphire,
Be as diligent sentinels guarding against the legions of the five poisons,[132]
Resting happily on the green grasses and sleeping on the cushioning
    leaves,
May the splendid alpine deer be my friends and companions!

The lush grasslands of the Northern Plains are free of human
    habitation,
There, without need of any exertion, the mother awareness of the
    limitless expanse (Tib. *dbyings)* joins in perfect union with the child
    awareness of the mind's own nature,
Calling out across the plains with a song recalling the kindness of my
    lama who has the three types of lineage,
May I frolic together with the handsome white-lipped Tibetan
    wild donkey!

With no attachment or obstruction, the vagabond wind blows free...
    where does it go?
With no fixed aim or goal, the alpine deer roams free...there he goes!

May I be like them, traversing the broad path of the wisdom holders
of old,
Like a celestial yogin who has abandoned all worldly deeds![133]

From this day forward, even at the cost of separating from this matrix
of flesh and bone,
I will never seek to support myself by relying on those who would lead
me to worldly distractions nor by any unseemly mode of livelihood,[134]
May I complete the goals of this life as a poor mendicant in a rustic,
remote region,
Far from any who know me or have any connection with me!

Although the twelve ascetic practices are not easy,[135]
May I adhere to them and thereby rise above the state of a superficial
Dharma practitioner who acts hypocritically and practices just for
show,
May I follow the broad path of virtue free of deceit and insincerity,
And thereby abide in the easy and happy state of mind that always
finds and rectifies one's own errors and shortcomings!

From now until samsara is entirely emptied,
May I always walk in the sublime footsteps of my peerless lama,
And thereby have the good fortune to lead to the state of complete and
perfect liberation,
All beings, my own mothers of past lives who have long protected and
nurtured me with their vast kindness!

If all these prayers and aspirations are fulfilled in accordance with my
wishes,
O, how wonderful! What greater joy could there be than this?
Having bound myself in this retreat to profound meditation on
uncreated, self-existent emptiness,[136]
I now go forth to encompass the ultimate benefit of my mothers, all
sentient beings.

Alas! These sorts of prayers and aspirations are just the work of the
mouth, like the shouted prayers of ordinary people at a smoke
offering.[137]

11. Accomplishing a Meditative Retreat in Sacred Places

Such a focus on words and elegant sayings just increases your
    distraction toward the senseless and the meaningless,
It is time, therefore, to abandon your words and writings, and to
    concentrate in silence.
O Padma Mati of Achak (Tib. *a lcags*),[138] do you understand this?

And so, from that day forward I ceased my daily production of quatrains, seeing such activity as an unwanted and unnecessary means of increasing my ties to the world of ordinary conceptuality with its attendant confusion. I continued to come out of my meditation cell only on the second day of the Tibetan month (i.e., the day after the full moon) to meet with Khenpo Rinpoche and his attendant. We would spend the day deep in conversation on the meditative experiences of the previous month. I would look to Khenpo for clarifications, and he would likewise consult with me. This was a marvelous opportunity for profound Dharma discussions with immediate practical application. It was our monthly celebration of the joy of the Dharma.

One day some people arrived from my hometown in Golok. They were on a pilgrimage to the sacred places in and around Lhasa. The news had reached them that Khenpo Rinpoche and I were on retreat in Tsering Jong and that we met with visitors only on the second day of the month. They came and waited. When I received their news, it was not good. I learned that my paternal grandmother Dzamlo, who raised me like a second mother and who was a precious treasure to me, had now embarked on the fifth path, the final period in the cycle of life and death.[139] This bad news of her passing struck me very hard. I was completely miserable. For the next forty-nine days[140] I engaged in the practice of the transference of consciousness (Tib. *phowa*) for my grandmother during the fourth (and final) meditative session of each day. Together with the *phowa* practice, I exerted myself with assiduous efforts of prayer and aspiration to invoke the powers and blessings of the enlightened ones and the Dharma protectors to free my grandmother from the difficulties and dangers of the bardo.

My grandmother's passing functioned as a strong incentive that stimulated and focused my efforts in the retreat. It increased my determination to detach from worldly involvements, to renounce worldly aims, and to pursue liberation with undivided devotion. It caused the reality of impermanence, of the transitory nature of all composite phenomena,[141] to appear vividly and continually in my mind.

A little over six months had passed since I sealed myself into this retreat. It was the twentieth day of the fifth Tibetan month of the Iron Horse year (i.e., early summer of 1990) and I had just finished the noon meal, which is the last meal of the day for the Buddhist anchorite. I went out the door of my shelter into the courtyard and began my meditation session. At once I felt a singular sense of focus on the goal of liberation whereby any interest I had in the things of this world simply fell away. In this aspect of Dzogchen meditation, the eyes are wide open and look upward at the vast expanse of endless space. As I looked upward in meditation, I remember how the summer sky was brilliantly clear, with the sun shining warmly above. A few fluffy white clouds drifted by in the otherwise clear empty sky. From them came a light warm sprinkling of raindrops that glistened in the bright sunshine. Suddenly there descended from high up in the sky one small bird brilliant with all the colors of the rainbow.[142] He was so perfectly beautiful, it was as if he was painted by a skillful artist. As he perched there directly in front of me, I saw his little eyelids slowly close, from the bottom up, and then open wide. Then, without a trace of fear or hesitation, he commenced to sing a wonderful song. The refrain was something like, "*Triii-oop, Chir-Chir-Chir, Triii-oop, Triii-oop!*"

I spoke to him thus:

Alas! Animals possessing such bodies, how heart-rending!
You are so beautiful, with your colors stunning as a peacock,
Your body and tail swirling with the five colors of the rainbow,
Your throat like a bouquet of white lotus blossoms,

The details of your body and limbs like the work of a divine artist,
Your voice a sweet song that enchants the ear,
But you lack knowledge of what to cultivate and what to avoid,
The opportunity to engage in meaningful dialogue eludes you,

Alas, the sad plight of those who take birth as animals!
Although your delicate feathered body is wondrous in its beauty,
Before long it will end up as a snack for a fierce predator,
Empty by nature, it is transitory, by tonight it may be gone!

No chance is there to explain to you the law of cause and effect,
You lack the good fortune to meditate on the profundities of Dharma,

Why is it that you come here and so confidently stand before me?
What meaning do you intend in your tuneful chirps and lovely chants?
What is the message in your eyes as you look at me so intently?

Having spoken to him in this manner, I reflected deeply on the conditions and circumstances faced by the various types of animals who are all basically in the same situation as this dear bird. There arose unbidden, from the depths of my heart, a fierce and unbearably strong feeling of compassion for them. All these living beings, in all their multitudinous forms and locations, are none other than my own kind mothers of past lives. My deep compassion for them hardened into a powerful resolve: so long as any of them remain in the dark prison of samsara, I shall also remain, and, for their sake, I will never abandon the vast and sublime deeds of the bodhisattva until they all have attained liberation. With these powerful feelings and deep yearnings, my tears could no longer be restrained. As for the young bird, he hopped around a bit and leisurely flew up into the pellucid blue sky.

In general, one enters an extended period during which attachments to the busy affairs and endless noise and activity of the outer world are assiduously cut off, and one focuses exclusively on the internal world in rigorous meditation. However, it is natural in this situation that meditative experiences sometimes reflect various aspects of one's physical constituents and mental processes including a variety of cognitive manifestations and emotions. With regard to these, it is necessary to maintain a mental discipline whereby the mind is undisturbed by hopes and fears, and by judgment, elaboration, and categorization. All such extraneous thoughts, feelings and images are simply allowed to dissolve into the vast space of pure meditative awareness. As it is said in the ancient precepts:[143]

In the fields of summertime,
There is nothing that will not grow;
In the yogin's meditative experience,
There is nothing that will not occur.

In the case of one who is striving to maintain the continuity of a Dzogchen practice, it is necessary to allow all appearances, perceptions and thoughts, be they good or bad, to unravel themselves naturally, and in that way make them a part of the path itself.[144] However, there may be some engagement, some attraction or repulsion, toward the fleeting impressions, appearances, and thoughts that arise in the mind. It is said in the ancient precepts that "these pose a danger to the cultivation of a good crop of meditative accomplishments and realizations." Such precepts I always took very seriously. As we say in Tibetan "I hold them in the palm of my mind."[145]

It is said that the best meditator improves by the day, the middling meditator by the month, and the lesser meditator takes a year to progress. The ideal situation is one where progress in meditative accomplishments and realizations is constant. Like the waxing moon, it continually increases. However, in my own case, I am unable to claim such steady progress or specific meditative accomplishments or realizations with any sense of confidence. Because of my own karma, *kleśa* (mental addictions), and unwholesome thoughts, I found myself under the influence of habitual fixations and attachments to the false appearances of the ordinary world.

On the other hand, with the passage of time spent in this meditation, there was a gradual increase in my inner sense of faith, devotion, and confidence in my lama and in the Dharma, and particularly in the teachings of the Dzogchen lineage. Over and over there arose in my mind the thought: "Oh how marvelous to be here, in this sacred place of meditative retreat where I can fully engage in this wonderful practice." With a lightness of heart and a carefree, serene mind, the days and nights passed by with remarkable speed.

In this manner, and in reliance upon my excellent companion and on my excellent retreat house, I was able to succeed in making some diligent and focused effort in my practice. When I then became a refugee and arrived at my place of exile, I was able to continue my practice under the wise and generous protection of His Holiness the Fourteenth Dalai Lama of Tibet who we Tibetans refer to with honorific terms such as the "the savior of men and gods", "our lord and protector", and "the supreme transcendent one". Under his protection, I had the good fortune to be able to remain in retreat for a number of years. In this way I have gone in this life from place to place, encountering all kinds of situations, and making my way steadily in accordance with tradition. I strive to never separate myself from the virtuous state of mind that arises from continually visualizing my lama and the Three Jewels upon the crown of my head. I try always to pass my days in a relaxed state of mind, endowed with serenity and happiness, neither attached to objects of desire, nor disturbed by objects of fear.

That year (1990), in the last weeks of summer, Khenpo Rinpoche and I made a journey to a place on a high, rugged peak that we could see from Tsering Jong. This was a pilgrimage site known as the Sacred Cemetery Playground.

It is located on a place called Overseer Mountain. In the past, many illustrious beings such as the omniscient Jigme Lingpa left their footprints at this site. It is a wide shelf near the summit set into the mountainside and sheltered from the strong swirling winds of the high Himalaya. From here you look out over a vast panorama in all directions. A few wild animals, such as alpine deer and the Tibetan snowcock,[146] can be seen roaming around. Otherwise there is no one to be seen. Wherever you look, you will see nothing of the busy world of men, no monasteries, no towns, no villages. This is a high rocky mountain that juts up into the sky, above the clouds and surrounding peaks. On the high mountain shelf is the sacred site mentioned by Jigme Lingpa in his eighteenth-century-CE memoir that inspired us to make the difficult journey to this place. Just as he described, there were a number of ancient rock dwellings whose walls were fashioned from carefully crafted stone, and whose roofs were made from panels of the flat black slate found in this area. Here we spent the next two and half months continuing the practices of our meditative retreat. The weather was cold—a biting, penetrating cold. Sometimes snow would blanket the landscape. Our supply of provisions was extremely limited. We certainly had to bear some external suffering at this time. However, the internal world of meditative accomplishment flourished more than ever. In this special place, meditations are vast and crystal clear, and even our dreams were extraordinary.

As it was the words of the omniscient Jigme Lingpa in his memoir that enticed us to come to this marvelous place on Overseer Mountain, I will quote them here:

A Song of Sudden Realization

Namo Guru!
Look upward, and there is the sky of the clear light timeless purity,
The spontaneous, unproduced illumination brighter than the sun and
     clearer than the moon,
Beyond this, there is no view, no meditation, no deeds to be done,
Young man,[147] your mind is freed in the vast expanse of the blue sky above.

Look down, below are the teeming realms of living beings trapped in the
     endless rounds of birth and death,
These are your own dear mothers of your countless former lives who
     suffer every misery in the toils of samsaric existence,

Dreams and Truths from the Ocean of Mind

Seeing all this, unending compassion spontaneously arises in your heart,
Young man, your mind is freed in this vast loving kindness of the sublime
    Dharma.

Look all around, from this lofty perch at this majestic mountain,
Clothed in shimmering garments of snow, rain, and swirling mists,
A beautiful shining palace, mantled with snows, but free of any
    attachments and desires,
Young man, your mind is freed in this exalted space of rock and snow.

With enemies there is aversion and strife, with family and friends there
    is compulsive attachment,
Whether in town or in the monastery such entanglements always arise,
    but now you must release them as soon as they appear in the mind,
This endless busyness is the senseless foolishness of the immature,
Young man, your mind is freed to be happy no matter what happens.

Eating meat, the sinful food, but never taking the life of a fellow being,
Spreading your wings and gracefully soaring on the wind both near and far,
Like the huge vulture who never fears falling no matter how high he soars,
Young man, your mind is freed in the sky of pure view and meditation
    and soars to the ultimate without any fear.

Possessing a virtuous state of mind even though born an animal without
    capacity for deep and complex thought,
The heavenly snowcock has no appetite for foods that entail the suffering
    of others,
She sings her sweet songs in the mountains and eats only grasses and
    sprouts,
Young man, your mind is freed in the ways of the divine snowcock.

Although born a deer because of past karma, he runs and plays across
    hill and meadow,
Swiftly escaping the predations of the shameless hunters,
Happily eating whatever leaf, grass, or berry there is to find,
Young man, your mind is freed in the ways of the musk deer.

Yesterday I saw a corpse chopped and scattered to feed the vultures,

In the mists of the mountains, the meaning of the illusory body of youth
was realized,
Young man, you will have no misery when your mind and your body
separate,
As your mind has been freed in the clear light of the dharmakāya.

Young man, there is no certainty that death will not come to you this
very night,
The heavy deeds of worldly life cause one to fall like a stone to the
infernal lower realms,
But once freed from the endless busyness of the world, the stages of
the sublime path are quickly surmounted,
And your mind is freed in the expanse of uncontrived reality.

There is no need to labor on the path for three countless eons,
The essence of the three sets of vows[148] is fully accomplished in state of
reflexive awareness,[149]
This is the ultimate realization, the realization of the Buddha himself,
Young man, your mind is freed in this clear light of the Dzogchen.

Here in the isolated mountain retreat on the lofty ledges of Overseer
Mountain, the strict regime of my solitary retreat is not disturbed by the
snows nor hindered by the rains.
In states of experience of ecstasy mixed with melancholy,
These verses were spoken by the yogin who has transcended illusion,
Khyentse Özer (Jigme Lingpa).

I have included this blessed *Song of Sudden Realization* by the omniscient
Jigme Lingpa because I believe that just as it inspired me, it may be inspiring
to all who wish to enter an isolated, solitary retreat and will help in their
practices and realizations.

In the future, I would very much like to return to this wondrous place of
pilgrimage. However, at this point it is difficult to imagine when and how I
might get there.

With the approach of winter, we descended from the mountain and began our journey back to Tsering Jong. We returned by a different route
which brought us to the gates of Palri Monastery, the largest of the Nyingma
monasteries in the Chonggye region of the Yarlung Valley, in the district of

Lokha. Palri is one of the three main Nyingma monasteries in Central Tibet. We made a formal visit there, complete with prayers and rituals. Continuing on to Tsering Jong, we arrived at the time of the autumn harvest. Everyone, man and beast alike, was busily engaged in tasks and duties to bring in and prepare the crops. As we passed through the area we encountered the most hospitable reception from the local people who treated us with veneration, devotion, and affection. We received from them an abundance of every provision we could use for our retreat. We then celebrated with the monks, nuns and laypeople an extensive offering feast on the tenth day of the lunar month (Padmasambhava Day).

As soon as the extensive Tsok offering ceremonies were concluded, we re-entered our respective retreat quarters and renewed our exertions as before. Now, be it day or night, our strict retreat practices were maintained without a break or interruption, and all our energies and efforts were concentrated exclusively on advancing our meditative practices.

It is said by the wise, "With sufficient practice, there is nothing at all that does not become easy." As the weeks and months passed in the retreat, all such things as boredom, weariness, and discouragement steadily slipped away leaving my body and mind in a state of exhilaration leavened by a deep sense of inner peace and profound happiness. At night, when the few inhabitants of the area were all asleep, and when the moon was bright enough to provide adequate illumination, I would go out the back of my retreat compound and ascend the rocky slope up toward the summit of the mountain and sit on a flat rock. There I would continue my meditation practices. I found this useful in gaining freedom from some subtle obscurations.

Gradually my need for sleep and for using a bed diminished. I became accustomed to spending the nights, when resting, in the seated, cross-legged position rather than laying down. My doctors now suggest that my occasional back problems have something to do with this pattern of sitting up all night without ever giving my body the chance to completely relax. Otherwise I had no difficulties, and benefited greatly from the kindness of the elderly lady Kyizom who came every day to bring me hot tea and special foods. How could I ever repay her for the effort and generosity of these benevolent acts?

12

Continuing the Retreat in the Crystal Cave of Yarlung and Other Sacred Sites in Yarlung Valley

ON THE fifteenth day (full moon day) of the second Tibetan month of the Iron Horse year (March 30, 1991) we finalized the retreat at Tsering Jong with an extensive tsok (Tib. *tshogs*), spiritual feast offering, prayer ceremony, and dedication of merit. We then set forth to continue our meditative practices at other sites in the Yarlung Valley that were made sacred and powerful by the presence of true yogins of the past. Arriving at these, we would engage in preparation rituals and aspirational prayers, do some of our meditative practices, and then dedicate the merit. There were a number of nearby sacred sites that we visited in this way, staying long enough to complete some brief rituals and meditations. We were determined to quickly reach the Crystal Cave of Yarlung[150] and spend as much time as possible there.

On the eighteenth day of that month (April 2, 1991), we arrived at this remarkable pilgrimage site, the Crystal Cave of Yarlung. It is a place where the meditative accomplishments of powerful yogins are extensively documented, and remain there as a spiritual potency. Entering the sacred space of this cave, I was overwhelmed with a vivid awareness of past times when Guru Rinpoche, a "second Buddha," lived here with his consorts. The accounts of his activities here, as well as those of other highly venerated yogins, are documented in a various biographies and hagiographies. The clear and immediate awareness of all of this affected me deeply as I entered this cave. My eyes filled with tears, and the tears became a torrent that I could not restrain. For a time, my mind was absorbed in a unique state of intense joy mingled with wistful sadness—joy to be in the locus of such powerful spiritual accomplishments and the enduring presence of the blessings and powers of Guru Rinpoche and the other famous yogins, and wistful sadness that these wondrous beings were no longer here in their human form.

The Crystal Cave of Yarlung is one of the three main places of pilgrimage in the Yarlung Valley. In it is a famous sacred treasure, a stone image known as "The master of Oddiyana in his meditation retreat in the Crystal Cave of Yarlung." It was from this cave that the renowned tertön (i.e., Dharma treasure revealer) Orgyen Lingpa (1323–?) promulgated his hagiographical study of the life of Padmasambhava entitled *The Crystal Cave Chronicles of Pema.*[151]

In general, it is necessary to understand the ways whereby the Dharma is accomplished, and the necessity of gaining subtle control of the mind. Without these, there is little value in a mere external practice of traveling to these isolated places. The heroic bodhisattvas who came to these places in the past and achieved success in their meditation practice made special arrangements with the local deities and mountain gods, enlisted their Dharma protectors, and supplicated the lamas and deities of their lineage to support, encourage, and empower any meditator who comes to these places to follow in their footsteps. Because of this, these special places possess unique powers and blessings that facilitate the meditative practices of those who go there to practice. These unique and propitious qualities are something that I have had the good fortune to experience directly.

Having arrived at the Crystal Cave of Yarlung, Khen Rinpoche and his niece set up his retreat in Sharling, the cave of the Mahaguru (i.e., Padmasambhava) on the eastern side of the mountain peak. I established my retreat in Nupling, the cave of Khandro Yeshe Tsogyal (757–817) on the western side of the peak.[152] In my cave, there was a spring that flowed from an opening in the rocks on one side. Other than the soft gurgling sound of the flowing water, there was nothing to be heard. Outside, there was not a single person to be seen in the high alpine landscape, only the occasional soaring eagle or lone Himalayan condor making huge circles in the pellucid sky above the lofty peaks. The vibrant goddess of summertime had just arrived in these high mountains, and she welcomed me with her colorful wildflowers and her opulent green robes covering the alpine meadowlands. The gentle breezes carried the scents of rare and precious medicinal herbs and the perfumes of a hundred kinds of alpine flowers. Every day the grass grew greener and the flowers more colorful. Such a place naturally engenders deep happiness, and spontaneously promotes a mind of clarity and virtue.

One day some unusual thoughts or sensations arose during my meditations. These caused me to temporarily suspend the resolve I made back in Tsering Jong not to write any more entries in my journal during the retreat. This is the first of a series of quatrains I recorded in the journal at that time:

> If impressions of the vajra words of that time long ago have not been
>   effaced,
> In the former part of the eighth month of this year,
> The flight of the feathered one toward Varuna (the West) is close
>   approaching.
> These secret words are held in the heart of Pema (Padmasambhava).

What exactly did this, and all the other such verses mean? I was not altogether certain at this time. Later I came to understand these first four lines to be a sign pointing to my leaving this area south of Lhasa on the fifteenth day of the eighth Tibetan month, and making my way toward the Land of the Noble Ones (India).

On the second day of the fourth Tibetan month we completed our retreat at the Crystal Cave of Yarlung. At the temple, next to Sharling, the cave of the Mahaguru, the resident monks showed us some of the Dharma treasures of the cave, including the skull bowl of a brahmin that is marked by a naturally occurring sacred syllable (not inscribed by human hand). This skull bowl was used by Guru Padmasambhava on the occasion when he drank five hundred pints of beer in one sitting.[153] Also among the treasures we saw was the crown jewel of Yarlha Shampo,[154] and the perfect rock crystal used by Guru Padmasambhava in performing empowerments and initiations. After meeting with these sacred treasures, we performed an extensive tsok offering, a prayer ceremony, and a dedication of merit. We were joined by monks and attendants of the temple and some other pilgrims. I recall the elderly resident monk in charge was called Gyalpo La. There were several monks on a retreat who were staying in small cabins or shelters near the cave, and some nuns and laypeople who had come on pilgrimage. It was with much difficulty that I parted from this very special place, and I was filled with nostalgia as we set out upon the path and journeyed toward our next destination.

On the eighth day of the month we arrived at the site of Zangri Kharmar, the monastery and hermitage of Machik Labdrön.[155] It was from this sacred site that the great adept (Skt. *mahāsiddha* and angel, Skt. *ḍākinī*) Machik Labdrön, promulgated her teaching of *Chöd* (Severance). We had journeyed to this place to continue our retreat, expecting to receive lineage transmissions of *Chöd* and Machik Labdrön's own texts, such as the *Great Exposition of the Machik Doctrine,* and precepts for its practice from the lamas of Zangri Kharmar. However, we received instead instruction from the cosmic teacher known as "impermanence," as the implacable winds of recent events had reduced this famous monastery and pilgrimage site to dust and splinters. There was nothing else remaining. When we enquired of monks in the area, they were only able to point out the place where the abode of Machik Labdrön had once stood. On that site some small shelters of branches and leaves had been erected. In these we resumed our daily four session retreat practices, and added to them the practice of *Chöd*. We spent a full month here, and found it to be meaningful and productive.

One day while we were there, two Chinese military officers from the Copper Mountain prefecture arrived and told us that public displays of religious practices were forbidden in this area. Listening to their instructions, we again felt the weight of oppression descend upon us. There was nothing to do but pack up our few possessions and leave. The people in this area were extremely poor. They lacked adequate resources to live a decent life, and were deprived of the knowledge and opportunity to practice Dharma. This made us very sad, but there was clearly little that we could do at that point to help them. It has been many years since I have been allowed to visit this place, so I do not know if there has been any change in those harsh conditions of oppression.

PART THREE

13

Continuing the Retreat at Chölung and Elsewhere in Ölkha Valley

ON JUNE 17 in the year 1991, being the fifth day of the fifth Tibetan month, we arrived on the sacred ground of Chölung (Tib. *chos lung*) in the valley of Ölkha in Lhokha. This is one of the important places of pilgrimage in Central Tibet as it is where Lord Tsongkhapa accomplished his own retreat. Here we found a wonderful lama in residence. His name was Geshe Chönzay, and he lived there with ten or twelve young monks who he was guiding in the study and practice of the Dharma. He welcomed us warmly, and seemed even grateful for our presence, indicating that it would be of benefit to his disciples to have us engaging in our retreat at this place. He took us first to the retreat cave of one of Lord Tsongkhapa's many illustrious disciples, Tokden Jampel Gyatso (1356–1428). Then he brought us into the sacred precincts where Lord Tsongkhapa had accomplished the accumulation of 100,000 mandala offerings. His stone mandala base was enclosed in a carved wooden enclosure and was partially obscured by the many offerings brought there by pilgrims.

Geshe Chönzay[156] was one of those rare individuals whose scope of insight and erudition encompassed both the verbal teachings and the inner realizations of the Dharma, as well as the complex affairs of Tibet and the world. He embodied the Dharma in such a pure way that he was altogether free of the stains of sectarianism. Gén Chönzay received us poor pilgrims with the open and loving manner of a father welcoming home his beloved sons. When we came to this place, we had nothing in our hands but a monk's staff and nothing in our packs but bags of *tsampa*. Gén Chönzay supplied us with everything we could possibly need to continue our retreat.

The retreat place at Chölung, surrounded by green meadows ornamented by colorful wildflowers, was opulent in its beauty. The mountains here are covered with emerald grasses that spread in all directions down the gentle valleys where they are dotted with the riches of the nomads—sheep, goats, horses, and yaks. Looking out at this lofty bucolic landscape, I was reminded of my own homeland in Golok. As before, we set about establishing the strict boundaries and practices of our isolated retreat. In this we were supported by the people of the area who welcomed us with kindness, and made certain that we lacked for nothing that was needed for our practices. The time of the summer retreat arrived while we were there, and so we joined the resident monks in the traditional monastic purification practices (Tib. *gso sbyong*; Skt. *uposadha*) on the appropriate days of the lunar cycle. The rest of the time we remained in our solitary retreats.[157] At the conclusion of the summer retreat, Khen Rinpoche and I determined that I should go down to the village below to solicit alms. We needed the alms in order to offer a traditional monastic feast to the monks at the end of the summer retreat.

Early the next morning I left the retreat alone and hiked down to beg for alms. I arrived at the home of one family and entered the gate of the enclosure that surrounded their house. There I found a woman who was tending to a cow, and I asked her for some alms. She said, "Just wait here and I will fetch you something" and disappeared into the house. It was taking her some time, so I looked around for a place to sit down. All I saw was a pile of dirt on one side of the enclosure. As I sat down on the ground and leaned my back against the dirt pile, I began to reflect upon the situation in this manner:

Alas! Whenever I traveled in my earlier days,
I always rode upon a fine horse or a strong mule.
I was always dressed in elegant monastic finery,
Surrounded by minions, servants, and myrmidons.
Look at me now!
Dressed in the rags of a homeless beggar,
A load of empty bags across my back,
In my hands only a crooked staff to aid my tired legs.
Should my dear parents and family see me now,
Their despair would be exceeded only by their grief.

Thinking like this, I reflected on the bigger picture. In former times Lord Tsongkhapa had walked upon this very land, dressed in the ragged clothes of a beggar, having abandoned all worldly concerns in pursuit of the sublime. The Lord Buddha himself, and the exalted masters who followed him such as Longchen Rabjam and Jetsün Milarepa (1052–1135), had all practiced in this austere manner. The life stories of these famous beings and their engagement in the hardships of the path filled my mind. I would not presume to compare myself with their high levels of realization and attainment. I was more like an unfledged chick in an aerie, dreaming that he was like his mighty father, the royal white eagle, circling above mountain peaks and diving like lighting to snatch a lamb or seize a goat in the valley far below. But then again, I knew that I had succeeded in setting foot on the glorious path trod by my spiritual forbearers, Lama Rinpoche and all the sublime masters of the Lord Buddha's sublime tradition. Even to possess the ability to make an aspirational prayer to follow in their footsteps was evidence of some extraordinarily good fortune. Therefore, in my heart was a mixture of deep trepidations and lofty exultations.

Soon the woman returned with a large plate of fresh *tsampa* and cheese, topped with a big chunk of butter that had been lovingly formed into the shape of an auspicious jewel. She offered it to me with an uncommon display of reverence. I took this as an omen that my efforts were in indeed pleasing to the Three Jewels. I carefully put the plate into the pot I was carrying to present at the offering ceremony.

For that entire day I went from house to house in the area to collect alms until all my bags were full and I could carry no more. The excellence of the first donor's offering, and her wonderful manner of offering it was repeated again and again. We call this "begging for alms." However, it is very different than begging done because of desperate need or destitution. In fact, I did not have to "beg" at all. Once the villager saw that I was a spiritual mendicant following the path of Dharma, I was treated as an object of veneration. In a country like Tibet, deeply imbued with the treasures of Buddhist civilization, ordinary people find much value in honoring and supporting monks in whatever way they are able. People would thank me for the opportunity to give, saying things like:

I myself am heavily burdened with the unremitting duties of maintaining family and home. Though I wish from the depths of my heart that I could devote myself to the study and practice of the Dharma, in this life I lack the leisure and opportunity to do that. Please accept these alms (i.e., food, money, clothing, etc.) offered with pure and virtuous intent. Please send me your blessings and include me in your prayers so that I have good fortune in the present life, and in future lives will be able to follow in your venerable footsteps.

And so, I returned from my rounds to the retreat at Chölung. There we paid our respects to the resident monks with the various offerings I had gathered, and treated them to a grand luncheon. With this the summer retreat came to an end. As is the old tradition, we then had a few days of relaxation. For this we traveled together to the famous natural springs of Olkha where in former times His Holiness the Dalai Lama as well as the Panchen Lama had come to relax.

We proceeded down the road, to continue our retreat in other sacred places. We went to the mountain retreats and hermitages of Chuzang, Samling and Dzingchi. At each of these pilgrimage sites we spent a week or so paying our respects and practicing our meditations.

On the eighth day of the eighth Tibetan month (1991) we departed from Olkha and made our way to Tsetang, the capital city of Lhokha. From there we set out for Samye. In accordance with our original plans, we went to Samye in order to continue our solitary retreat in Padmasambhava's Chimpu hermitage in the mountains above Samye Monastery. This was to be the place of our long-term solitary retreat. However, other events intervened. The word by now had reached my homeland that I was in this area. Messengers from my two monasteries started to arrive with requests that I return. Their pleas and adjurations soon began to create obstacles to my retreat practice. Around this time, I began to perceive many indications that I should not remain in Tibet, but should travel on to India, the Land of the Noble Ones and on to other lands.

These indications became more and more difficult to avoid, as I could not return home nor stay in this area if my spiritual quest was to proceed. And so, I made the difficult decision to undertake the lengthy and dangerous journey into exile in India, traversing the mighty Himalaya with its endless ice, snow, and wind, its narrow passages and sheer precipices, always struggling to avoid the menace of the ubiquitous Chinese soldiers and secret police who haunt the roads and byways of the border region like agents of Yama, lord of death. After more than a year meditating in retreat, eating little more than roasted barley flour and water, my body was rather weak. I am amazed that I managed to cross the high snow-covered mountain passes and avoid succumbing to the thousand dangers that confronted me every day. I had no energy left for worry or panic, but simply placed one foot in front of the other, following the inexorable pull upon my heart of the sacred places of the Lord Buddha awaiting me on the other side of the Himalaya in the holy places of India, and in the living presence of the Lord Buddha that is His Sublime Holiness, the Dalai Lama. In this manner I proceeded step by step, over the treacherous and icy mountain paths, protected by the objects of my faith and veneration from fear and misadventure until I finally crossed into the free lands of my exile.

During the period of my intensive retreat in Central Tibet, I spent one year and two months at the sacred precincts of Tsering Jong, over a month at the Overseer of the Snow Mountain, over a month and a half at the Crystal Cave of Yarlung, a month at the hermitage of Zangri Kharmar, over two months at the retreat of Chölung in Ölkha, and several weeks in the hermitages of Chuzang, Samling and Dzingchi. In total, I spent almost two years in these sacred sites and holy places exerting all my energy in pursuit of the sublime Dharma. I had such good fortune to be able to take advantage of this opportunity to engage in a meditative practice that allowed me to accumulate some merit and eliminate some of my defilements. I look back at this as a time when I was able to extract real benefit from the good fortune of gaining a human form in this life.

14

Leaving the Sacred Places of Southern Tibet and Entering Exile in India

ON THE fifteenth day of the eighth month of the Tibetan Iron Sheep year (September 23, 1991), I was once again led off to another land. However, the rope through the nose ring this time was in my own hand. And so, I led myself along the path traversed by the supreme head of both the sacred and secular societies of Tibet, our lord and protector who came this way in 1959 with his disciples and devotees, both gods and men. I traveled on, to follow in the footsteps of His Holiness the Dalai Lama, when he was obliged to escape from the invading forces and cross over the ranges of high, glacier-mantled mountains that encircle his homeland. After trekking across the dangerous passages of the high Himalayas and slipping through the guarded border into India, I continued on to follow the steps of His Holiness to the principal sites of Buddhist pilgrimage in India and Nepal.

From my close acquaintance with Khen Rinpoche, I knew without hesitation that he would support my decision to leave Tibet. However, it was clear that notifying him in advance of my departure would not be good. He would then be implicated in my flight, and could be held responsible by the authorities, and even by my own family and monastery who trusted him to look after me. When I departed, I left behind a letter for Khen Rinpoche explaining the reasons that led me, with my limited vision of the truth, to set forth on this journey to the center of the world (Bodh Gaya) and the other sacred sites.

Rather than continuing on to Samye with Khen Rinpoche, I quietly went off on my own once we reached the town of Tsetang. As I first set out on the road, I saw three women coming toward me carrying buckets filled with water. I knew this to be an auspicious sign that suggested my activities in both the short term and the long run would be accomplished without major difficulties. I was most relieved, and in my happiness presented each of these ladies with a choice apple from my bag. I soon procured a ride to Lhasa in a truck used to carry stone. The bed of the truck was hard steel, and the road was filled with ruts, rocks, and holes. It was a rough ride, with me bouncing up and down all the way to Lhasa. There I went to the house of my friend Lungtok Tenpay Nyima. I had to stay there for a little over one month until suitable arrangements could be made for the journey to the Nepal /Tibet border.

While waiting there, I composed a letter in the form of a poem called "The Song of the Distant Traveler" and sent it to my family and associates back home.[158] It went like this:

As the summation of the enlightened deeds of myriads of Victors,[159]
O peerless lama, you are the buddha who knows all,
From the mighty clouds of your compassion and vast kindness,
Send forth the fertile rain of your constant and unfailing blessings!

Alas! Beloved families and friends, please listen to my words,
Don't be sad or worried, but relax and think of me happily,
Moved by the inexorable power of my own karma and aspirations,
I have walked the paths that have now taken me to another land.

At this time, we lack the good fortune to be together,
However, the lucky day when we meet again may not be far off.
For now, I seek only some remote and isolated place,
Hidden in the folds of an icy mountain or rocky ridge,

A tiny hut or sheltered space just enough for one person,
A place conducive to meditative concentration,
Where my mind can relax and continue to expand, that is what I seek.

I pray to my lama who holds the threefold lineage: "Please provide
    what I need to make it so."

Dear vajra brothers,[160] beware of short-sighted viewpoints,
Never deviate from the precious traditions of our predecessors,
Cultivate with diligence the crops of the Dharma and our monastic
    teachings,
In this way, flowers of pure gold will come to adorn your crown.[161]

Dear friends, countrymen, and beloved family members,
Please do not worry about me,
With the eyes of the buddhas and bodhisattvas as my witness,
Wherever I wander, I go with constant prayers for the benefit and
    happiness of each of you and of all the limitless beings,

Dear brothers and sisters, no matter what changes and what stays the
    same in your life or abodes,
Never, ever let the luminous radiance of the Dharma in your heart grow dim,
Maintain always the good effort in your chosen field of endeavor,
In this way, the purposes of self and other, the goals of this world and of
    the Dharma, will surely be accomplished.

My two dear brothers and three sisters—to insure your happiness and
    success in this and future lives,
Continue to seek guidance at the feet of our peerless lama,
And like a tree and its shadow, never leave our dear parents and family,
But always follow the exemplary deeds of the most excellent ones.

My respected and dear friends in the Dharma—so that your minds are
    ever peaceful and happy,
Never defile the precious wish-fulfilling jewel of our lama's vast and
    profound (Dzogchen) teaching,
With the dust and filth of dark and unwholesome deeds,
But always keep it clean and bright by applying yourselves to your
    practice with constancy and reverence.

Dear parents, elders, and teachers, please don't worry about me,
The young cuckoo bird in the forest of foot drinkers,[162]

14. Leaving the Sacred Places of Southern Tibet

Flies south to the land of Mön[163] when winter time approaches,
He is not gone away forever; after a while you will see him again.

Although the young fish loves to play in warm and familiar waters with
his dear companions,
He fears the guile and sharp hook of the merciless fishermen,
So, he follows circuitous and difficult passageways to the deep, cool
waters of the vast ocean,
Where a secure place free from fear will be found.[164]

Never is there a day that I do not think of each of you,
However, the seeds of the prayers and aspiration of my former life were
germinated by the warmth and moisture of present circumstances,
And I grew to turn the blossoming lotus of my heart and mind,
To the sun, the benefactor of all, in the sky of universal longing.[165]

Now as my early years have passed, and the sun of this life begins to move
toward the far horizon,
There is no longer time and leisure to waste on a myriad of plans and
possibilities,
So now, in whatever I do for myself or for others, wherever I go, wherever
I stay, in all my thoughts and activities,
I will follow exclusively the course set for me by the Sublime Lord of the
Land of Snows.

These words are the traveling song of a distant traveler,
Arising clearly in his mind as he wanders far away,
His fingers dance across the pages to record them,
As his feet step across the land on his solitary journey.

This traveling song of the distant traveler is the work of Padma Mati
(Sogan Rinpoche), an itinerate wayfarer who wanders like the wind without attachment or fixed destination. It is written and sent with a virtuous
attitude on the banks of the Kyichu River that flows gentle past the environs of the Jokhang Cathedral of Lhasa, on the twenty-fourth day of the
eighth month of the Iron Sheep Year (1991).

After writing this letter, I gave it to a pilgrim from my home region who
was preparing to return. Later I learned that it safely reached its intended
recipients.

On the twelfth day of the tenth Tibetan month, I departed from Lhasa. Traveling by car, in three days I arrived at the town of Dram on the Tibetan/ Nepali border. The border crossing was closely guarded by Chinese soldiers. Therefore, I engaged the services of two Nepali guides who knew hidden pathways that crossed the border in areas not frequented by the occupation forces. On that day I had to put aside concerns for the safety and preservation of my cherished human body, and forced it along a path filled with deadly, spine-chilling dangers and daunting physical demands. It was on that day that I finally parted from my cherished homeland, the wondrous land of glacier-mantled mountains and lush emerald valleys, and entered into a life of exile. In my journey through the myriad events of this dreamlike existence, what I experienced that day remains ever vivid and unforgettable; it has left an impression in my mind that cannot be erased.

In this wide world with all its many cultures and communities where human beings struggle in their various ways to survive and flourish, it is well known that those who fall into the status of refugees have particular challenges and difficulties. There are the difficulties associated with the particular circumstances that drive them to seek refuge, and the difficulties encountered in the process of fleeing from that place to a new location where they may find safe refuge. There are the dangers faced in the home country, as well as those to be faced on the road to refuge and the challenges to be faced in the new location.

As for the particular situation of Tibetans, we look back on the long history of our homeland and culture. Over 2500 years ago there was a teacher who was born in India, the Land of the Noble Ones, who bestowed a marvelous doctrine and way of life that was free of any harm and that led to true peace and happiness. This was Shakyamuni Buddha, the Lion of the Shakyas. As recorded in the *Saddharmapuṇḍarika-sutra*, at one time, while he was residing in the Bamboo Grove hermitage, the Lord Buddha proclaimed to his followers:

> Arya Avalokiteshvara, in the presence of over a thousand buddhas,
>   made this prayer:
> "May I go to the glacier-bound land of Tibet,
> A remote expanse where none of the buddhas of the past have set foot,
> There may I establish those beings, who are so difficult to teach,
> On the path of liberation and enlightenment."

Tibetans have lived for thousands of years under the pellucid skies of their vast alpine realm. In modern times, archeologists have found physical remains of Tibetan culture on the Tibetan plateau that date back at least 35,000 years.[166] The historical record reflects how the first king of Tibet, Nyatri Tsenpo, ascended the throne the year 414 B.C.E.[167] Following the time of King Nyatri Tsenpo were many groups or dynasties of kings such as the seven "sky kings," the six "earth kings," the eight "between [heaven and earth] kings", the five "period kings," the thirteen "good time kings," and the five "very good time kings."[168] During the reign of the twenty-eighth king of Tibet, Lha Thothori Nyentsen (circa third–fourth century), the Buddha Dharma first spread to Tibet, and the foundation for its flourishing was established. The Dharma king (Skt. *dharmarāja*) Songtsen Gampo was the thirty-third king of Tibet. During his reign, he built the Jokhang temple in Lhasa and many other Buddhist temples such as the Ramoche. He also provided for the inner objects of worship in these temples, including the Jowo Rinpoche image of Lord Buddha in the Jokhang, and the image of Lord Buddha at the age of eight (Jowo Mikyö Dorje) in Ramoche Temple of Lhasa.[169] Dharmaraja Songtsen Gampo's Minister of Dharma, Thonmi Tengpo Sambhota (circa seventh century), did much to create the causes and conditions necessary for the development and spread of Dharma in Tibet such as creating an alphabet and writing system for the Tibetan language.

The thirty-seventh King of Tibet, Devaputra Trisong Detsen (755–797) caused the light of Dharma to burn brightly and illumine the entire land by bringing from Buddhist India mighty teachers such as Shantarakshita and Padmasambhava—the sun and moon luminaries of the Dharma. King Trisong Detsen also sponsored many distinguished translators such as the sage Vairochana (Berotsana) to study Sanskrit and translate texts from the treasury of the Buddhist canon, including sutras, shastras, and tantras. In this manner many treasures of the Lord Buddha's teachings were rendered into the Tibetan language.

In these ways the Dharma-endowed realm of Tibet truly became the Dharma field of the Lord Avalokiteshvara. Throughout Tibetan history he manifested as many of the most influential religious and secular leaders who did whatever was necessary to spread and support the sublime Dharma in Tibet and in the hearts of its inhabitants. In the present time he has manifested as our glorious national leader, the personification of pure and limitless compassion, the refuge and protector of all beings, the master of enlightenment, none other than the Fourteenth Dalai Lama of Tibet. He is known by other names such as Vajradhara-vagindra-sumati-shasanadhara-samudra-shribhadra, Sovereign of the Triple World, He Who is Unrivaled among Gods and Men, Sublime

Goodness, and He Who Acts in All Ways without Obstruction throughout All Mundane and Transcendent Realms.

Historically, Tibet's Buddhist civilization comes from India, the source and wellspring of the teaching of the Lord Buddha. Tibet's styles of sartorial splendor reflect those of the Mongolian lands. Its manner of preparing food and drink is influenced by its commerce with Chinese people. However, over the centuries and millennia, Tibetan culture developed its own unique characteristics based on devotion to the study and practice of the Dharma. The laws and customs, both within the family and in the larger society, integrated the Dharma in almost every way. Visitors and chroniclers from the East and the West observed the uniqueness of Tibet and described the remarkable harmony and happiness of Tibetan people. Accounts of "Shangri-la" developed and spread throughout the world so that Tibet became known as a place of vast beauty, harmony, kindness, and happiness. Tibet was the one place in the world where the sublime spiritual and literary treasures of the Buddha's Dharma had been transmitted and transplanted in their entirety. Tibet became the center of Buddhism in the world for nearly one thousand years. Devotees and scholars from other lands where Buddhism had been persecuted or had never spread could come to Tibet, learn the language, and enter the grand monasteries and institutions of higher learning.

Blessed by gods, and surrounded by rings of the world's highest mountain ranges, Tibet's peace and happiness was protected throughout its history. While its spiritual and literary treasures were available to any individual dedicated enough to make the journey, its material treasures, such as its vast forests and its tremendous mineral wealth, were too hard for rapacious foreign invaders to reach and transport. This all changed in the middle of the twentieth century. With the development of advanced military vehicles and aviation and other modern technologies of war and conquest, even the highest mountain ranges in the world were no longer an insurmountable barrier. When these weapons and technologies were combined with the aggressive policies and imperialist ideology of the People's Republic of China, the ancient nation-state of Tibet had no effective defense.

When the Chinese invaded in the 1950s, it was like the heaven and the earth were turned over. They devoted their huge military and police resources not just to conquering Tibet but also to annihilating its culture and its history. The thousands of monasteries and ancient temples that covered the Tibetan plateau were not just outlawed and closed, but were mostly bombed or burned to the ground. The unique art treasures of Tibet were tossed into fires if they burned, or melted down if they contained metal. Precious religious images were transformed into bullets and bayonets. The teachers, lamas, intellectuals were imprisoned and killed. The huge libraries were burned to the ground. Medical and educational establishments were completely destroyed. The possessions and wealth of the people and the public institutions were systematically looted. Vast numbers of Han Chinese people were moved into Tibet from China to transform Tibet into a Chinese province.

By the late 1950s and early 1960s, any chance that Tibetan culture could survive in its homeland was quickly disappearing. For thousands of years it had been a beacon of enlightenment and a source of salvation and happiness to people everywhere. Now it was on the edge of annihilation.

At the age of sixteen, His Holiness the Fourteenth Dalai Lama took over the reins of power, both political and spiritual, as the leader of Tibet and the only hope for the survival of Tibetan culture. He stood up to the advancing Chinese army and confronted its generals. In a heroic effort, he managed to evade their bullets, bombs, and battalions and crossed the Himalayas into India. Over 100,000 Tibetans soon followed His Holiness into exile, accepting the generosity of the Indian people and government who granted them sanctuary in the homeland of the Lord Buddha.

In the decades since His Holiness came to India, Tibetan refugees have continued to follow him into exile, fleeing the unremitting oppression. His Holiness continues to be the light of hope and the source of refuge to Tibetans in Tibet and in their places of exile throughout the world. He has re-established so many of the monasteries of Tibet, one after another, in India and elsewhere. He has built schools, welfare agencies, hospitals, temples, and homes for the orphans and the elderly. He has established institutions for the administration of a Tibetan government in exile to serve the needs of Tibetans in Tibet and around the world and to represent them in international assemblies and in world capitals. He has been, for over sixty years to date, the academic and spiritual teacher of the Lord Buddha's teaching for Tibetans and for people in every corner of the world.

Under the leadership of His Holiness the Dalai Lama, many Tibetans in Tibet, and in exile in India and all over the world have done well. New generations of Tibetans are learning the ways of the lands where they now live, and are continually gaining in their knowledge of Western arts and sciences. They have become successful participants in the societies, schools, businesses, and governments of countries around the world. However, at all times the deepest and most fervent wish in the hearts of all Tibetans is to come together again in a free Tibet.

This goal can only be achieved by following the "Middle Way" approach as consistently taught by His Holiness. This is the path that refuses to harm anyone else in the pursuit of one's own aims. It seeks to overcome all difficulties, all disagreements and hostilities by understanding the concerns of the other party and finding some way to address them without losing one's own principles and essential priorities. It is a path that might take longer, but in the end, it is the only effective way to attain peace and happiness for all. In this manner His Holiness continues to seek a way to come to terms with the Chinese regime.

This is certainly possible. Historically, Tibet and China have shared a long and peaceful border with the lofty perimeter of the world's largest and highest plateau providing a dramatic and unambiguous boundary between Tibet and its neighbors. Trade with China and, for most of our history, the shared heritage of the Dharma made the two countries largely harmonious and often mutually beneficial. However, in this century there are new pressures and exigencies that put strains on countries and societies. Increasing population and pollution, with increasing demand on decreasing resources exacerbate ethnic and religious tensions. We must recognize and honor the many ways in which we are all the same. These include our desire for human rights and freedoms including religious liberty, and our need for a healthy environment and sufficient food, clothing, housing, and health care. We all want these for ourselves, and must respect others' needs for these same things. As long as one ethnic group denies these things to another, there can be no peace between them. Tibetans are therefore at odds with the Chinese regime and whoever supports their imperialist policies that deny Tibetans all that is most important to them: their land, their rights, their religion, and their history. So long as His Holiness the Dalai Lama, our refuge and protector, is not allowed to return to his historic home and role in Tibet, there is nothing that can remedy the situation.

I feel profound gratitude to all the people throughout the world who have become friends of Tibet and of the oppressed people of Tibet. Their help and support are of vital importance at this time. Among these friends are many Chinese people, both in mainland China and in so many other countries. I pray that all of us keep up our efforts for the survival of Tibet and all that it represents. I pray with my hands pressed together that the leadership of the Chinese regime comes to see more and more how we have many interests in common, and how treating Tibetans, as well as China's own people, with respect and kindness will benefit them and their country, whereas the continued cruelty and oppression will only bring harm to themselves and their country.

As long as the Chinese regime continues its oppressive policies, we will have more and more Tibetans attempting to escape over the treacherous trails that lead across the Himalaya. So many have died and continue to die in the attempt to escape. Men, women, and children die on these trails that are the only feasible route to freedom. Walking all night and hiding during the day, it can take several months to cross the border for those who do not lose their lives along the way. They die or are badly wounded by falling off the narrow mountain trails and plunging into the abyss, or by drowning in the hundreds of treacherous mountain streams and rivers that must be forded to avoid the bridges guarded by Chinese border police, who shoot refugees on sight. Many are maimed by frostbite or succumb to hypothermia due to the sub-zero temperatures at night. Others fall victim to disease, or from lacking the minimal amount of food and drink necessary to keep a human being alive. Some are shot or beaten to death by the police, soldiers, and border guards stationed to prevent Tibetans from fleeing the "motherland." The accounts and documentations of these ongoing deaths are well known after more than fifty-five years of such tragedies.

I myself only barely survived this journey. My body was weak and emaciated. I experienced the powerful freezing winds that pervade the Himalaya, the swift, icy waters that must be forded, the near escapes from the soldiers that haunt the routes through the mountains, the near starvation, and so many other deadly threats to life and limb that are the price that Tibetans must pay for any chance of freedom. If not for the rare privilege of having good helpers and some transportation for a good part of the journey, I would have certainly lost my life.

15

Arriving in Nepal After Escaping Across the Border

I ARRIVED in Kathmandu on the November 28, 1991. There I found my good Dharma brother, Lingtrul Rinpoche Kadak Chöying Dorje (b. 1955), as well as other friends. They provided me with everything I needed—food, clothing, lodgings and bedding. I will not forget all the kindness and generosity they showed me at that difficult time.

My habitual diet of simple vegetarian food, devoid of any type of animal flesh, together with the added austerities and deprivations of my retreats and difficult journey over the Himalaya, had all left my body rather weak and emaciated. Upon seeing me like this, my vajra brother Lingtrul Rinpoche said, "You have certainly pushed your body to the limits. In such a precarious condition one will readily attract diseases and can become extremely sick." He gave me good advice from his kindness and experience. One night he took me to a local Tibetan restaurant. There he ordered a large quantity of rich foods made from the bodies of cattle and goats. He presented this to me with the urgent injunction that I consume every morsel. Under the power of his kindness and concern, and not wanting to displease him, I ate what I was given.

Having finished this heavy meal, I said to him:

Dear Rinpoche, following your wise counsel and urging, today I have interrupted my long commitment to a strict vegetarian diet. I now ask your

176

15. Arriving in Nepal After Escaping Across the Border

Sogan Rinpoche on his arrival in
India—1991

permission to immediately reestablish my vow to avoid all foods made
from the flesh of living beings.

I told him of my vow to eat only vegetarian foods and dedicate the merit to
my sister who had urged me to adopt such a diet. I told him of the shame I
would experience if I returned to a meat diet. In respect for Rinpoche's feelings, and those of the other meat-eaters in our company, I did not mention
the other two reasons for my abstention from consuming meat. First, I had
eaten much of it as a child, relishing the taste of bloody flesh like a hungry
wolf. Second, I had realized that the path of selfishly supporting my life force
through the consumption of flesh would lead to involvement in the deaths
of countless living beings, each of whom had shown me much kindness in
many former lives. Thinking in this way, I long ago had realized that eating

the flesh of my fellow living beings in order to satisfy my own appetite was unsuitable. This realization, combined with my vow to dedicate the merit of this virtuous diet to my late vegetarian sister, made it impossible for me to eat meat any more.

A long, long time ago, the Peerless Teacher, the sublime Lion of the Shakyas, took birth here in Nepal, in a place called Lumbini. In a former life, long before that, he was born as the great-hearted prince who gave his body so that a tigress and her children might live. It was in this sacred place, called Takmo Lüjin (Giving His Body to the Tigress) that he generated the spirit of enlightenment (Skt. *bodhicitta*) in his heart. These and other sites of pilgrimage associated with the Lord Buddha are here in Nepal. In addition, there are other pilgrimage sites such as Maratika, the mountain cave where Padmasambhava, a "second Buddha", accomplished the immortal state of Vidyadhara in union with his consort, and the pilgrimage site known as Yanglesho, where he accomplished the exalted state of Vajrakila. There is also the site where the four brothers of low caste, being the former lives of the three dispellers of darkness in Tibet—Shantarakshita, Padmasambhava, and King Trisong Detsen, together with the King's prime minister, built the Boudhanath Stupa helped by the power of their profound prayers and virtuous wishes. In addition to these, there are many other historical sites of pilgrimage in Nepal associated with the life, teachings, and prophesies of the All-Compassionate Buddha, such as the great stupa of Swayambhunath. A pilgrimage to any of these many sacred locations can bestow upon the pilgrim both blessings and spiritual powers.

The palace of the father of Queen Belza Tritsun (569–650), the first wife of Tibet's Dharmaraja Songtsen Gampo (seventh century), now lies in ruins, serving only as a noisy, crowded assembly hall for pigeons. Elsewhere there are many places with pieces of ancient pillars, obelisks, and steles lying scattered on the ground, ancient temples to various gods, and crumbling palaces of various potentates abandoned to their desolation. These serve us now as eloquent memorials to remind us of the principle that all compounded things are transitory.

One day, in the late afternoon, I was circumambulating the Boudhanath Stupa on the upper level walkway toward the top of the stupa. Coming around to the western side of the stupa, I sat down to rest on one of the corners. It was a peaceful, beautiful evening. The high clouds, shining their whites and silvers and pale greys, now started to glow with the yellows, reds, and purples of the setting sun, all against a lovely turquoise sky shading to deep blue in the eastern horizon. Caught up in this peaceful display of daz-zling beauty, I forgot myself and fell into a sense of luminous perception that seemed to encompass the vastness of space.

Slowly my thoughts turned reflective. All my life up to now had been lived under the shadow of alien oppression, filled with the hardships of occupa-tion and harsh rule. Now, like the clouds of good omen that ornamented the sky, I had been carried as if by a fortunate wind across the heights of the Hi-malaya, and found myself now in this beautiful land of Dharma and freedom, beyond the reach of the dark forces that continue to torment my homeland. Here I was, seated upon the very stupa that embodies so much of our ancient history, a sacred shrine frequented by so many of the true bodhisattvas of past and present times, worshiped by powerful kings and by multitudes of pilgrims across the ages. It is a shrine also to the close fraternal relations between Nepal and Tibet, loved and honored by all our peoples. Most of all, the great stupa is a sublime monument to our Teacher, the Lord Buddha, who came here to dispel the darkness of this world. He was born here and walked upon this very ground. How wondrous to be here now. But how sad to have failed to be present then to learn directly him and all his glorious disciples.

I thought of the lives of so many of the enlightened masters who had passed this way in order to teach us the path of the bodhisattva that leads to the state of ultimate liberation. I thought of our teacher Shantarakshita, our guru Padmasambhava, and our Dharma King Trisong Detsen, who in former lives had built this Boudhanath stupa. I thought of the heroic translators, such as Vairochana, who were embodiments of compassion and wisdom. They passed through this very place on the way to carry the treasures of the Dharma to the eager ears of fortunate disciples in Tibet. We study the his-tory of each of these illustrious ones. We treasure here their mighty works, but we no longer have access to their living presence. Even in recent times, many true bodhisattva teachers have come to this place to benefit living be-ings and to propagate the sublime Dharma. The fragrance of their spiritual presence still perfumes this land. That their manifest presence is no longer available leaves me feeling a little sad.

As I sat there on the high step of the great stupa, this feeling of sadness would not leave me. Thinking of my tormented homeland, I felt like a lone survivor of a terrible disaster. I wept. My tears fell like a summer rain. The tragedy of Tibet, and the pervasive tragedy of this world of impermanence and pain filled my heart with sorrow. So, I chanted the powerful verses of the *Prayer to the Distant Lama*[170] that always bring me comfort in hard times.

Immediately after, I practiced the four initiations that culminate in meditative stabilization on the non-dual state of *dharmakāya*.[171] This is of tremendous benefit in freeing the mind from the illusions of the ordinary world. As I completed this meditation, it seemed as if the veils of random thought and worry fell away. I felt free to rise above my personal concerns like an eagle gliding over the peaks of the Himalaya. For the next few days, wherever I went and whatever I did, my mind was filled with a sense of lightness and happiness.

My journey out of Tibet to this very different land and culture made me consider the similarities and differences among people. In this age of modern transportation, we can go to different countries with relative ease. Some travel around and take photos to recall the exotic sights they see. Others go to gain an understanding of the people and cultures they encounter. Travels provide a good opportunity to do both. However, it is especially valuable to learn new things from various cultures and traditions. This can change the way we perceive the world, broaden our horizons, and help us find deeper meaning in life.

Although there are differences in such things as language, customs, clothing, and diet in the different cultures, human beings are not so different in our fundamental nature. Every living being, human or non-human, shares the very same desire to find happiness and comfort, and to avoid misery and pain. In this, there is no distinction between any of us. Furthermore, due to the interdependence and interconnectedness of all beings and all things, the search for our own happiness and freedom from suffering necessarily depends upon others, and can never succeed through selfish action based on the illusion of an independent, inherently existent self. Thinking like this, I appreciated more the opportunity to experience this wonderful place and its people. It is an ideal place for a spiritual pilgrimage.

For those who would undertake a pilgrimage to a religious site, I believe it is important to first gain some knowledge about the history of that place. One should visit with a state of mind that rejoices in the wondrous deeds and teachings of the distinguished people who came here in the past, and whose presence imparted to it a sacred status. A pilgrimage should be based upon an awareness of the particular ways in which the distinguished people followed a path that contributed to the physical and mental benefit of other living beings. If one goes on the pilgrimage in this manner, and cultivating aspirations and increasing one's faith and devotion, it will bring significant benefit. On the other hand, going to these sacred places with the attitude of a tourist or a hiker can only yield good photos and some exercise.

Regarding the way to go on a proper Buddhist pilgrimage, Katok Situ Chökyi Gyatso (1880–1923) wrote the following verses in his *Precious Necklace of Lunar Jewels: A Guide to Pilgrimage.*[172]

> Abiding free of attachment, clinging, and objectification,
> Without favoring disciples close to you, but with impartiality to all,
> Going to all places, without discrimination, for the sake of beings and
> their welfare,
> This is the way of the superior pilgrim.

> Without concern for sect or lineage, avoid unseemly guidance,
> Without concern for religious perspectives, avoid unseemly views,
> Without concern for the name of the holy person, avoid unseemly
> stinginess in offerings,
> This is also the way of the superior pilgrim.

> With faith in all embodiments of the Enlightened One's body, speech,
> and mind,
> Traveling to every isolated place, monastery, and shrine without weari-
> ness or grief,
> Without unnecessary assistance, without annoyance, accumulate merit
> with purity of perception,
> This is the way of the ordinary pilgrim.

> What then is the way of the inferior pilgrim?
> In the beginning he decides to go on a pilgrimage to a certain sacred
> place,
> Then subsequently abandons the effort when seeing how far or high it is,
> In the end he has just gone to the general area, but has no real encounter
> with the sacred place.

> Firstly, such a pilgrimage is merely superficial, with no real value,
> Secondly, it can be a pilgrimage of sin, that increases his demerits,
> If he fails to appreciate the good qualities of the lamas and monastics,
> And just perceives their faults,

If he fails to engage with the sacred images and holy scriptures, and
    just glances at them from a distance,
If he begs for food and objects if others are around to see,
Or just steals them if there are no witnesses.
If, having difficulties in the course of the pilgrimage, he belittles the
    sacred place,

If, as soon as he walks out their door,
He forgets everything within the sacred precincts,
If he thinks himself to be a brave man for having quarreled and fought
    with others along the pilgrimage journey,
Then all of his efforts on the pilgrimage are made in vain.

These precepts of pilgrimage show the nature of the superior, the ordinary, and the inferior pilgrimage. It is important to bear them in mind.

For the next several weeks, I went on a pilgrimage there in Nepal in the company of Lingtrul Rinpoche, Tulku Pega, my cousin and assistant Lama Chönam (Chöying Namgyal, b. 1964 C.E.), and several others. We went to the two main stupas (Boudhanath and Swayambhunath) and other sacred sites. In those sites we paid our respects and made offerings and prayers. In our travels in Nepal, we were dismayed when we saw the stark contrast between the manner in which Tibetans had historically gone on pilgrimages to these places, and how they have now been reduced to homeless, impoverished refugees in a foreign land.

There are many Buddhist monasteries in Nepal, as well as many sacred monuments, stone and bronze images of buddhas, bodhisattvas, and gods. There are many Buddhist libraries, stupas large and small, as well as a large number of monks and nuns, tantric adepts, and devout laypeople. All of these fill the land with the warmth and light of the Lord Buddha's blessings and powers. It would have been my desire to slowly bask in this supernal light, and absorb these blessing at my leisure. However, I had made the long journey and hazardous escape from my besieged homeland thinking always of finding my way into the presence of our Lord and Protector, His Holiness the Dalai Lama. This being my priority, I set off on my travels once more, proceeding on to India in the company of my cousin and helper, Lama Chönam.

16

My First Glimpse of the Golden Face of the Supreme Lord of the Glacier-Mantled Realm and a Pilgrimage to the Sacred Places of India

FROM KATHMANDU I traveled to India on a large public bus in the company of Lama Chönam and other refugees from Tibet. Arriving at the Nepali-Indian border, we were subjected to the usual delays, bureaucratic complications, and demands for fees or bribes by officials and police. It then took several days and nights of constant travel, but with little difficulty and in the best of spirits we finally reached Dharamsala, the "Second Capital of Tibet."

Arriving in Dharamsala, we asked for directions to the home of Tseten Namgyal (circa twentieth century), a pharmacist in the Mentsee Khang (Tibetan Medical Center) in the Gangchen Kyishong section of town. Tseten Namgyal was married to the sister of Lungtok Tenpay Nyima's wife. Lungtok Tenpay Nyima was the gentleman in Lhasa who hosted me during the weeks I spent in Lhasa preparing for my escape from Tibet and pilgrimage to Dharamsala. He had told me that Tseten Namgyal would take care of me once I arrived. I stayed for a few days with Tseten Namgyal and his wife. He then suggested the we go to the Tibetan Bureau of Security, where he introduced me to the Secretary of the Bureau, who listened intently to my story and asked me to put its salient points into a letter to the Private Office of His Holiness the Dalai Lama. He said that this would start a process whereby I should eventually gain an audience with His Holiness. He had the letter delivered that day. The next morning, we received a message from the Secretary saying that His Holiness sent a reply and that I was to present myself for an audience that very day. I hurriedly showered and shaved, and dressed in my cleanest robes. The Secretary sent a taxi, and I was deposited at the gates of the Palace. There Indian and Tibetan security police frisked me, put me through the metal detectors, and sent me up to the audience waiting room.

As I sat there awaiting the audience, I recalled something from the past that gave me a sort of reverential confidence. When I was a small child at home back in Amdo, my grandmother, Dzamlo, would sit by the western window every afternoon as the sun approached the western horizon. Pressing her palms together in devotion, she would say, "O Lord Avalokita—Your Holiness Tenzin Gyatso (b. 1935), our Dalai Lama who is abiding in the western Noble Land of India...." Tears filling her eyes, she would pay homage to him, tell him of her troubles, share her thoughts, her fears and hopes, and request his support and blessings. I remembered how, as a small child I had thought that His Holiness the Dalai Lama was perhaps an ancient buddha of former times in India like Shakyamuni Buddha, or maybe a legendary master like Guru Padmasambhava. Never did I consider the possibility that he could be a living bodhisattva who could been seen by an ordinary human being in the present time. As the years passed, I gradually gained a bit more knowledge about the situation in Tibet and the outside world. In particular, I learned His Holiness the Dalai Lama had been forced by an implacable invader to flee his homeland and seek refuge in India. Understanding this situation more and more, my sadness deepened. Subsequently, I learned that it was His Holiness who had recognized me as a tulku, the rebirth of an important lama. With this high position came many responsibilities and perquisites, and an ever increasing need to seek the guidance and blessings of His Holiness. This became my personal quest. I did not discuss it with others. It was my own inner need to see His Holiness face to face and receive the nectar of his precepts. That drove me on, eventually causing me to abandon my high thrones and devoted followers, my comfortable home and loving family, and risk life and limb on the dangerous road into to exile. Without fulfilling this goal, I felt my life would have no real meaning or value. Therefore, knowing the journey to be hard, the goal to be remote, and the danger to be great, I had set out with determination on the path that now brought be to this seat in the palace awaiting an audience. Now, on this twenty seventh day of the twelfth month of the year 1991, the wish that had lived for so long in the depths of my heart was about to be fulfilled.

16. My First Glimpse of the Golden Face of the Supreme Lord

Sogan Rinpoche's first meeting with His Holiness the Dalai Lama,
Dharamsala—1991

These early childhood memories now blended with my present situation
of good fortune such that I scarcely knew whether I was awake or deeply
immersed in a dream. The feelings I now experienced, feelings of happiness, of faith, and of deep pleasure were so powerful that I could not keep
my body still. It trembled with excitement and anticipation as I sat there
waiting. Suddenly, a small side door opened and a monk, who turned out to
be Ku-ngo Jampa Tsultrim, His Holiness's personal secretary, quietly motioned with his hand for me to come forth. Entering the next room, I was
touched by the lovely, fragrant cleanliness of everything. I could see now on
my right, through the glass doors of the inner office, the physical form of
limitless compassion, the universal Lord and Protector, His Holiness the Dalai Lama. He was seated on a chair, in the manner of Maitreya, with a small
desk in front of him, upon which were papers he was reading. Immediately
I offered the homage of my body, speech, and mind. Then I offered the small
image, cast of pure silver, of the Four-Armed Avalokiteshvara that my father
had found in a garbage dump near a Chinese army encampment. He gave

it to me and I had carried for all these years in a *gau* reliquary around my neck. With it I offered a thick woolen monks seat (Tib. *gding ba*) of the size, shape, and color specified by ancient Buddhist tradition and *Vinaya* law. I had sewn this with my own hands. Next, I offered a special greeting scarf of the finest white silk. Saying, "This is an excellent omen," the Great Compassionate One picked up the silver image and touched it to the crown of his head in the gesture of blessing. The red woolen monk's seat he took in his hands as he stood up, then placed it on his chair and sat down with a radiant smile. He then looked at me, and speaking as a loving father to his dearest son who was just arriving back from a distant journey, said "How was your trip? What difficulties or remarkable things did you encounter on the roads and mountain trails?" His gentle manner of speech, and the love flowing from his all-seeing eyes banished completely the fear and trepidation I had upon presenting myself to the Lord Protector of the World. "Your insignificant servant comes from the Manyin Valley in the Akyong Bum province of Amdo." I heard myself say. I gradually began to speak with a little more confidence, saying:

> On the journey here, this inferior but reverent person encountered no particular difficulties or obstacles worth mentioning, but has come of a purpose, to offer you from this day forth the totality of his body, speech, and mind. Please, Lord Protector, use them as you will! I have no other source of guidance and protection, so please hold me in the firm grip of your limitless compassion, and guide me with the bright light of your all-penetrating wisdom.

These words flowed almost spontaneously from the depths of my heart.

His Holiness's face was as radiant as the harvest moon on a cloudless night. He smiled and touched the crown of my head with his hand. My body and mind overflowed with the nectar of his blessings as he accepted my offer. "Now," I thought to myself, "my acquisition of this human life has found its purpose and has achieved true significance." My copious tears of joy could not be restrained.

These days, it seems that most people, monks or laymen alike, make extensive efforts to appear prosperous and impressive in the way they live. They have a sense of competition in the richness of their abodes and accouterments. Even those who are leaders of small status, in small towns take much pride in the opulence of their offices and the numbers of their underlings and servants. One might imagine that the beloved leader of Tibet, the protector of peace and purveyor of happiness on this planet Earth, His Holiness the Fourteenth Dalai Lama would have a residence and executive offices commensurate with his exalted status. If that was what he desired, he could have readily obtained it, and no one would be in a position to criticize. However, His Holiness has always turned away from such things as they just increase attachment to the eight worldly concerns. In every aspect of his public and private life, His Holiness maintains the pure and simple lifestyle of an ordinary Buddhist monk. An example of his approach is seen in the manner in which he maintains his private office within the Tibetan government in Dharamsala. Although it is from these very offices that the light of the four types of enlightened activity[173] radiate out to bring benefit and happiness to the entire world, and include numerous bureaus and agencies with Tibetan, Indian, Chinese, and English language sections, and security sections, as well as reception offices and audience rooms, they all appear to be simple clerical offices and meeting rooms, without any special embellishments or impressive façades. It is remarkable that the distinguishing feature by which one knows one has arrived at the headquarters of the Wish Fulfilling Lord of Universal Compassion is not gleaming golden roofs, intricately carved pillars, or colorful, bejeweled balustrades. Rather one finds only an unobtrusive gateway festooned not with opulent gems, but with a group of Indian and Tibetan military guards.

A few days later His Holiness left for Dzogchen Monastery in South India. I followed him there, departing Dharamsala with Lama Chönam, and the Lamo Tsangpa oracle and his family. We traveled to Delhi, where we caught the train that would take us down to South India. Traveling day and night across the hot plains of central India, the black smoke and soot of the train's engine blended with the smog and pollution of the industrial zones along the route. We stopped at all of the many little towns and villages along the tracks. Never in my life had I seen so many people. When I was small, there was a place near our nomadic home where we would stay in the summer time. You could pick up a large flat rock and see millions of little insects swarming this way and that, over and under each other. It was like that here in India, only these were not ants, but human beings just like me.

Going among them, I realized that I did not possess so much as a single word of their language. The weather was hot. It was a heat beyond any I had known outside of a blazing furnace or cook stove. The food these people ate was also beyond my experience. The lentils and strange vegetables on their plates stimulated in me a sense of alarm rather than appetite. The terrible heat, the heavy, unfamiliar smells, the relentless press of the swarming multitudes made me long for the vast open spaces, the sparse population, the clean, pure waters, and the cool mountain air of the valleys of my homeland. I felt homesick for the familiar things of home, for my dear parents, relatives, and friends, and for the delicious foods of our people, the *tsampa*, fresh butter, cheese and so forth that always graced our table.

However, this slowly changed. Gradually I became accustomed to India, and began more and more to admire Indian ways. India has a deep respect for the freedom and human rights of the individual. It is a democracy that truly distributes ruling power to the entire population. This is seen in the peaceful ways of the people, in their natural friendliness and warmth, in their morals, and in their sense of responsibility for the welfare of each other and society in general. India has a multitude of ancient spiritual traditions, and Indians have always respected any religious path that does no harm to others. Where else in the world is there such diversity and tolerance? Of all these good qualities of Indian society, one has special meaning for me. India has a vast array of nutritious and very tasty vegetarian foods. In particular, the lentil and vegetable dishes that, on first encounter, had made me rather queasy, soon became my favorite food.

After a few more days of travel, we arrived at the Dhondenling Tibetan settlement in Kollegal, in the Chamarajanagar District of the State of Karnataka in South India. Nearby, we found the Dzogchen Monastery that had recently been established there. We joined a gathering of thousands of monks and laymen who had come on hopes of seeing His Holiness in person. The monks were from Sera, Drepung, and Ganden monasteries, as well as from a large variety of other monasteries affiliated with every school and lineage, Nyingma, Sakya, Kagyu, Geluk, Jonang, Bon, etc. There were foreign people gathered here from all corners of the world. There were Tibetans who had traveled here from all over India, Nepal, Bhutan, and other countries. All had come to hear the Dharma directly from His Holiness Dalai Lama. His topic on this occasion was Dza Patrul Rinpoche's work on the philosophical view, the meditative practices, and the compassionate activities that are the basis of the Dzogchen.[174] He then gave initiations and teachings from the Great Fifth Dalai Lama's work on the *Kagye* text known as the *Oral Instructions of the Vidhyādhāra* from the cycle of his secret teachings based on his own pure perception.[175] Having given all these teachings together with the ceremonies to inaugurate the new Dzogchen Monastery and to bestow blessings and powers on all attendees, His Holiness set out on his return journey to Dharamsala.

After the teachings, Lama Chönam and I spent ten days at Dzogchen Monastery. During that time we received teachings from Nyöshul Khenpo Jamyang Dorje (1932–99) on several texts, including the *Mountain Retreat Manual*[176] of Kyabje Dudjom Rinpoche (1904–87). Nyöshul Khenpo was closely related to the lineage of Lama Rinpoche and Khenpo Ngagchung. He was very kind and generous to me at this time. Khandro Tsering Chödron (1929–2011), the consort of Jamyang Khyentse Chökyi Lodrö, also took an interest in me, giving clothing, money, and whatever could be useful on my journey and at my destination. She invited me to come whenever I could to Sikkim, where she would take care of all that I needed for an extended retreat. For my return trip from South India back to Varanasi and the North, the leaders and lamas of Dzogchen monastery took care of all my travel arrangements and expenses. Their kindness to me is something I cannot forget.

During this time at Dzogchen Monastery, I was visited by a delegation of monks from Sera Je Monastery's Jadrel House, and also by a delegation from Drepung Gomang Monastery's Zungchu House. Each delegation ceremoniously presented me with an elegant greeting scarf and said that they looked forward to my attending their college. I accepted their gift, but in each case said that I had not yet decided on my next move, and would be returning now to Dharamsala to sort things out. Each of the three biggest and most influential monasteries of Tibet, Drepung, Ganden, and Sera, is divided up into numerous college houses (Tib. *khang tshan*). When you enroll in one of these monasteries, you reside in one or another of these houses according to the location of your birthplace, or for later refugees born in exile, according to the birthplace of your parents. The monastery and the houses are anxious to enroll as many tulkus as possible, as this increases their connection with the homeland and gives the people from that area an incentive to contribute to that institution and receive the spiritual help from it. Later on, I learned from a friend familiar with the customs, that I had made a mistake in accepting the ceremonial greeting scarves from both delegations. The acceptance of the greeting scarf in this context is taken as a pledge to join that monastic house and enter that monastery. I had not understood that, and had just thought that these were groups of nice monks presenting me with a greeting scarf just like so many others wherever I am recognized as a bona fide tulku.

As I was preparing to leave Dzogchen Monastery, my attendant and cousin Lama Chönam fell ill in the unbearable heat that was oppressing that region.

He was quite sick, and I was very concerned. We engaged the services of both a traditional Tibetan doctor, and a modern Western physician. Between them, they gradually managed to return Chönam to his usual robust health. I come from a very large family, with many siblings and a large number of close relatives, aunts, uncles, and cousins, each one very dear to me. However, Lama Chönam has always had a special place in my heart. From our early childhood to today, Chönam and I have shared our lives and experiences, both good and bad. We have traveled together across the mountains and valleys of Tibet, across Asia and beyond. We have gone on pilgrimages together and shared in audiences with wonderful lamas. Much more than a cousin or attendant, Chönam has always been my best friend and closest confidant.

On January 31, 1992, the twenty seventh day of the twelfth month of the Tibetan Iron Sheep year, I departed from Dzogchen Monastery. We went first to Bangalore, and from there traveled north for several days to the holy city of Varanasi. It was in the environs of Varanasi that the Lord Buddha first taught the sublime Dharma. It was here, in the Deer Park of a place called Sarnath, that he "turned the Wheel of Dharma," teaching the Four Truths to his first human disciples, known as the Five Fortunate Protégés.

In Varanasi we came upon a group of Tibetan refugees who had come here to go on a pilgrimage to the sacred sites of Buddhism. We met on a public bus that had been hired for the purpose. By good fortune, there were two empty seats on the bus, and the people there, our fellow pilgrims, welcomed us. These Tibetans were all from the Lhasa area. The Indian bus driver and the Tibetan guide were accustomed to taking Tibetans on a quick circuit of some of the main sites, with some simple comments about their significance. We had other ideas about the proper way of conducting a pilgrimage, and I had with me the famous book by Amdo Gedun Chöphel (1903–1951), known as the *Guide for Pilgrims to the Sacred Sites of India*.[177] When the driver tried to bypass an important site to speed up the trip, or the guide's comments were too brief or superficial, I was able to redirect the driver and supplement the guide's comments. Soon, by the demand of the pilgrims on the bus, I took charge of the routing and gave detailed explanations of each sacred site. In addition, I was kept busy giving offering ceremonies and bodhisattva vows as appropriate to the various sacred places we visited. In this way we were able to fulfill the requirements of a true pilgrimage to the extent of our ability. The pilgrims on the bus now treated me with deference and appreciation.

We made our way, without undue haste, to many of the most important sites. We traveled to Shravasti, site of the Lord Buddha's display of miracles.

We visited Samkasya, the site where Lord Buddha returned to Earth after spending his summer retreat in the Trayastrimsha heaven tutoring his late mother Mayadevi in the Abhidharma teaching. Next we went to Lumbini, the site of the Lord Buddha's birth. Next we visited Kuśinagari, from where the Lord Buddha departed at the time of his parinirvana. From there we went to the temple of the famous monastic university of Nalanda, and from there to Rājgṛha, capital of the ancient Magadha empire and site of many of Lord Buddha's teachings. Nearby we visited the cave where the elder Kashyapa accomplished his meditations. We went on to Gridhrakuta (Vulture Peak), where the Lord Buddha taught the *Heart Sūtra* and other *Prajñāpāramitā-sūtras*, the *Lotus sutra, Shurāṃgama-samādhi-sūtra* and many other teachings found in the Theravada and Mahayana canons. We then proceeded to the premier site of Buddhist pilgrimage, a place near the banks of the Nairanjana River, the bodhi tree and sublime temple of the Vajrāsana at Bodh Gaya, where the Lord Buddha manifested the attainment of highest, perfect enlightenment. After making extensive prayers and offerings there, we went next to the site of the Vishuddha Stupa, marking the place where the Lord Buddha, after abandoning his princely throne, cut off his long hair and entered the life of a forest ascetic. Not far from there, we found the cave where Shavaripa gained his accomplishments (Skt. *siddhi*). Then we went to the sacred Sitavana charnel ground not far from Bodh Gaya, and on to the other frightful Bhayanaka charnel ground. At every one of these many sacred places we took as much time as necessary to generate a profound sense of devotion out of which flowed our fervent prayers and aspirations.

India, known as the Land of the Noble Ones, is the historic place toward which all Buddhists direct their prayers. It is both the place of origin of the Dharma and the land of the most sacred sites of Buddhism. It is the land where, in former times, the Supreme Teacher, the unequalled Lord of Sages, was born and where he demonstrated the twelve great deeds of a Buddha[178] and all his other sublime activities. After the Buddha's attainment of nirvana after death, his compassionate actions in the world continued in the works of his disciples who compiled and published the vast canon of his sacred speech, and in the works and teachings of his mighty followers such as Nāgārjuna, Asaṅga, Āryadeva, and the others among the Six Ornaments and the Two Superiors,[179] and the Eighty Mahasiddha Great Adepts,[180] as well as others such as Padmākara (i.e., Padmasambhava), who is known as a "second buddha." It in this land of India that all of these illustrious beings walked, taught, wrote their texts, and built the temples, stupas, hermitages, and monasteries that we visited on the present pilgrimage. Long before the present time, these sacred edifices and monuments were largely destroyed by invaders whose hatred was inflamed by intolerant doctrines and guided by profound ignorance. Now all that remains of many of these sacred places are broken foundations, fragments of walls and toppled pillars. However, I can testify from my own direct experience that if you have some knowledge of the history and special nature of these places, and if you have sufficient respect and faith, then by merely visiting these sites you will satisfy your deep desire to receive the blessings and powers associated with the illustrious beings whose presence made these places sacred.

Having accomplished the pilgrimage in this manner, we next proceeded to the Dehradun area where we were able to find a number of our relatives who had also come here as refugees. We then went to meet, establish a Dharma connection with, and receive blessings from the three illustrious lamas who resided in this area: Mindroling Trichen Rinpoche (1930–2008), Sakya Trichen Rinpoche (b. 1945), and Drikung Kyabgön Chetsang Rinpoche (b. 1946). This was the first month of the Water Monkey year, and the time of Losar, the Tibetan new year. His Holiness the Dalai Lama was planning to visit the nearby sacred site of Tso Pema for the New Year celebration. He was to arrive on the tenth day of the month, so we proceed there immediately. We joined there an assembly of thousands of pilgrims who had gathered from all over to receive teachings and blessings from His Holiness.

Among this gathering were people of many ethnic groups in this area of North West India, including people from all over Ladakh, Zangskar, Jammu, Kashmir, Himachal Pradesh, and the Punjab. Large crowds lined both sides of the road up which His Holiness was to travel on his way to the monastery. Bowing reverently, we all held in our hands long white greeting scarves, flowers of every color, and auspicious offerings of every sort, and sticks of incense filling the air with clouds of the finest fragrances. As crowded as the streets were, everyone stood there reverently waiting for His Holiness in even, orderly rows. After some time, ten official Indian military honor guard vehicles came down the road, heralding the arrival of His Holiness. Then came the motor coach of our Lord and Protector himself. As he approached, we could see his smiling face turning this way and that, acknowledging the devotion of the vast assembly. As he came near us, His Holiness noticed me, and gave me a special gesture of acknowledgement. A cousin from our homeland, Uncle Gyalpo, had joined me and Lama Chönam. Upon seeing the wonderful way in which His Holiness had singled me out from the huge crowd, he was quite astonished.

Over the next several days, His Holiness gave the initiation of Hayagriva, together with other Dharma teachings. After that, he gave an audience and special teachings to all of us who were the most recent refugees from Tibet. His Holiness then when to the Nyingma Zahor Monastery at Tso Pema, seat of the Dudjom Rinpoche, where he celebrated the tenth day festival according to the rites of Vidhyadhara Dungdrub. In addition to this, His Holiness invited several oracle gods who watch over the Tibetan government, as well as some Dharma protecting gods. In all, this was a most wonderful occasion during which we received so many blessings from His Holiness.

In former times, the master of Oddiyana, Padmasambhava lived here at Tso Pema. There came a time when the local leader, the King of Zahor, turned against Padmasambhava. He was unhappy that Padmasambhava had taken his daughter Mandarava as a tantric consort, and condemned him to death for violating traditional marriage customs. He was taken into custody and placed on a high pile of wood where he was to be burned alive. However, as he had manifested his body out of the dharmakāya, it was not subject to the five elements, and fire, no matter how hot, had no effect upon it whatsoever. Guru Padmasambhava, having attained mastery of the five elements, simply transmuted the huge mass of fire around him into water, which formed here a deep mountain lake. This is the lake of Tso Pema.[181] Having transformed fire into water, Padmasambhava next transformed his enemy the King of Zahor into a close disciple and generous patron. The King then bestowed upon him his own crown, which is the distinctive hat worn by Padmasambhava and seen in sculptures and portraits of him. The King of Zahor then gave his daughter, Princess Mandarava, to Padmasambhava. Later, Mandarava and Yeshe Tsogyal, the queen of Tibet, became his chief tantric consorts.

Above the lake of Tso Pema is the mountain peak on which is the cave where Padmasambhava practiced his meditations. Nearby is the secret cave of his consort, Princess Mandarava, and various other places of high spiritual valence for pilgrims to this area. It is said that the bushes and small trees that flourish around the lake are the descendants of the lotus upon which Padmasambhava sat in the middle of the lake after creating it from the fire. On the ritual days of each month, these bushes are said to sway in accompaniment to the chants of Padmasambhava's "Vajra Guru Mantra" when the entire lake rings with the voices of devotees reciting this mantra. This is especially true when the Khunnu people of this region gather by the hundreds to join in the recitation of the mantra. They have a special bond with Padmasambhava, the

Vajra Guru, from the time when the King of Zahor commanded the people of the region to bring gallons of sesame oil to pour on the pyre so as to make to fire burn more fiercely. They bravely refused, and by doing so formed an everlasting bond with the illustrious guru. Sitting on the banks of Tso Pema, listening to the people of Khunnu chanting the Vajra Guru mantra, was one of the more moving experiences of this trip.

PART FOUR

17

Establishing my Strict Retreat
in Dharamsala

I COMPLETED the circuit of most of the major pilgrimage sites of India, and then returned to Dharamsala. It was the first month of the Tibetan year, and the time of the Monlam Chenmo, the religious and cultural festival that marks the New Year celebrations. The festivities were in full swing as we arrived in Dharamsala, with thousands of monks gathered from Drepung, Ganden, and Sera, as well as from hundreds of smaller monasteries near and far. The local people of the Kangra area in which Dharamsala is situated came in droves, monks and laymen, nuns and laywomen. The Tibetan people, and many from other ethnic groups, arrived from every direction, filled with joy and anticipation, carrying their babies and leading their children, helping the elderly and calling out to brother, sister, friend and acquaintance. This gathering of thousands assembled here to bask in the light and warmth of the Dharma teachings of His Holiness the Dalai Lama.

His Holiness began with a series of teachings on the *Jātaka*, the canonical accounts of former lives of Shakyamuni Buddha. As the days of teaching continued, His Holiness gave teachings on two of Sakya Pandita's main works, the *Differentiation of the Three Moral Codes*, and the *Clarification of the Intent of the Buddha*.[182] On subsequent days he taught Atiśa's *Lamp of the Path to Enlightenment*. After that, he bestowed the initiation empowerments of Chakrasaṃvara and the Thousand-Armed Avalokiteshvara. He bestowed the bodhisattva vow together with extensive teachings on its meaning and practice. He concluded the ten days of teachings with the longevity initiation of White Tara.

After that, I again had the good fortune to have a private audience with His Holiness. He asked me for a report on my pilgrimages in India, in particular, he asked about my inner feelings as I encountered each of these sacred places. After expressing myself as best I could on those topics, I took advantage of the situation and asked His Holiness for his advice on how I should be thinking about my present activities and plans for the future. Where should I go, and what should I do?

His Holiness responded to me, saying:

> You have received teachings from some well qualified lamas, and up to the present time you have worked hard and undergone many difficulties to practice and accomplish their teachings in meditation retreats. It would be good for you to continue these efforts as much as you can. There are sacred sites hereabouts in India and Nepal where meditators and mahasiddhas have accomplished wondrous things since ancient times. However, if one goes on a meditative retreat in such places, it may be difficult to obtain the necessary food and water. The weather may be harsh, and sustaining your health and avoiding sickness will be a challenge. In this way, many obstacles to the success of your meditations will arise. For the time being, it would be better for you to engage in a retreat here in Dharamsala. Do not be concerned with finding a suitable place, food, clothing, and any other requisites for staying in a long retreat. As long as you are in the retreat, I will take care of all these things.

The next day I was shown to a retreat dwelling. It was a meditation cell on the roof of the Namgyal Monastery. These accommodations, together with a supply of food, clothing, and anything else I might need was provided by His Holiness and delivered to me by his attendant Tenzin Damchö. Thus it was that I began my first Dharamsala retreat. Before my audience with His Holiness, Lama Chönam and I had decided that if he recommended that I return to Tibet, then we would go there together. If he advised me to stay in India, then Chönam would return to Tibet by himself. So two days after I began my retreat, Lama Chönam was on his way back to our homeland.

Having made the decision to enter the retreat, I now solemnly promised myself to pursue the accomplishment of my meditations with all my strength, allowing no obstacle to disturb my mind. I began the retreat on the fifth day of the second month of the Water Monkey year (April 8, 1992). As I had done before in my solitary retreats in Tibet, I first posted a notice on the gate leading to my quarters that required others to keep out for the duration of the extended retreat, and informed them that I would be on a silent retreat, not interacting with others except on the second day of each Tibetan month when I would emerge to take care of any exigencies. As His Holiness, in his limitless kindness, had provided for all of my external needs, the only worldly actions left to me were eating, sleeping, and disposing of bodily waste products. Under these conditions, my mind became very peaceful, clear, and free of trivial concerns. My meditative states became deep. My pure and virtuous states of mind gradually increased. All this caused me to become uncommonly happy. On my monthly breaks, if he was in town, I was granted a private audience with His Holiness to review my progress and remove any doubts. The gift of the room and requisites allowed me a remarkable freedom from worldly involvement, and my meditations flourished.

Although I lived in solitude, I was still situated within a community of people. Some were no doubt curious about who I was and what I was doing. Nobody there knew anything of my background. I was like a rock that

Sogan Rinpoche on retreat in Dharamsala—1994

mysteriously fell from the sky. I lived like a rabbit in a solitary warren, rarely emerging, always silent, and never engaging in social interaction. On my monthly ventures out of my solitary retreat, some of the monks and laymen in the immediate vicinity would ask questions to satisfy their curiosity. I would answer as briefly as civility allowed, remain close to my silent meditative state, and providing very little information in an effort to avoid senseless talk and distraction. One time I remember a certain monk from Namgyal Monastery came to talk to me. He said, half seriously:

> If you continue to sit in meditation all day and night, month after month, your legs will forget how to walk, and you will become crippled. If you remain silent like this, your tongue will forget how to speak, and you will become mute.

He then asked me, "Don't you ever read books?" I said that I do not. He responded, "Can you read or write?" When I said, "Not so much." He asked, "Can you at least write your signature?" When I said, being less than forthcoming, "What is a signature?" he became agitated and called me an idiot. "You fool," he said, "You can't read and you can't even sign your own name! Why do we have such a stupid bumpkin in our midst? This monastery is a respected institution of higher learning." Then he advised me further, "You are a young man. Why act so senselessly? Go out and enter one of the schools in Dharamsala. Learn to read and write. Make something of yourself!" I answered only by saying, "Yes, sir!" and returned to my quarters. At this point, efforts expended in trying to convince him that I was not an entirely worthless person would likely have been in vain, and would have used up valuable time on this one free day of the month. A year or so later I ran into this monk after my background and position had become widely known. He seemed a bit embarrassed. "Thank you for your advice last year" I said, "You will be pleased to know I have now learned to sign my name."

The eastern door of my retreat opened to a vast panorama. The first rays of the morning sun would fall on the distant peaks, and gradually spread their golden mantle over the ancient emerald forests that covered the hills and valleys. This expansive vista enhanced my meditative states and contributed to my continually positive and productive mental state.

Something should be said at this point about this special place known as Dharamsala. Dharamsala is identified with Jalandhara, one of the most important of the twenty-four sacred mandala sites in the world, according to the Chakrasaṁvara and Vajrayogini Tantras.[183] In recent years, Dharamsala has become the abode of the Living Treasure of the World, His Holiness the Fourteenth Dalai Lama of Tibet. Since His Holiness has come to abide in Dharamsala, it has become famous throughout the world, as if the gods came down from their heavens and beat their divine drums to celebrate his presence. It is the place where all peoples of refinement and high culture, of every ethnicity, come to gain insight and spiritual sustenance. Dharamsala has become the spiritual capital city of Tibet. Nestled in the emerald green hills backed by the majestic snow mountains of the Himalaya, it is the incomparable spiritual retreat of the world. From the deep forests surrounding Dharamsala come the cries of arboreal monkeys and the barks of wild dogs. In the depth of the night one can hear the distant growls of slinky leopards and the howls of exotic denizens of the thick alpine woods. This is a paradise for so many kinds of animals who fly in the clear mountain air, swing through the forest canopies, or swim in the sparkling mountain lakes and streams. Trees of every type, evergreens, deciduous trees, fruit trees, ferns large and small, flowering bushes, berry bushes, clingy vines, exotic herbs, and alpine meadows all offer opulent habitat for the animals and rare pleasure for the fortunate human visitor. The fragrant flowers proliferate everywhere, attracting the most beautiful and diverse butterflies, dragonflies, and hummingbirds. Colorful birds of every size and species put on an endless fashion show. The cuckoo, the five-color bird, various kinds of woodpeckers, and many different types of songbirds fill the air with their distinctive calls and wondrous songs. Then there are beautiful ravens everywhere. Their loud and raucous calls sound a bit like the sacred syllables, E Vam. The colors of the other birds are like the palette of a divine artist. They travel and play together in their bird communities, flying here and there, in flocks or one by one, making you happy just to see or hear them. Some, like the peacock, display their finery as they dance with fluid and well-practiced steps. The songs of the birds deepen one's meditative concentration when heard during retreat sessions. This really helps the mind to enter into deep states of samadhi. The sounds of nearby waterfalls and other natural sounds can make one think of one's own lama with much clarity. It always brings awareness of the transitory nature of all things. All of these natural features make this the ideal environment for the meditator to quickly achieve the peaceful, relaxed, and deeply integrated state of mind that is the basis for higher meditative attainments. Above and beyond its peaceful, natural splendor, this is the blessed realm of Dharamsala, the true Potala of the cosmos, as it is the abode of Lord of Infinite Kindness,

Avalokiteshvara himself, in the form of the lord protector of Tibet, His Holiness the Dalai Lama. Here the important work of the Tibetan government is carried out in institutions of education, meditation, and administration. There is the cathedral known as the Tsuklag Khang, various monasteries and sacred shrines, and the main and branch offices of every bureau of the Tibetan government to provide for the welfare, health, education, and protection of the people. It is as if Indra had moved the entire Trayastriṃśa Heaven from atop Mt. Meru to this sacred ground in northern India.

After meditating for several months in retreat, it was announced that His Holiness was going to bestow the Kalachakra initiation in the Khunnu Valley in an area some distance from Dharamsala, but in the same region. His Holiness arranged for me to travel there with the Namgyal monks. As soon as the initiation had been completed, I returned to Dharamsala and resumed the solitary retreat.

An interesting thing occurred in the preparations for the Kalachakra. During the preparatory rites leading up to the initiation of Kalachakra, the monks in the monastery preformed the sacred dances, prayers and music to invite the deities associated with the ritual. Outside the monastery, in the public square, people gathered from throughout the Himalayan regions to partake of the opportunity to receive this high initiation from His Holiness. Dressed in their best costumes and finest jewelry, each according to his or her local region and custom, the people played their music and danced in big circles around the square. A representative of each area would be encouraged to come forward and sing a song or ballad characteristic of his people and locality. A gentleman from Ladakh came up and sang a beautiful yak-herding song, the song of the Himalayan cowboy. How closely it resembled the songs of the Golok nomads of my homeland. Not only that, but so many features of his clothing and ornaments were similar to those of Golok, so far away. Then I remembered. As a child, the older people in our village used to talk amongst themselves about the ancient times. They would say, "We were not always poor and downtrodden folks suffering the oppression of a harsh alien occupation. We are the descendants of the mighty kings of the highlands of Ladakh, who extended their dominion to the far corners of Tibet." This may well be the reason for the similarity of the dress, language and music.

18

Returning to the Glacial Valleys of My Homeland for a Quick Visit

IN THIS manner I spent over five months in Dharamsala in my solitary retreat. At an audience with His Holiness the Dalai Lama, the Omniscient One gave me this commission:

> It would be good if you return to your homeland at this time to consult with your lama. While you are there, you should go to the Jonang monastery and receive their lineage teachings and precepts on the six-branch Vajrayoga of Kalachakra. You should return here in one year. You will have my protection on this journey, and will encounter no serious obstacles going there or returning. I have also arranged for all the supplies and other requisites for your travels.

In accordance with these precepts from the His Holiness, I took a bus to Delhi, and from there flew to Nepal. Friends in Katmandu facilitated my transit of Nepal, but I had to cross the dangerous and heavily guarded border alone, relying only on the powerful, unseen protection of His Holiness to avoid the brutal border guards. It had not been my idea to go to Tibet, but I had entered into the broad river of His Holiness's guidance, so that with his powers and blessings, I now traveled easily into and across the vast Tibetan plateau, all the way to the home of my parents. This journey was almost effortless, like a voyage in a dream. Almost miraculously I reached my destination with no significant obstacles.

Not a single person among my family and friends in my hometown had any idea that I was coming. As I reached the area of my family home, I saw my mother. She had gone outside to tend to the needs of the yaks, sheep, and horses. I called to her, "Ama!" Seeing me there, she froze in momentary shock, unable to believe her own eyes. Recovering her faculty of speech, she said, "My son! My son," as we ran into each other's arms. She embraced me tightly as tears of joy streamed down her beautiful face. My own tears I could not restrain.

After that initial reunion, I quickly found my father and siblings and gradually met with all my relatives and hometown friends. This was an exceedingly joyous time. After a week, I left there and went to see Lama Rinpoche, my lord of refuge from the toils of birth and death. As I was traveling to his hermitage, I reflected on the years that had passed since last I had seen him. I became keenly aware of how much I had missed him, of how strongly I wanted to sit again in his presence, and of how much I had feared that I would not see him again in this life. Once we were alone, I told him in much detail all that had transpired since we last met. I carefully described the proceedings of my solitary retreats in southwest Tibet, my pilgrimage to the sacred places in India and Nepal, and my solitary retreat in Dharamsala under the tutelage of His Holiness, who had now sent me on this mission to Tibet. All these things and more I told Lama Rinpoche, and then presented him with the various sacred objects that His Holiness had sent to him. With all of this, Lama Rinpoche was extremely pleased. I stayed in his presence for about one month. This gave me an excellent opportunity to ask him about the various issues that had arisen in the course of my solitary meditations. He gave me detailed instructions that cleared away obstacles I had encountered, and facilitated much future success in my meditative practices.

During my visit with Lama Rinpoche, a messenger came to see me from Awo Sera Monastery. The message he brought was a strong exhortation to return to the monastery, as I was its enthroned founder and leader. I had to refuse the request for the time being, as I had promised to return directly to my home.

Upon my return, I spent several months in retreat nearby my family home. It was wintertime, and the weather was quite cold. This was not a strict retreat as before. Rather than the usual four sessions every day, here

18. Returning to the Glacial Valleys of My Homeland

I only did two sessions. After the second session, I spent the evenings and early mornings visiting with family and friends. I had some disquieting concerns that I kept to myself. These arose because I did not know if I would see any of them again in this life. They did not know that I was to return to India before the end of my one-year errand. Now the New Year festivities were upon us. The first day of the new Water Bird year (February 22, 1992) found me celebrating the occasion with my mother, father, sisters, brothers, cousins, and friends, enjoying the rituals, both sacred and profane, the local customs, costumes, and delicious foods. Losar, the lunar New Year, is an especially joyous time for all Tibetans, as we all turn one year older on that day. It is the birthday of all Tibetans, so we must necessarily throw a very big party.[184] After spending the first day of the Losar celebrations with my family, I went on to Bayan Monastery on the second day of Losar to be with all my Dharma friends. We passed the time pleasantly rehearsing our childhood memories. Happy though it was, I had much on my mind. I was now thirty years old. For us this is an important milestone, when we evaluate the passing of our youth, and the prospects for the later stages of life. Beneath my joyful holiday demeanor, I was a little sad as I realized that I may not see these dear friends again, or if we meet again, they may be very much older. Also, I knew that my upcoming journey would be fraught with dangers. Once again I must trek across the entire Tibetan plateau, then over the highest mountains in the world, hiding during the day, moving stealthily at night, braving the high winds and constant snows of the Himalayan cold season, taking the most dangerous pathways, climbing up and down sheer cliffs on narrow paths above dizzying precipices, and crossing at the most frightful places in the mountains to avoid detection by the border guards of the Chinese regime who shoot refugees like me on sight.

Knowing I would not be there for the next year, but unable to speak openly about my plans, I wrote a poem and read it as a contribution to the Losar festivities at the monastery. The purpose of the poem was to share my thoughts and feelings, as well as to give some Dharma teachings in an exaggerated way to be a little entertaining, but without losing the underlying significance. It gave a hint of my plans for the future. Nobody would understand the hints then, but later on, reflecting on my exit from our homeland, they would recall key words in the poem that suggested my intention. Each line of the poem began with a different letter of the Tibetan alphabet, in order from the first to last.

Alas, my hair is no longer thick and black, but has become dusty grey
    and sparse,

Beard, mustache and nose hairs grow long, but memory and wisdom
    grow short,

Callow youth with its vigor and beauty is seeping away,

Decline and disability of old age are slowly overtaking me,

Empty activities fill my days and keep me distracted,

For others, I appear to be practitioner of Dharma, but thirty years of
    practice have failed to subdue my mind.

Good tea, tasty meat, all objects of the five senses are my obsession,

Happily distracted and lethargic, I am unaware of the approach of death,

I have all but ignored the precious teachings of the Tathāgata.

Joyfully I have been shown the mystic truth of the nature of the mind,

Keeping busy with trivial activities, I have done little to meditate on it.

Leisure and opportunity so difficult to find, I have heedlessly squandered,

Moment by moment death approaches, as sickness and old age pursue me.

Never have I been able to repay the limitless kindness my dear parents,

Or to accomplish much Dharma practice or benefit to other living beings.

Presently I am becoming decrepit in body, and slow of mind,

Quickly I am putting an end to the opportunities of this life,

Rapidly destroying them as if plunging a phurbu into the heart of an
    unseen demon.

Silently the sinister soldiers of the hot and cold hells sneak up on me,

Terrifying hell-beasts from the land of the dead scream "Dza! Bhyo!
    Phat!"

Unable to resist, I will be pulled underground to face Yama, King of Hell.

Vain and vacuous are my vestments and special hats,

Worthless are my high ecclesiastic titles and high honors,

X-actly what good will they do me when I appear before Yama?

You should know that the eight worldly motives are the source of all
    obstacles,

Zero progress will be made on the path of Dharma until these motives
    are eliminated.

The horned auditor demons of Yama keep a perfect record of all my
    thoughts and deeds,[185]

The long-tailed livery demons of Yama will come for me with their
    iron chains to drag me to the courts of the dead.

When will they arrive, in a year? A month? A moment?

This illusion-like body is a contrivance of infirm flesh and unstable blood,
When death arrives, these physical elements will be left behind.
Who knows where I go then? Only the lama knows.
There is no sense in making many clever plans for the future,
The sun of my present life is moving onward, to set in the West,
My sublime father, the King of All Dharma, to you alone do I turn for all
answers in the present and future.[186]

After the Losar celebrations were concluded, I travelled with my younger brother Guru to a Jonang monastery, Thubten Choglé Gyalwa, in the Ngaba region of Amdo. The lama of this monastery was Thukje Pelzang (circa twentieth century). His Holiness had advised me to ask Lama Thukje Pelzang for the unique Jonang lineage teachings on the Kalachakra vajrayoga. After receiving these teachings, I remained in this monastery and entered a strict silent retreat with sixteen other monks for fifty days on the Jonang preparatory practices called "the six branches of preparation" (Tib. *byor ba yan lag drug*). Here my meditation practices and state of mind improved notably. We all stayed and practiced in one big hall. This lama, Thukje Pelzang, was a little overweight. However, he was quite impressive and grand in appearance and demeanor. He was an accomplished yogin who had mastered the literature of the Kalachakra and its associated practices of the secret channels and winds (Tib. *rtsa rlung*). Because of this, he was widely considered to be a true master of Buddhist yoga (Skt. *siddha*). He was also fully accomplished in the yoga of mystic fire (Tib. *gtum mo*), and could comfortably stay outside on windy, subzero winter nights without any warm clothing, wearing just a thin cotton sheet for modesty. He was never concerned with the wealth or standing of his disciples, but only in their ability and determination to practice diligently and uphold the sacred precepts for the stability of the Lord Buddha's Dharma in this world, and the concomitant benefit of all sentient beings. He was one who exemplifies the very best lamas, who are dedicated exclusively to the three principles of the monastic tradition of the Lord Buddha: the study, accomplishment, and activity[187] of the Dharma. In this way, Lama Thukje Pelzang continually enhanced the flourishing of the Dharma in general and the practice lineage of the Jonang tradition in particular.

No one but my parents and a few others knew that I would be leaving after one year. My father would say, "It is so good that you came back home this year. From the time you were a small child you always stayed with the lamas, travelled with the monks, and hung around in the monasteries. You risked everything just to see the golden face of His Holiness the Dalai Lama. Now you should not have so many plans and ideas. Just stay here in your own homeland. Bayan and Awo Sera monasteries need you. There is much good you can do here." My mother had a different viewpoint. She said, "Going back across the border is fraught with danger. My heart would break if any harm was to overtake you. But following the words of His Holiness is most important of all. Your dad and I are getting old. Please do not stay away long. Come home again soon." She would cry and weep often. I reassured her that I planned to return before long. However, it was not to be that way. I travelled far away, and always thought of returning home, but the opportunity to return stubbornly evaded me. In the end, the terrible news of my mother's passing was to reach me in a cold and remote place of exile.

As the autumn began to give way to winter, I went to see Lama Rinpoche. He was sick and had to travel to Pema Dzong for medical treatment. Although old and sick, he spent almost a month giving me precious precepts and special teachings. I was so sad, knowing I would not see him again in this life. He knew I was going India, and that there would be no opportunity to meet again. So he gave me a series of very special teachings. When I saw him earlier, I told him that I was returning to India the end of the year. My mother and brother Guru accompanied me on a short visit to Awo Sera Monastery. The townspeople and monastics welcomed me with celebrations large and small. They did not know I was just visiting and would again be traveling far away. They had made many preparations and plans for me staying there for a long time. There was indeed so much I had to do in fixing up Awo Sera, not to mention rebuilding Bayan Monastery from the ground up, after its total destruction by the Red Guards of the "cultural revolution." But where was the time and opportunity to do such things? This was but a quick, fleeting respite from the bitter exile forced upon me by the terrible circumstances prevailing in my unfortunate homeland. Now it was as if I was led like a yak with a rope through the nose, out of Tibet and back into exile.

19

Once Again Establishing My Strict
Retreat in Dharamsala at the Palace

AFTER WHAT seemed like a short time, the visit to my beloved homeland was over like a fleeting dream. I flew from Chengdu to Lhasa by plane, then with the help of some friends, I traveled by land to the Tibet/Nepal border. Having safely crossed the treacherous border, it then took one week of hard walking to arrive in Kathmandu. From there, I managed to reach India safely. When I reached Dharamsala, I met with His Holiness the Dalai Lama and related in detail my travels and adventures in Tibet. He seemed pleased with my account, and gratified by my return. Then, in accord with his advice, I resumed the solitary retreat on the top floor of Namgyal Monastery. Soon it was time to celebrate the arrival of the New Year of the Wood Dog in Dharamsala.

My cousin Lhodrak was one of the monks studying at Namgyal. He contracted tuberculosis and was very sick, but with medical treatment at the Tibetan hospital and the Western clinic in Dharamsala, his health was restored. On occasion I would have the opportunity to meet with His Holiness and also to attend his teachings. Other than that, I continued my strict retreat, emerging from it only once a month. Other than that, I would never see, meet with, or communicate with anyone. In this manner, my practice became stronger and more rewarding.

One day, a traveller from Tibet brought the terrible news that Lama Rinpoche had departed this world. It felt as if my heart had fallen right out of my chest, and my misery was profound. Immediately I went to His Holiness and informed him of Lama Rinpoche's passing. I offered a special mandala in request that he recognize Lama Rinpoche's reincarnation.

That summer His Holiness went to give the Kalachakra initiation in Garzhar, known as the land of heroines because in former times there were many women living there and very few men. I left my retreat to attend this initiation. On the way back, I visited the special holy sites and places of pilgrimage in that area. I engaged in the ancient practice of Nedrel, which means to not simply visit a pilgrimage site, but to actually spend time there to meditate and make offerings in order to really connect with the special qualities of each sacred place. These places include the site of the self-arisen, talking image of Avalokiteshvara, the holy mountain of Ghantapa, a famous practitioner of the Chakrasamvara Tantra,[188] Tso Pema (the Lotus Lake of Padmasambhava), and several other sacred sites. I visited and meditated in these sites on the way back to Dharamsala where I re-entered my retreat. Later I joined the retinue of His Holiness when he travelled to Mundgod and Bylakuppe in South India. At these places, I had the good fortune to hear His Holiness's profound teachings on Madhyamaka including Nāgārjuna's

Sogan Rinpoche with family photos in his new quarters, Dharamsala—1995

Mūlamadhyamikakārika with commentaries, and Je Tsongkhapa's *Essential Clear Explanation.*

On March 1, 1995, I moved into my new quarters in the Phodrang compound of His Holiness the Dalai Lama in Upper Dharamsala. There I spent most of my time in solitary retreat. On some occasions His Holiness or one of the several official oracles such as the Nechung, the Tsering Che-nga, or the Tsangpa oracles would commission me to officiate at ceremonies such as the ritual cake (Tib. *gtor ma*) offering rites of the various manifestations of Hayagriva. It was quite peaceful around my quarters and no one disturbed the serene silence except maybe the macaques or the gibbons. In this manner my practice continued to go well.

During this period of residence in the Phodrang, I had the good fortune of participating in some of the lengthy and meticulously produced rituals of the Great Fifth Dalai Lama's *Twenty-Five Hidden Terma* on the *Manifestations of the Peaceful and Wrathful Deities,* and also his treasure texts of Hayagriva, Vajrakila, and other deities. These practices involved millions of mantra recitations, each with their unique meditations, and days of fire offering pujas to finalize each ritual invocation of these gods.

On July 18, 1996, I travelled to America in the retinue of His Holiness the Dalai Lama. We landed first in Los Angeles. I was welcomed at the airport by my old friends Lingtrul Rinpoche and Lama Chönam. At the teachings, it seemed like most of the audience was composed of Chinese students. His Holiness lectured on Tsongkhapa's famous epitome of the Buddhist path, the *Three Principles of the Path* (Tib. *Lam Tso Nam Sum.*) He also gave an Avalokiteshvara initiation. We travelled to some of the other communities around Los Angeles, and visited attractions such as Universal Studios. This being my first journey west of the Himalaya region, I was overwhelmed by the sights and sounds of the modern Western city, the technological wonders, skyscraping buildings, and so forth. It was like some mechanical city of gods. Our journey took us on to Canada where His Holiness gave various teachings, and then to Sydney, Australia, where His Holiness bestowed the Kalachakra initiation.

During this time I had some problems with my right ear and needed medical help. His Holiness did a divination and found that the best thing would be to get treatment either there in Australia or in America. Further divination revealed that treatment in America would be more effective. His Holiness said that medical expenses in America are extremely high, but that I need not be concerned as he would arrange with the Tibetan diplomatic office in New York to make all arrangements and take care of the expenses. The clinic that was recommended to me is located in Milwaukee, and there I met an excellent and kindly doctor, Thomas J. Haberkamp. He skillfully performed the surgery, and refused any payment. The results were good, so I could return to India in fine condition. However, before going on an airplane, I had to give the ear one month to heal from the surgery. This month I spent in Boulder Colorado at the home of my friend David Bolduc.

I was then put on a plane for New York, and from there, after a stopover, I was to proceed back to India. In New York, my cousin Thubten Jigme Norbu (1922–2008) picked me up and showed me around. When the time came to fly to India, a funny thing happened. For all this time since leaving the company of His Holiness's retinue, I had been traveling alone. Not knowing a single word of English, I was like a person bereft of the power of speech. This led to some awkward moments. For example, from New York to India I was to transit three countries and four airports. Thubten Jigme Norbu gave me a card on which he had inscribed a selection of odd dots and squiggles that he said were words written in the English language. I was to show this at each point of transit, and whoever read it would know who I was, where I was going, my flight information, my vegetarian diet, and my lack of language skills. Thanks to this card, I had no problems moving from plane to plane. Everyone to whom I showed it was kind and helpful. The final leg of the flight was a nonstop from Paris to New Delhi. Once the plane left Paris, I felt relaxed, knowing there would be no more transits. After a few hours the plane landed. Looking at the people in the airport and the nearby city, I was surprised to see nothing familiar—nothing looked at all like Delhi and no one looked like the people of India. I turned to ask other passengers about this place, but was foiled by my linguistic limitations. We were all taken from the plane and directed on to a bus. I was led here and there in the manner of a dog on a leash. The bus arrived, after half an hour or so, at a beautiful high-rise hotel. I was led to a remarkably opulent private room on the twenty-eighth floor.

I felt a twinge of panic. But how bad could my situation really be if I was being ensconced in such luxurious quarters? When we were leaving the airplane, a young Caucasian couple had read my card, taken an interest in me, and indicated how I was to proceed by way of primitive sign language. Once in my room, I opened the door and was relieved to see my friends were in the room across the hall. They would knock on the door when it was time for meals, time to go to sleep, and eventually, time to leave for the airport. This really helped me to relax. Alone in my suite, I had a marvelous view from all the many large windows. I could see the sky filled with brilliant stars, and below all the lights of a big city looking like stars that had descended to earth. What city? What country? Why was I there? I had no idea. But why worry? I was fine. We had a wonderful dinner, and in the morning a fabulous breakfast. My friends indicated with signs that I should pack my things and that we were going to fly (or at least, to flap our arms). The bus took us back to the airport, and we flew away. I had no idea of our destination, but hoped it would be India. When we landed at the familiar New Delhi airport, I was relieved. I kept the elegant little card from the grand front desk at the hotel. Later I found it among my things, and was able to discover that I had been a guest in the Kingdom of Kuwait. Someday I would like to go back, this time as an English-speaking American citizen. Back in Dharamsala, when I visited with His Holiness, I told him of my travels and my unexpected sojourn in Kuwait. He suggested that I should learn at least a little English.

Later that year, in the eleventh Tibetan month, I traveled with a large group of monks from Namgyal monastery, attendants to His Holiness, to the town of Siliguri in Eastern India to receive the Kalachakra initiation. Siliguri is in the area where India's borders meet with those of Nepal, Sikkim, and Bhutan. The tens of thousands of people attending this initiation had come from these four countries, from Tibet, and from all over the world. After around ten days, this most auspicious initiation was concluded.

The next day I was walking through the big outdoor market place of Siliguri with the whole troop of Namgyal monks. Suddenly we heard the desperate cries of someone at the height of terror and panic. As we turned the corner we saw a reddish and yellowish goat with a long grey beard. He was straining at the end of a rope tied to a thick pole sunk into the ground. The ground was covered in the blood and entrails of his friends and relatives. An angry looking butcher wielding a long, gleaming knife was now approaching. The goat cried and looked this way and that for any source of refuge. I could see how he shook and trembled all over in abject terror. Suddenly his eye caught mine, and it was as if he saw something in my eyes, some last shred of hope, some possibility, some chance, however small, of succor. I immediately asked my companions, some of whom spoke Hindi, to stop the butcher and ransom the goat. The butcher was in the mood for killing, not for talking with monks. He roughly told us to go away, and to do so very quickly. We insisted, and he then said that the goat would cost us plenty. He named a price well beyond the normal cost of the finest goat or goat carcass, probably thinking that would get rid of us. The monks told me to forget about it. Though I did not have so much money at that time, I agreed to the inflated price.

Wading into the puddle of blood, entrails and mud, I then took the bloody rope and led the goat away. He immediately became docile and followed me like a faithful dog. I took him back to our compound and washed the blood and filth off his long hair. I too needed washing, as my hands and clothing were all bloody from contact with the ground and the rope. All the while I had to endure the criticism of some of the younger monks. "What are you going to do with your big goat?" they said:

> We are all returning to Dharamsala in the morning. Are you going to stay here and live with him? You are going to end up getting rid of him. You can't take him back with us, in the cars and buses and trains. This shows your failure to think before you act.

Some of the more senior monks, however, were happy to see what I did, and complimented me for putting compassion before logistical considerations.

What to do? I asked around, and fortunately His Holiness's ritual attendant, Ven. Tenzin Drakpa (also Tashi-la), responded to the need saying, "Don't worry. We will find a way." He located an old friend, a senior monk from Sikkim known as Yuthok Gelong, whose hermitage was located up in the Sikkimese hills beyond Siliguri. When told of the ransomed goat, Yuthok happily told us that he would help. He said that his disciple's place was surrounded by broad meadows filled with deep, sweet grasses and bubbling mountain streams. The goat, to whom I had given the name Tenzin Tsering (Long-Lived Upholder of the Doctrine) would be safe and happy there, and Yuthok Gelong's disciple was glad to have a new companion. I gave him a good sized donation as a stipend for Tenzin Tsering's upkeep and expenses. So the next morning he arrived in a commodious truck, ensconced Tenzin Tsering in a bed of fresh grasses, and took him to his new home in the beautiful hills of the Sikkimese Himalaya.

Feeling forlorn upon saying goodbye to my friend Tenzin Tsering, I wrote this poem:

> On the floor of the sinful butcher's house of slaughter,
> Scattered with the blood and guts of his friends and relations.
> Trembling with fear and crying for help,

Is a bearded goat desperate and with no source of succor.

My friend, if you knew how to speak and understand like a human,
Then you and I, harmonious in thought and deed could join together
And proceed on path of Dharma,
However, you do not now have the karma or fortune for this.

So you ended up in front of a murderous butcher,
You were tied up in preparation to be killed,
You stood there just staring in panic, not knowing how to get away.
How very sad is animal life with such lack of resource and strategy.

But the ambrosia of His Holiness's words of Shri Kalachakra,
Entered into your ears from the speakers in the market place.
With this powerful blessing and predisposition,
You will soon obtain the precious life of a human or god.

O Tenzin Tsering, the pain of our parting,
Lies heavily on my heart,

Sogan Rinpoche with Tenzin Tsering in
Siliguri, India—1996

But in the next life, or a life thereafter,
We may well meet on a happy day of reunion.

Until then, in the company of Ven. Yuthok Gelong,
You now go to live in the Dharma-blessed land of Sikkim,
Where you will enjoy a relaxed life of safety and comfort,
Free from the fear of having your life cut short.

From the highest pinnacles of the upper worlds,
To the lowest pit of the infernal regions,
There is not a single being who does not desire happiness in life,
And all are the same in recoiling from misery and death.

How is it that some do not understand this,
Killing their fellow beings,
Rushing to eat their flesh while it is still warm?
How can people do such things?

Alas! In this world of men,
When will all other living beings, just like you,
Be free from such threats to your life?
I pray that such a time comes soon!

By means of the virtue of saving your life,
I pray that the wish to truly benefit others—the precious *bodhicitta,*
Arises within the hearts of all beings,
And that those who are in fear or in danger become free.
May they all live long and happy lives,
Passing peacefully and going on to attain true liberation.

Thinking in this way, I have long rejoiced in a pure vegetarian diet, and
have managed to generate in my heart maybe a little true, unfeigned compassion for living beings which face death at the hands of butchers.

There was another time during my travels in Nepal when I was able
to ransom the life of a goat from the hands of a butcher. At that time, I
was staying in the house of a Dharma friend in Kathmandu. I brought the
goat there, and with Getse Rinpoche's help and guidance, we performed
on his behalf the ritual of ransom from being killed (Tib. *tshe thar cho ga*)

and the prayers for his eventual full liberation. We then took him to the compound of the most venerable Kyabje Trulshik Rinpoche's (1923–2011) monastery, where he would be comfortable and cared for. Unfortunately, he was not to enjoy a long life, and after a brief period he quietly passed from this world.

This practice of considering the welfare of threatened and oppressed beings of the sky (i.e., birds), the ground (goats, etc.), and the water (i.e., fish), and freeing them from the butcher's knife has long been one of my favorite

Sogan Rinpoche at Trulshik Rinpoche's Thubten
Chöling Monastery in Nepal—1998

practices of virtuous deeds. I do it as much as I am able wherever I travel. Also, I do my best to encourage others to take up this practice or contribute funds to others who do it.

Following the advice of His Holiness, in the Earth Tiger year (1998), at the time of Saga Dawa, the anniversary of the birth, enlightenment, and the Lord Buddha's attainment of nirvana after death, I traveled to Nepal in the company of the Khen Jhado Rinpoche in order to receive the cycles of initiations, precepts, and oral transmission of the Jangter—the treasure text of Jangdak Tashi Topgyal, especially the *Three Cycles of Teachings on Spiritual Attainments.*[189] This is a rare teaching and only Kyabje Trulshik Rinpoche and maybe a few other lamas are qualified to transmit it. We received the *Three Cycles of Teachings* and a few other teachings from the Jangter. The *Three Cycles of Teachings on Spiritual Attainments* is a tantric meditation and offering ceremony for worshiping Padmasambhava in his outer, inner, and secret modes. The initiations, precepts, and oral transmission of this threefold teaching cycle involve also a meditation retreat that must be led by the officiating lama immediately following the ceremonies. We therefore stayed with Kyabje Trulshik Rinpoche at his monastery, Thubten Chöling, for about one and a half months. In the breaks during the meditation retreat, I composed a main point outline (Tib. *zin bris*) as an instruction manual on the practice of the *Three Cycles of Teachings on Spiritual Attainments* according to the instructions of Kyabje Trulshik Rinpoche. He was very pleased with my manual. Upon reading it at the conclusion of the retreat, he gave it a long title.[190] I have heard that he published it for use in his monastery.

Reflecting on our time with Kyabje Trulshik Rinpoche, I composed a song of commemoration with Khen Jhado Rinpoche that we called *The Clear Bell to Memorialize Our Journey*:

In the middle of a cloud to the east of Kathmandu,
Soaring in a helicopter of beautiful color and shape,
Relishing the amazing panoramic view,
Khen Rinpoche and I flew to Trulshik Rinpoche's monastery,
By means of the wondrous kindness of His Holiness the Dalai Lama.

Without effort we flew, without difficulty we landed,
Arriving in Phablu, a place previously unknown to us,
After a cup of tea, and a change of sky-vehicles, we again took off,
Proceeding like a bird over a remote and jagged landscape,

19. Once Again Establishing My Strict Retreat in Dharamsala

To our destined meeting with Trulshik Rinpoche.[191]

Landing at Thubten Chöling, Trulshik Rinpoche's monastery in the sacred
    land of Tara,
We were greeted by over three hundred of the resident monks and nuns,
Standing in long, orderly ranks, dressed in glorious religious robes,
Wearing high yellow hats, holding auspicious umbrellas and sticks of
    incense,
And accompanied by a legion of new refugees from Tibet.

Leading the welcoming procession was Migan Tsering, a monk dressed
    as the spirit of longevity with a long staff, long white hair, and a long
    white beard.
The smoke of large ritual offering fires billowed and rose in the pellucid
    sky,
Auspicious snow lions danced to the music of huge Dharma drums.
Then, as we approached the monastery gate, monks stood on both sides
    of the road, and proffered auspicious offerings of incense, greeting
    scarves, fresh yogurt and fragrant tsampa,

The illustrious lama, protector of each and every being,
Was seated on the lion throne in the buddha hall of the monastery.
The monastery was set in a most beautiful place, just like Tsari in Tibet,
Wondrous with high peaks, flowing waters, deep woods, and flowers
    everywhere.
The weather was ideal, the air clean and pure, the crystal streams
    descended from the sparkling glaciers above.

We stayed here in this mystic mountain retreat,
A place to please the buddhas and delight the gods,
The peace and happiness of mind and body that came over me here was
    amazing.
Trulshik Lama, who I revere with all my heart, mind, and spirit,
Bestowed initiations, transmissions, and profound meditation
    instructions.

He kindly provided the two of us with ideal food, drink, and lodgings,
We were thus able to pursue our generation and completion meditations,

With mind and body in happy and vigorous condition.
The wondrous sound of "HŪṀ" filled the air with the mystic vibrations of
    the perfect wisdom of ultimate awareness,
Freeing the mind from even the slightest trace of the object of negation.

This is the pure awareness of profound emptiness,
Not to be found in this world by traveling near or far away;
Emptiness is the inalienable essence of the mind itself,
Like blood is the essence of living flesh.

This amazing yoga is the very essence of the thought of all buddhas.
However, in a few months of meditation, with the four daily sessions,
It is not feasible to attain much deep and vast realization.

However, by studying the sutras and tantras,
By receiving the precious precepts of an authentic lama,
And by making consistent and assiduous effort to understand them
    and fully integrate their meaning,
I am confident that the welfare of all my mother sentient beings will
    be served.

Although the two of us may have insufficient merit,
And may be too much caught up in worldly concerns,
If we continue to make efforts in these meditations,
We may achieve some progress by the end of this life.

Therefore, we make now a sacred commitment to accomplish the bound-
    less purposes of the sublime Dharma and all living beings,
In accordance with the precious precepts and teachings given us by His
    Holiness the Dalai Lama.

This completes *The Clear Bell: A Memorial of our Journey*, a composition of our shared thoughts by Sogan Rinpoche and Khen Jhado Rinpoche.

While we were staying in the Kathmandu Valley, it happened that Jadrel Sangye Dorje (1913–2015) was staying nearby in the Asura Cave of Yangleshö.[192] This wonderful lama and my own precious teacher, Khenpo Münsel, were fellow disciples of Khenpo Ngagchung. Because of this he took a particular interest in me and treated me with special kindness. "If you are the rebirth of the Sogan Rinpoche," he said, "that means you have a very special relationship with the Sera Khandro."[193] He advised me to seek her out and connect with her by way of her unique Dharma treasure text teachings. I followed his advice and had an especially good opportunity to clear away various doubts and questions concerning my Dzogchen meditation practice.

And so it was that I passed over six years in Dharamsala. By the divine grace, limitless generosity, and profound personal kindness of His Holiness the Fourteenth Dalai Lama of Tibet, I was able to receive from him the transcendent blessings and powers of the Kalachakra initiation six times, as well as receiving many essential cycles of Dharma teachings, of inconceivable value, from illustrious masters of the Nyingma, Kagyu, Sakya, and Geluk, lineages, and, in particular, had the opportunity to study and extensively practice the profound secrets of the Dzogchen. It would be hard to have the good fortune to receive all of this even if one had spent many eons amassing a vast store of merit.

20

The Highs and Lows of My Life on the Shore of the Pacific Ocean

THE PRIVATE Office of His Holiness sent an official request to the Rigpa Fellowship to provide arrangements for my travel and accommodations for a year in America. Accordingly, on October 22, 1998 I left India on a flight to the USA. Sogyal Rinpoche (b. 1947), the head of Rigpa, asked two of his students, Jeff and Kirsten, to host me in their house for one year. In this manner, Rigpa Fellowship sponsored me to study English language in San Francisco for one year.

In the beginning of this year, I had very few acquaintances, and no knowledge of the language and customs of this country. I felt some homesickness for my own land, my parents, and so forth, and suffered a bit from what they call "culture shock." However, I was usually able to maintain a rather serene and happy state of mind wherever I went, and in whatever situation I found myself. This was due to the fact that at an early age I encountered a lama who gave me the profound precepts and teachings of the sublime Dharma. Having received these, I was blessed with the good fortune to be able, in some small degree, to accomplish them in meditative practice.

In recent times, it seems as if everyone wants to come to America. They have many hopes that by coming to this country, they will have the chance to enjoy its legendary freedom, opportunity, and wealth. America has always been known for its natural wonders and vast resources. It is now also known for its many advances in science and technology, as well as its huge military power. The Constitution of the USA, with its Bill of Rights and other amendments, provides for the free practice and expression of many religious traditions, for freedoms of speech and of the press, and for various other freedoms that promote human rights. Not only are these rights and freedoms asserted by the Constitution, but the government and its legal system try in many ways to protect them in practice.

America's natural beauty is found in its vast landscape of forests, plains, mountains, rivers, lakes, and oceans. With its large economy, the largest in the world, the people of America are generally active and busy. However, it is also a place where many people pursue the inner treasures of the mind through religious practices and various spiritual and philosophical studies. With all of its attractions, America is a place where tourists come from all over the world to see its sights and experience its many diversions such as sports and entertainment. In America every person can aspire to many opportunities for advancement, and can demand the same rights regardless of race, religion, ethnicity, gender identity, and so forth. The people have many reasons to be proud of and loyal to their country.

When I arrived first in America, I could not speak a single word of English. Also, having grown up in the remote highlands of Tibet among the nomadic herdsmen, I had no acquaintance with any big, congested, complex urban area like the modern city where I had arrived. I had no concept of a map or a public transportation system, and getting around the city was rather challenging. After a while I learned a little English and was able to find my way to school and back home. The teacher and students at the school for immigrants were very helpful. Wherever I went I was often recognized as a Tibetan. I believe it is because of the respect and love that people everywhere have for His Holiness the Dalai Lama that I have always been treated with kindness in my travels. Now in school, my fellow English language students were eager to befriend me and learn more about Tibet.

San Francisco is certainly among the most famous and attractive cities in the world. It is in the "Golden State" of California, a place rich in natural beauty and resources. Around the middle of the nineteenth century, many people of European ancestry flocked to California in search of gold that had been discovered there in large deposits. Charmed by the beauty and other good qualities of the area, and the lack of effective military opposition from its indigenous citizens, many eventually settled there. As this process continued, cities expanded and people of European background became the dominant ethnic group. Eventually they allowed people of other races and ethnicities from all over the world to settle here. In recent years California, and especially San Francisco, became a unique society where people from all over brought their customs, their foods, their skills and their ideas to produce a vibrant international community. The offerings of restaurants and theaters rival any place on Earth, and it would certainly take years to sample them all. In 1967 there were major gatherings in San Francisco of young people, called "Hippies," who rejected much of the material and nativist culture of the time and many sought various kinds of spiritual awakening.

I found the people of San Francisco to be characteristically friendly and easy to approach. There is an openness and diversity here that I have not found elsewhere, with people from all over the world living together in harmony. I lived right by the beach of the Pacific Ocean, where the sound of the waves is like music to my ears, and the blue expanse of the sky blends seamlessly with blue of the vast ocean, as if the sky itself had come down to join the earth. The Pacific Ocean is connected to San Francisco bay by the Golden Gate, which is spanned by the famous Golden Gate Bridge. The bay is ringed by cities and its waters are ornamented by boats of every size. Four mighty bridges cross the bay here and there, allowing for the constant traffic of swift, brightly colored vehicles strung out along the broad highways and boulevards like prayer flags waving in the wind.

In San Francisco there is always a breeze blowing the cool, clean ocean air over the hills and across the bay. The weather is marvelous—it never gets hot and it never freezes. Looking down from any of the many hills of San Francisco at night, the lights of the city sparkle and twinkle as if the stars of heaven came down to lend their brilliance to the beautiful city by the bay. At times the mist and fog will creep softly into the city climbing the hills and filling the streets with coolness and mystery. The lofty spires of high buildings, and the towers of the mighty bridges rise up above the swirling vortices of fog creating a scene of intricate beauty as if painted by a fanciful and skillful artist.

San Francisco is seven miles north to south, and seven miles east to west. In these 49 square miles are 49 named hills. Among these are seven famous hills. Among the highest of these, around 1000 feet above the waves of the ocean are the "Twin Peaks." A nice road takes you up to the summit of Twin Peaks, where you can stroll along a walkway and look down at the spectacular vista of the city, the ocean, the bay, and the distant mountains.

20. The Highs and Lows of My Life on the Shore

In the oldest part of the city are the "cable cars." These were built in the late 1800s, and travel up and down the hills by cables running just beneath the roadway. You can get on them whenever they stop, and enjoy many marvelous sights of the city as they take you up the steepest hills and down the deepest valleys. Although on the map, you can see that San Francisco is very small in size, just a little finger of land surrounded by water on three sides. However, it is among the biggest cities in the world in its contributions to science, technology, commerce, arts, culture and so forth.

On Sundays we had a day off from English classes. From my house I would walk up to the top of Bernal Heights and sit in the little park. From there you have an excellent vista of the city and surrounding waters. I would do my recitations while observing the sights below. You can see the crowded, busy streets with people rushing here and there pursuing their concerns. I would think:

Alas! Harried inhabitants of this big, bustling city,
Pursuing very different activities and driven by different desires,
But in the end everyone, human or non-human, is doing exactly the
    same thing—
Avidly attempting to find happiness and continually trying to avoid
    misery.

However, the activities in which they engage, the activities of the sam-
    saric world,
Are just like the waves of the ocean—always in motion, but never getting
    anywhere,
The possessions, wealth, and pleasures of the world, no matter how much
    you accumulate,
Cannot possibly bring any real satisfaction.

All my fellow beings and I may find a little pleasure in this world now
    and then,
However, our only certainty is that our lives in this world never last more
    than about one hundred years,
And when the end comes, we will not even have the ability to glance back
    for one last look,
At all the things—the prized possessions, the good friends and dear
    relatives gained through a lifetime of hard work and dedication.

Without any doubt one will then be off alone on the long and dangerous
journey through the unknown territory of the bardo.

All of this brings up the fact that a human life, endowed with the opportunity and ability to effectively engage in the practice of the Dharma, is
of inestimable value. Why? Because such a life, lived with wisdom and discretion, brings about the transcendence of this samsaric world of troubles
and the attainment of a state of true and immutable happiness for oneself
and others. A happy state of mind arises only from cultivating a peaceful
and well-subdued mental state. No real contentment can ever come from
pursuing and amassing external things and pleasurable sensations. Not only
do such things not yield happiness in this life, but they are of no benefit
whatsoever for future lives. Alas, most of us ordinary people are not cog-
nizant of these facts. Instead, from our early childhood until we draw our
last breath at the end of our life, we spend all of our time caught up in the
illusions, the dreamlike illusions of this world. We continually pursue the
ephemeral things of this life just like a sleeping person frantically pursues
the phantoms of his dream. Very few of us ever expend the effort to consider how to make adequate provision for our future life. Therefore, when
the time arrives that our consciousness must release its hold upon our body,
there is nothing we can do to avoid the iron grip of terror, despair, and most
bitter regret.

Take me, for example. In my early years, I grew up in the beautiful highlands of Eastern Tibet. However, I had no opportunity to enjoy the huge
advantages of freedom and formal education that is the birthright of young
people in other lands. I grew up at the time when Tibet was being devastated by foreign invasion and oppression in the greatest cataclysm ever to
overtake our ancient and lofty land. Needless to say, this was a time when
we suffered a great many traumas, deprivations, and indignities. Later,
these circumstances forced me leave behind my beloved mother and father, and follow the harsh and dangerous road into distant exile. Ultimately my solitary path of exile took me to the furthermost limit of the Western
continent, where I knew not a single person nor one word of the language.
Now, as I look to the future, there is no possible doubt that all too soon I
will be blown by the relentless winds of karma to some new life, I know
not where. As for this body of flesh, blood, and entrails, it is but a temporary abode, a borrowed shell. There is no way to know in what country or
what place I will cast if off. Nevertheless, this is a very fortunate situation

20. The Highs and Lows of My Life on the Shore

Robert W. Clark and Sogan Rinpoche in Tibet at the village of Taktser

for me. Due to some meritorious actions in former lives, and due to the profound kindness of my mother and father, I was able to obtain a serviceable body and a life blessed by the presence of the leisure and opportunity to engage in Dharma practices. I was then able to cultivate a measure of faith in the words of the Lord Buddha, and a bit of knowledge about the distinction between propitious and unwholesome deeds. Most especially, I was able to receive the treasure of profound precepts of practice from my singular refuge, the incomparably kind Lama Rinpoche, and to internalize these to some small extent through meditative practice. Whenever I think of the good fortune of obtaining all these rare blessings, tears of gratitude and devotion fill my eyes.

During the week, Monday through Friday, my days were spent in school that first year in America. Sometimes on weekends I would be asked by Rigpa or some other Dharma center to teach Buddhism. My lack of English would have prevented this. However, I had the unique good fortune to meet a brilliant scholar of Tibetan language, Dr. Robert W. Clark of Stanford University. Dr. Clark speaks the most elegant English and is amazingly fluent in both spoken and written Tibetan. With his generous and tireless help as my translator, I was now able to communicate even the most complex and poetic teachings of Buddhist philosophy and Tibetan lore to my students in both lectures and writing from that time forward. With his indispensable help, I regained my voice. I could now communicate effectively in this new world, and teach a multitude of students in America and Europe.

Most of my students are college graduates who have a real thirst to receive the Lord Buddha's teaching. They tend to read all the books they can find on Buddhist topics, and come to class well versed in many aspects of the Dharma. Western students typically seek knowledge avidly and broadly, never hesitating to ask questions about whatever is on their mind. Some pay little heed to whether or not their question has anything to do with the topic of the lecture or with the Dharma in general. Others are caught up in their own personal problems and transitory troubles, and believe somehow that by practicing Dharma they will solve these mundane difficulties and obtain some worldly advantage. Fortunately, a growing number actually understand the basic ideas of the Dharma and sincerely seek to practice it correctly and attain its lofty goals.

It seems that in the world of today, there is a bewildering variety of different worldviews, philosophies, and religions, each with their own myths and rituals. Among these, the Dharma system of Lord Buddha is distinct in certain ways. It is commensurate with modern science in that both privilege evidence over belief and empirical knowledge over any sort of revelation or commandment. In both cases an idea or theory must be capable of being verified or disproved by direct observation, experiment, or logical analysis. The fundamental view of Buddhism is dependent arising (Skt. *pratītyasamutpāda*) whereby reality is understood as depending upon an inexorable process of cause and effect. All phenomena exist only in dependence upon causes and conditions, and therefore do not exist inherently.

Unlike science, however, the Buddhist view of reality (i.e., dependent arising) entails the fundamental interconnection and interdependence of all beings which creates the necessity and indispensability of loving kindness and compassion for all. The actions and behaviors of a Buddhist must therefore do no harm to any living being. All aspects of Buddhist ethics are rooted in this loving kindness and compassion. By engaging in the practices of the Dharma that combine and integrate the sutras and the tantras, the *kleshas* (the mental states that are the source of every misery and ailment that afflict sentient beings) are fully and permanently eradicated from the mind. As a result of these factors, Buddhism, especially the Buddhism passed down from the Lord Buddha himself in the unbroken lineages that have long been nurtured in Tibet, is gaining in adherents. We can see that interest and study of Buddhism is increasing around the world. Many followers of Communism who have said that Dharma is poison, and others who have thought that science will in some way nullify Buddhism, or that social progress might be hindered by Buddhism, are finding themselves becoming admirers of Buddhism once they take the time to examine what the Lord Buddha actually taught.

At the beginning of January of the year 2000, I moved to my new apartment in the southwestern part of San Francisco, near the ocean beach. Several of my students got together to pay my rent and supply me with food, furniture, and every other thing I needed to be comfortable. Among them my main sponsor was Mr. Jay Su, a generous individual who has deep faith in the Lord Buddha's teachings, and who has learned well the way to do good in this world. Thanks to him and the others, I was able to stay happily in that apartment and engage in various activities for the benefit of living beings and the flourishing of the Dharma. Then there came the day that I received the unhappy news that my dear mother had been taken ill. The illness was serious. The more I heard and investigated, the clearer it became that there was little hope that my mother would remain long in this world. I desired desperately to visit her one more time, like one who is lost in a burning

Sogan Rinpoche's mother, Konchok
Drönma (1938–2000)

desert desires a drink of water. However, permission to enter Tibet was not to be given to me. I consulted doctors in my mother's hospital in Tibet and other doctors here in San Francisco to determine if there was anything to be done. It happened that a new, very expensive medication was available here, but was not available in the hospital in Tibet. My mother's doctors asked me to obtain it, and with the help of my friends in San Francisco we were able to supply it. But the die was cast, and my mother's condition gradually deteriorated. Alas! The day arrived when I got the terrible news that she was gone. With that, the fragile link between loving mother and son was severed, and the hope of seeing her once more in this life was now lost.

With the passing of my dear mother, my heart was broken, and I experienced deep sadness. Considering the situation carefully, I saw that the very nature of samsara, the vicious cycle of life, death, and rebirth, determines that everything that comes together, must one day fall apart. This was no different. I realized that the deep suffering I was experiencing over this loss could keep me in misery, or could possibly be an inspiration to deepen my practice of the Dharma. In this way I was inspired to redouble my efforts in meditation and other Dharma practices. Accordingly, I travelled to India, and returned to my place in Dharamsala where I could engage in various extended funerary procedures and Dharma practices for the benefit of my dear departed mother. His Holiness the Dalai Lama helped me to invite a number of distinguished lamas from India and Nepal to perform a great requiem for the guidance and salvation of my mother in the afterlife state.

At this time, while I was in India, I spoke by phone with my brother Guru. He requested that I send him a letter of condolence and spiritual instruction. He said that he was in need of spiritual support and advice. As he repeated his request several times, I saw nothing for it but to produce a composition of my best advice and send it on to him. This is what I wrote:

A Letter of Advice
Summarizing the Fundamental Meaning

O Lama of infinite kindness, you are the lord and master of all the spiritual
  adepts of the Plateau of Snowy Peaks (i.e., Tibet),
In an instant you clear away the stygian darkness in the hearts of your
  multitudes of disciples

20. The Highs and Lows of My Life on the Shore

With the incorruptible glory of your perfect ethics that shines like sun
    and moon together,
Upon the high summit that crowns the majestic mountain of the Lord
    Buddha's sublime teachings.[194]

O Lama, your true form is the boundless dharmakāya, truth body
    changeless throughout time and space,
Your nature is the miraculous manifestation of the saṁbhogakāya, body
    of bliss,
Your compassionate heart emanates in countless nirmāṇakāya emanation
    forms and bodies,
Therefore, please now bestow your living legacy of unerring insight and
    profound realization.

I pray for the skill to fully appreciate the four aspects of impermanence,[195]
And to always use that skill to develop renunciation of worldly values,
And to combine that with the full development of the bodhicitta spirit
    of enlightenment,
So that the view of Dzogchen, pure throughout both samsara and nirvana,
    is attained without effort in a single session.

Dear brother Guru, high are the many mountains, wide the deep
    valleys, vast the windy plains that separate you and me,
But our hearts remain linked together, ever inseparable;
So listen carefully with every one of the hundred petals of your ear,
Listen with care and confidence to the beautiful words of truth that
    I now give to you.

Although I have received so many profound precepts, I have not
    managed to put them all into practice,
Therefore, I can only repeat a lot of these fine words without having fully
    taken them to heart
In this epistle of advice in which the essential meaning is summarized.

Big brother Padma Mati is merely beating the beautiful drum
    of Dharma so you can hear it clearly even at such an immense
    distance.

This body of mine, a branch of the glorious wish fulfilling tree,
Grew up in the lovely emerald mountains of the Amdo region of
  Golok,
But the leaves of the branch, the years of this life, find me scattered to the
  ends of the earth,
The pain of this separation from home and family, like a burning heat,
  made me cry out in misery.

However, the Lord of the Potala sheltered me with his cooling shade,
Allowing me a corner of the sublime palace of the Ganden Podrang,[196]
Giving me real happiness with mental and physical comfort,
And the good fortune to engage freely in my religious and worldly
  work.

However, as the processes of this degenerate age progress,
This world is gradually losing touch with the wondrous doctrine of the
  Lord Buddha,
So that the teachings given by the likes of me are but the repetitions of
  sounds, like a parrot.
Nevertheless, I cannot refuse your request, so I will speak now the
  precious words that express the sublime Dharma.

After we are born into this world, from one moment to the next we have
  no real ability to remain,
Some die in old age, others die young,
The messengers of death come for you in the midst of your unfinished
  business and unaccomplished goals,
Though we don't want to leave this life, we have no way to turn back this
  inexorable process.

Having struggled so hard to live in each of innumerable lives,
In this life you and I had the good fortune to have an incomparably
  kind mother;
She gave us life and she gave us our physical bodies.
Whenever she looked upon us, her face was always like the full moon,
  filled with radiant love,
Her passing now fills us with much sorrow.

However, all physical life is transient, even for the exalted Buddha
  who attained the indestructible vajra body,
We see that his physical body, blazing with the auspicious features
  and
Characteristics of a fully enlightened being, passed from the world.
If we think about this clearly, then we will not be confused about the
  transitory things of this world,
But will resolutely achieve the deathless dharmakāya that combines the
  clear light of mother and son.

Waiting until after you die to address your failings is the way of the fool,
Only the accomplishment of the Dharma now will bring benefit at
  the time of death.
Therefore, consider well how you and all beings, your own mothers in
  former lives, are always subject to death,
And make continuous effort to accomplish the sublime Dharma as long
  as you live.

From the summit of the highest heaven, to the lowest pits of hell,
There is not the remotest chance of attaining true happiness;
And so, my dear and most excellent brother, you must rely properly
  upon the precepts of a true spiritual master of the Mahayana,
Only in that way will you complete the journey to true and lasting
  happiness.

In the luxuriant warmth of summer, the beautiful garden is filled with
  flowers of every color and redolent of lovely fragrance,
A place so delightful that it seems as if the divine paradise of Indra arose
  here on Earth,
But when the frosty tiger of winter arrives, the frozen landscape turns
  gray with desolation,
As if destroyed in the conflagration of an atom bomb.

Although we know with certainty that one day we will die,
Somehow we think, "Not this year, this month, this day," and
Spend all our days making plans, preparations, and arrangements.
Is this not the ignorant play of fools?

The opportunities of this life are more valuable than all of Vaishravana's
   treasuries,
But upon passing from this life we enter the unknown realm of Yama;
With no possessions, friends, or clothing, we are driven on by the inexorable
   winds of our own karma,
Empty-handed, with no power to help ourselves, we are driven on with no
   benefit from all the plans and possessions of our last life.

In a luxuriant garden filled with flowers of every bright color and hue,
Bees hum their happy songs as they fly from blossom to blossom collecting
   the fragrant nectars.
See how later the fine essence of all those nectars, skillfully transformed
   into honey by the bees,
Is appropriated and enjoyed by others in distinct contradiction to all their
   plans, arrangements, and desires.

As we approach the end of this eon of the fivefold degeneration,[197]
The things of this world change faster than an actor changes costumes,
The dear friend becomes an enemy, the closely guarded secret is openly
   broadcast for all to hear.
Realizing this instability, put your trust instead in a true and unwavering
   spiritual friend.

You must fervently go for refuge, with powerful faith based on
   thorough analysis,
To the root and source of the path to sublime liberation—the state of
   unchanging, perfect happiness.
This is the Three Jewels, the only refuge that has the power and ability
   to protect you from the samsara,
Whose very nature is inescapable misery and endless trouble, pain,
   and fear.

If you do not wear the powerful armor of the bodhisattva's attitude
   and deeds,
You cannot progress upon the supreme path of the Mahayana,
Therefore, mount the stallion of the aspirational and operational
   bodhicitta,

20. The Highs and Lows of My Life on the Shore

And with unyielding determination and effort, speed across the
noisome plains of samsara and encompass the welfare and happiness
of all beings.

If you desire to taste the sublime fruit of accomplishing the two types
of siddhi,[198]
Which is to be found on the topmost branch of all the teachings of the
exalted esoteric Vajrayāna,\
You must cultivate the seed of that tree, which is the sacred vow of
samaya held with constant and unwavering commitment,
And continually watered and nourished with the fertilizer of mindfulness
and circumspection.

My excellent brother, you have accumulated much good karma, merit, and
lofty aspiration in former lives, so listen now with clarity and focus!
If you wish to look upon the face of the Enlightened One, who blazes
with the glory of all the supreme qualities and characteristics,
And who is the lord and master of all that that exists in samsara
and nirvana,
Then you, most kind and excellent brother, must search nowhere but
within the depths of your own mind.

Once you determine to seek this ultimate truth wherever it may be,
You can first eliminate the body—there is nothing ultimate there as it is
merely a composition of physical substances,
Speech is merely the movement of air, so there is nothing to be found there.
It is mind, dear brother, your mind is the supreme creator of all.

But where is the mind itself to be found? If you look for its origin, its
abode, or its movement,
First, it has no place of origin, no basis or foundation to be found;
Second, it has no place of abiding, its nature is unproduced;
Third, dear brother, it has no movement as it neither comes nor goes.

The nature of the mind itself is emptiness, as from the very beginning it
has never been created,
This empty nature manifests as uniquely unobstructed awareness.

Dear brother, without any doubt, you will realize this supreme truth
of the ultimate,
Once you fulfill the precept of merging the lama's mind of perfect
realization with your own mental continuum.

However, even though you have a direct realization of the non-difference
of the subject that realizes and the object that is realized,
If you do not then stabilize and integrate this realization in a continuous
stream of non-dual meditation,
Then your experience of realization will fade and disappear like a rainbow
in the sky.
Therefore, dear brother, always exert yourself in mindfulness and
circumspection.

In the meditative state when you focus on this natural, uncontrived,
ultimate nature of mind,
If you are too loose and relaxed, you will tend to fall into a heavy, sleepy
state of lethargy and obscuration;
If you are too tight and rigid, you will tend to get scattered into states of
distraction and endless conceptual activity,
Therefore, dear brother, in meditation always keep to the middle way—
not too tight and not too loose.

Whatever arises in meditation, whatever image or thought of any
object of the six senses,
Never cling to it, but rather remain just like a perfect mirror,
Reflecting every image clearly, but never clinging to anything at all,
Dear brother, in this way you will completely destroy all clinging and
attachment.

When you are able to maintain the continuum of this meditative
stabilization which is the ultimate mind, it flows like a river,
So that you are continually covered with waves of awareness that are
blissful, perfectly clear, and totally free of conceptuality.
Then rely on the precepts you have been given to clearly evaluate the
various experiences and realizations that arise.
In this manner, dear brother, you can maintain and sustain the pure,
unalloyed, supreme awareness of profound emptiness.

20. The Highs and Lows of My Life on the Shore

Within this meditation, dear brother, beware of subtle obstacles,
Associated with any meditation that holds to any kind of object,
Or a meditation wherein you merely sit in a state of equanimity.
Though in general these techniques are beneficial, I think that in
Dzogchen meditation they may become subtle faults.

So then, dear brother, when you get to the point where you can maintain
    the continuum of your undistracted mindfulness indefinitely,
Within the state of pure, unembellished, transparent lucidity,
Which is the essential nature of the uncontrived mind itself from
    beginningless time—

At that point you have nothing further to worry about.

This wondrous and powerful system is the precious patrimony from our
    peerless, unbroken lineage of sublime teachers,
It is the priceless gift that must be handed down in this way, master to
    disciple, to all future generations,
It is the unbroken chain of purest gold that connects us directly to all the
    enlightened ones,
It is this, dear brother, that is most suitable and proper for you to now
    take up and practice to completion.

Furthermore, driven by deep devotion and powerful faith,
And combined with the assiduous practice of guru yoga and the four
    initiations,
Engage in one-pointed prayer, and then the blessings and powers of this
    precious lineage of thought
Will flow freely into the vast space of your inner mind, dear brother.

Unwavering faith of the three types and the two accumulations are like
    messengers of the dawn in the eastern sky,
That bring forth the glorious morning sun of the perfect, original,
    inherent wisdom,
When it shines forth, without obstruction, in the sky which is like
    meditative equipoise,
Your perfect realizations, dear brother, will bloom like the lotus blossoms
    in the summer lake.

Although I have no such sublime experiences myself,
I have experienced the heat of proximity because of being immersed
 in the teachings of a peerless master of this sacred lineage,
And can explain them to you in detail with much affection, keeping
 nothing secret,
Do not forget any of this, but fully embrace it in the depths of your heart,
 dear brother.

Having exhorted me to give these teachings many times with your
 gracious requests,
Take them now, take them to heart, make them meaningful by your
 diligent practice, and accomplish their very essence,
In this way you will please the illustrious lamas of the lineage before you,
 and they will bestow their blessings upon you,
O mighty assembly of wisdom holders of the three transmissions,[199]
 please grant all your blessings!

As your older brother who lives in a land so very far away,
I have taken all that I hold most precious within my heart,
And withholding nothing, present it all to you in this gift of versified
 teachings,
I pray that they be pleasing to you and satisfy your aspirations and
 needs.

May the virtuous stream of all that I have said here with pure virtuous
 intent,
Merge together in the limitless ocean of universal enlightenment,
And extricate all beings, my kind mothers of the past, from the endless,
 fetid swamp of samsara,
May I become the skillful pilot who transports them all to the land of
 supreme liberation.

In a small corner of the beautiful country of India, land of the
 Noble Ones,
Is a second homeland for Tibet, a pleasure garden of peace and happiness.
Here, from the "Soaring House of the Play of Meditative Concentration,"[200]
I send this letter to you on an auspicious day of the Chutö month of the
 Horse year.[201]

20. The Highs and Lows of My Life on the Shore

Sogan Rinpoche and his father with his
mother's picture in India—2002

That was the letter of advice I sent to my dear brother Guru, younger child
of my own beloved mother and father. I wrote it for his sake, with the pure
motivation to provide some accurate guidance and indispensable advice for
attaining the supreme goal. Therefore, I am including it here in my narrative
for the sake of all my friends who may benefit in some way from carefully
contemplating its meaning.

Three years after my mother passed away, my father was finally able to
visit India. I joined him there for a pilgrimage. First we went to the Three
Great Stupas of Nepal[202] and other pilgrimage sites there. Returning to India,
we went on a pilgrimage to Bodh Gaya and all the major Buddhist holy places
there. We then went to receive the Kalachakra initiation and other teachings
from our refuge and protector, His Holiness the Dalai Lama. We had audiences with Kyabje Drubwang Pema Norbu (Penor Rinpoche, 1932-2009), Kyabje

Trulshik Rinpoche, Sakya Daktri Rinpoche, Gyalwang Karmapa Rinpoche Orgyen Trinlay Dorje (b. 1985), Drikung Kyabgön Chetsang Rinpoche, and the hundredth Ganden Tri Rinpoche Lozang Nyima (1928–2008). In this manner, and in the spirit of non-sectarianism, we had the good fortune to have audiences with these heads of the four main lineages of Tibet, and with many more living masters of the Lord Buddha's doctrine.

My mother and father met and married in a time when their homeland of Tibet was being torn apart by a merciless invader and conditions were more terrible than at any time in Tibetan history. Soon after their marriage they began having children; one after another we came. Our lives were characterized by desperate poverty and physical hardship. In addition, we were continually devastated by the horrible news of the ongoing destruction of our homeland, our society, and our people. These mental and physical hardships were unbearable and unthinkable. Yet we had no choice but to face up to them and find some way to survive. Often we had no food and no adequate clothing and were often close to freezing to death and dying of starvation. My mother and father, having given up their own food and warm clothing for us children, were tormented more by worry over our condition than they were by their own hardships and deprivations. Often my mother's weeping and crying over this terribly painful situation could be relieved only by my dear father's unfailing kindness and compassion for her. Although I was young at the time, the terrible memories of these years are sharp and clear as though they happened yesterday. As for my mother and father, their marriage continued for over forty years, through the good and the bad times, until my mother's untimely departure from this world.

Later, when my father joined me for the pilgrimage in India, he took with him his only photograph of my mother. It was her official ID card. Whenever we came to a holy place, he would take it out of his breast pocket and hold it lovingly against the temple, stupa, or other sacred object so that she, wherever she would receive an infusion of the blessings. He wore that picture next to his heart, so that at no time, day or night, would it ever get cold. The love of my mother for my father, and my father for my mother, was as vast and as deep as the ocean.

My father was able to stay with me in India for one year. This was a very happy time. We made up for years of separation, discussing everything good or bad; visiting sacred places and meeting with exalted beings. I wanted my father to remain with me in India and then return with me to the USA. However, the family back in Tibet needed him. Eventually he could no longer resist their entreaties and returned to the remote mountains of Golok.

21

Some Thoughts About the Busy and Pressured Life in the West

AFTER THAT period in India, I returned to America. For several years I was supported by Ed and Valerie Tansev, a generous couple endowed with deep faith. They ensconced me in a nice new apartment in the center of downtown San Francisco. Unlike the area out by the ocean beach where I lived before, this part of town is crowded and bustling. This was also an unusually busy time for me, crowded with many activities.

With a number of my devoted American followers, I started two organizations: Thubten Osel Chökhor Ling, a Buddhist center, and the Sogan Foundation, a charitable organization. With these two organizations legally established, there was much work and many duties to accomplish. For my Buddhist teaching and ritual duties, I was kept busy not just in San Francisco and elsewhere in California, but also in other parts of the USA and Canada, as well as a number of trips to Europe and India. Then there were my own efforts to learn English language and computer skills, and public and private meetings early and late. I had to keep a daily calendar with space for each hour of the day and evening. I would quickly fill it up until there was no space left. My duties were like the waves on the beach, coming one after another, endlessly and without a break.

Engaging in activities simply to fulfill one's own needs and appetites for food, clothing, amusement, and so forth is not a meaningful way to spend one's life. Therefore, I always wished to work for the benefit of the Lord Buddha's doctrine and for the happiness and welfare of all beings. It would have been good if it had been possible for me to stay in Tibet and to engage freely and effectively in beneficial activities to help the impoverished people of my devastated land. However, that was impossible given the political situation. So my karmic allocation was to go off to foreign countries far away, and do whatever I could in those remote locations.

In America and some other locations in the West, I found a modern world of power, wealth, and scientific/technical accomplishment unrivaled elsewhere. However, these days there are also many people who seek inner peace and happiness by looking within their own hearts. They are more and more turning to the wisdom cultures of the East, and especially to the ancient Buddhist culture maintained in the lineages of Tibet. When such people come to me with sincerity and good faith, I cannot turn them away. I must share with them whatever I know of the Lord Buddha's doctrine from my own direct experience and my own practice. In such ways as this I felt I must make effort to benefit others. I set this as the task I must always strive for: in whatever land or place I find myself, my fundamental goal shall be to act with the sincere desire to benefit others. Therefore, whenever I get some donation for anything I do for the living or the dead, I must not misuse that donation. I must use it for the benefit of others, for the unfortunate and the oppressed. I may use it to ransom the lives of beings condemned to death, like ducks or fish, or for anything that will bring comfort to those who suffer and guidance to those who have lost their way. In general, I must always do whatever I can, as much as I can, to relieve the misery of others in all ways large and small.

In the Spring of 2004, His Holiness the Dalai Lama bestowed a cycle of Dharma teachings on a large gathering of Golok people in Dharamsala. Some of them lived in exile, and others came all the way from Golok for the occasion. His Holiness gave a number of teachings to us, including Dza Patrul Rinpoche's seminal text on Dzogchen preliminaries, *The Words of My Perfect Teacher*, and Longchen Rabjampa's epitome of Dzogchen theory and practice, *Perfect Repose of the Inner Mind*.[203]

On this occasion, the disciples of this degenerate age gathered before the His Holiness, the Lord of Limitless Compassion, to receive the blessings of his teachings. This called for many ceremonies with strict protocols. I had the good fortune to function as the master of ceremonies. I was charged with many responsibilities including composing supplication to His Holiness. This was the formal request for the teachings where I composed and publicly recited a lengthy versified offering of praise to His Holiness elucidating his vast and unique qualifications to bestow these profound and transcendent teachings.

From my earliest years, I always enjoyed various types of leisure and recreation. In particular, as a son of nomads in the remote mountain vastness of Tibet, I loved to wander in the open spaces of nature, in the quiet places of forest and grassland, among lakes, streams, and waterfalls, where birds fly and sing, and wildflowers turn their multicolored faces to the sun. I was very happy whenever I got the opportunity to be in such places. Therefore, I would sometimes accept invitations from Dharma friends and students in California such as Greg and Teri who would take me out of the busy urban area to places where I could enjoy the sounds of the countryside and the natural beauty of the mountains and valleys. Sometimes I would camp overnight in my tent, hike up and down the mountains, or go for bicycle rides through the wilderness. Other times I would go swimming, or in the winter go skiing, just like anyone else in this land of leisure and beauty. I enjoyed this kind of recreation and revitalization. My deeper happiness, however, was not dependent on a pleasurable external situation. It was rather the result of practicing of the meditations I had learned, meditations that give rise to inner happiness that does not change with the vicissitudes and exigencies of external circumstance.

After a number of years living in San Francisco, I moved across the Bay to an apartment in Oakland with the help and support of some of my Dharma friends. There I continued my work and teaching of Dharma at my Buddhist center, Thubten Osel Chokhor Ling, and through the Sogan Foundation, accomplished things such as building and furnishing a large (1,000-student) Tibetan language school for science and technology in Golok. The school was named *The Pleasure Garden of Full Knowledge*.[204] The Sogan Foundation built a clean water system for the Village of Elderly Tibetans on Bayan Mountain, raised over $50,000 US dollars to help the young scholar/monks at Bayan Monastery, and engaged in other charitable works. With these activities, I was able to be of some benefit to Tibetans in Tibet and in exile as well as indigent peoples in India and victims of natural disasters in Indonesia.

As the autumn of the year 2012 approached, my father told me, "Dear son, it would be good if you could come home for a visit now. I have had a serious health problem recently, and we have not been able to determine the nature of the illness." I made preparation to leave. However, numerous attempts to

Sogan Rinpoche's father, Konchok
Chöphel (1936–2012)

obtain a visa from the Chinese consul were unsuccessful. I therefore began
efforts to bring my father to San Francisco for medical treatment. I made
efforts to obtain an exit visa so he could come to America. The Chinese consul required a large number of documents, fees, and forms, all of which I
quickly submitted. However, the Chinese regime still refused to allow him
to leave. As the days and weeks went by, my father's condition deteriorated.
For quite a while he had been going to the best local doctors in Golok. They
did all they could to treat his illness, However, they had limited resources to
work with. We had him transferred to the best hospital in Amdo, a twelve-
hour drive from Golok. This was the University Hospital in Ziling. My father
stayed for over a month in this hospital. Although he received good medical
care, his illness did not improve, but got worse and worse by the day. At this
point, my many efforts and appeals at the Chinese consul finally resulted in
my obtaining a visa. However, it limited my stay to only twenty days in Tibet.

The fortunate day finally arrived when father and son could once more
unite. Under the heavy weight of his illness, my father was scarcely able
to speak. However, his expression of joy upon seeing me was unmistakable.
He said to me and my brothers and sisters, "It is now time for this old man
to go. Don't be sad. This is just the natural way of the world. Dear sons and
daughters, please always act in accord with the Dharma, and you will have

good and happy lives." This message he gave to each of us with certainty and serenity. How could we ever repay the limitless kindness that he had always shown us? I wanted so much to stay, knowing that the end was approaching. However, my appeals to the Chinese authorities were rejected, and the end of my twenty-day visa had arrived. I said my goodbyes, and departed. I had spent only thirteen days with my father, as travelling from Peking takes over three days each way. On October 8, 2012, two days after I left him, all efforts to extend his life having failed, my father Konchok Chöphel departed from this world. When this sad news reached me, it felt as if my heart had shattered into pieces.

I immediately sent offerings to His Holiness the Dalai Lama and to other lamas in India, without regard to lineage or affiliation, in request for a series of ceremonies and rituals to benefit my father. I then travelled to India from California. On the way I went to Italy where I had some Dharma duties to perform at the Jangchub Chöling Center.[205] At this center, I was able to enter a retreat for the three weeks remaining of the forty-nine-day bardo period

Sogan Rinpoche with his father, brothers, and sisters several days before his father passed away. October 3, 2012

after the day of my father's passing. In order to benefit my father, I engaged in a mani retreat of the Great Compassionate One, Arya Avalokiteshvara. On the forth-ninth day I conducted the *Door Closing Ceremony* to close the doors of samsaric rebirth for my father. Along with that, I arranged for concordant ceremonies to be conducted for my father at several monasteries in India, as well as by a number of my closest teachers, mentors, and associates among the lamas, without any distinction of school or lineage.

In this way, one after the other, my two kind parents, loving source of my life, direction, support, and security, were separated from me and they left this world for the one beyond. From this point on I am an orphan, and must make my way alone in this world, always sad because the bright sun of reunion will never again rise to banish the darkness of our separation. All our unions with loved ones must end in parting. This is the natural course of the world. There is no one who can change this sad reality. We can never really repay the love and kindness of our parents. We can only strive to fulfill their kind aspirations for our goodness and success. We must keep their best advice and wisest counsel in our hearts and let it be our unfailing guide. For me, that means to always cleave to the precious teachings of the Lord Buddha and seek nothing more nor less than to fully accomplish them.

I had the opportunity to attend the twenty-sixth conference entitled "Mind and Life," led by His Holiness the Dalai Lama. These are discussions between Buddhist teachers and scientists who address issues of interest in creating some sort of interface between Buddhism and science. This took place in January of 2013 at Drepung Monastery in Mundgod, in Karnataka State. The Buddhist lamas and scholars in attendance presented their view of "mind and life" from the perspective that a happy and peaceful state of mind can only be achieved by engaging in practices based upon a view that encompasses dependent origination (Skt. *pratityasamutpāda*) and activities that do no harm to other living beings. The scientists propounded propositions based upon the view that the development of excellence in "mind and life" comes through the thorough analysis of material objects and the propitious manipulation of those objects based on the results of such analysis. There was much discussion back and forth between the two groups of scholars searching in good faith to find some useful areas of agreement and perhaps useful augmentation of knowledge and views. I believe there was some progress for many of the participants in gaining a better understanding of the theories and practices of others, as well as a determination to

Sogan Rinpoche's meditation at the Deer Park in Sarnath—2006

work together to promote the common goal of improving the minds and lives of ourselves and others. The goals we could all agree on included bringing about a better world, increasing peace and happiness for all, and working in large and small ways to help others. I certainly felt that I benefited from the conference as I learned many new things of significance. It seemed that, beyond the happy generalities, many participants were finding specific ways to work together on these goals and to integrate what they had learned in their work, research, and teaching.

All of these chapters contain a rough presentation of my actual memories and reflections without including anything unfounded, but also without giving more complete detail that would have extended this account beyond what seems a reasonable length. I think this is enough, so I will now bring the book to a close.

As suggested in these chapters, I have been wandering here and there for a long time. Not just in this life have I done this, but from time immemorial I have wandered from life to life, taking rebirth in limitless bodies and in numberless places. In the present life, I was born and grew up in Tibet, the

Land of Glaciers, a place of wondrous natural beauty. Due to karma accumulated in past lives, I was unable to stay in that good land, but was obliged to flee into exile far away, to strange lands that were unknown and bewildering to me. At length, I came to the United States of America and became a full citizen, joining with my fellow Americans who came, or whose forebears came, from every county on this planet to build this country of freedom and opportunity. I feel fortunate to live in this country where I can contribute with all the efforts of my body, speech, and mind to the welfare of my fellow citizens and can enjoy the freedom to follow my own conscience, practice my own religion, and do my best to help my friends and students all over the world. Accordingly, I dedicate my life, my resources, and all my merits to benefit all beings, each of whom has been my own kind mother in some former lifetime. In order to truly be of benefit to all of them, I vow never to cease my efforts, for as many future lifetimes it requires, to achieve the perfect state of peace and happiness for all, free of any trace of misery. And in all of those lifetimes, I pray from the depths of my heart, taking a sacred pledge that I will always be able to serve, and be guided in all things by the supreme embodiment of perfect wisdom and compassion, Padmapāṇi himself, His Holiness the Dalai Lama.

Sogan Rinpoche hiking in Yosemite Valley—2006

In Taktser, Tibet, birthplace of His Holiness the Fourteenth Dalai Lama, with California students and friends (left to right) Gabriel Alexander; Dr. Robert W Clark; Sogan Rinpoche; David Benedict (in back); Dr. Victoria Chen; Laura Batie; and Teri Herrigan—2007

With his family at home in Golok, standing left to right: his sisters Dolma Kyi and Tsepo, his father, and his brother Kunga Jamyang. Seated are Sogan Rinpoche and his brother Guru—2007

Sogan Rinpoche with older sister Dolma Kyi on Riwo Tsenga (Wu tai shan) the abode of Mañjuśri in China—2007

Sogan Rinpoche on the throne at Bayan Monastery during an offering
ceremony—July 27, 2007

Sogan Rinpoche at home in Oakland, California, with his best friend Kyi Kyi
(小牛貓)—2010

Sogan Rinpoche at Bayan Monastery with the Machu in the background—2011

Sogan Rinpoche with Bayan Monastery monks on Bayan Mountain—2011

Sogan Rinpoche (top center) with Bayan Monastery monks at Bayan Monastery—2011

L to R: nephew Rigzin Dorje, brother Guru, Sogan Rinpoche, and Namté, with Bayan Mountain and Bayan Monastery behind them—2011

Sogan Rinpoche skiing with Massimo Dusi, Cortina Italy—2011

Sogan Rinpoche at Tiger's Nest, Padmasambhava's mountain retreat
in Bhutan—2013

Sogan Rinpoche meditating on the site of Guru Serlingpa (ca. tenth
century C.E.) and Atiśa's abode in Muara Jambi, Indonesia—2014

22

Some Concluding Thoughts

THIS BOOK speaks of how, in this transitory world that is like a dream,
I have had many different identities and roles in this one birth,
I have been blown by the winds of karma to many strange lands,
And have had many different experiences, both good and bad.

The biography of a true sage is filled with wonders and amazing deeds,
Like the way he or she progressed on the path to high states of true
    realization,
This book gives no such fabulous accounts of the amazing and sublime,
Though there is certainly no need to speak here of such wondrous things.

However, during the course of a human life in this world,
I have had a range of experiences that, if examined carefully,
May have significance to those in future generations,
As they are touched by the sublime teachings of my mentors that I hold
    always in my heart.

Also, I write here of my experiences and impressions as one born in Tibet,
For those who want to know about the conditions of life in Tibet,
Or are interested in some of the Buddhist views and practices in Tibet,
And for the many Dharma friends who have a real appreciation of Tibet.

Encountering the teachings of the Lord Buddha, and meeting with authentic lamas,
Happens only as the result of accumulating merit over the course of
   many eons,
By their wondrous kindness, my mind has found some small measure
   of true peace and happiness,
Therefore, I mention here a bit about the way this occurred.

First, when I was young my parents nurtured me and I then received the
   title of "lama,"
Then I was guided and trained by a bona fide lama, and practiced in strict
   retreats,
After that I wandered alone on endless paths throughout this wide world,
This is my life story, the tales of a child of the land of glaciers.

If one does not know how to control and tame one's own mind,
Even possessing all the power and wealth of a god will be but a vanity,
Fame and celebrity, without taming one's mind, will cause only worry
   and grief,
This is why real happiness is so hard to find and rare in this world.

There is a true method that brings about enduring happiness,
It is that which benefits all: the precious, supreme bodhicitta,
May it be internalized by every living being, oneself and everyone,
And then the true benefit of self and other[206] will be spontaneously
   achieved.

Whoever reads through these sincere words,
Or thinks of me, touches me, interacts with me,
Or even despises me, slanders me or beats me,
May that be the cause of their quick attainment of highest enlightenment.

Throughout this wide world, and on every other inhabited planet,
May sickness, violence, war, famine, and natural disasters cease,
May perfect peace and happiness reign in the hearts of all living beings
   and in their environments,
And may the light of all that is good and auspicious pervade all worlds.

22. Some Concluding Thoughts

With this poem as a final ornament, the accounting of my thoughts and recollections reaches its end, for now. In my wanderings in the Western countries, I have encountered many sincere Dharma students and other well-intentioned people who are curious about Tibet and its traditions. Many of them have urged me again and again to write a detailed account of my life and experiences. Unable to refuse their sincere requests, I have written this book in a manner meant to be easily understood, but is not without nuance. As mentioned before, there is no intention here to present a systematic treatment of Buddhist teachings and philosophies, nor any emphasis on politics or history. I have chosen instead to gather together my impressions of what I have experienced in the different phases of my life to date, and to present them without distortion or exaggeration. May it be of benefit to all who read it.

This book was written in the Tibetan language by the wanderer Pema Lodoe, known also as Sonam Dawé Wangpo, who bears the title of the Sixth Washul Sogan Rinpoche. It was completed on the eighteenth day of the twelfth Tibetan month of the Water Dragon year of the sixteenth Rabjung Cycle, being the Tibetan year 2139 and the common year 2013, in the supernal palace of His Holiness, Arya Avalokiteshvara, the town of Dharamsala in the Northwest of India, Land of the Noble Ones.

May it all be auspicious!

* * * * *

This book was translated from the Tibetan into English by Robert Warren Clark, Ph.D., Coordinator of the Tibetan Language Program at Stanford University, known in the Tibetan community as Lotzawa Jambel Drakpa. The translation was completed on the twenty-fourth day of Tamuz, 5774 (i.e., July 22, 2014) in the hermitage of Tardo Ling in the village of Broadmoor in Northern California.

Sabbadānaṁ dhammadānaṁ jinati

(The greatest of all gifts is the gift of the Dharma)

Notes

1. Padmamati Publisher, 33040 Torreano, Udine, Italy. ISBN 978-88-908586-1-1.

2. A *tulku* is someone who is recognized, by someone in authority, as the rebirth of a distinguished lama or other Buddhist luminary or divinity.

3. Short for "Venerable."

4. The auspicious eight substances are: the mirror (Skt. *ādarśa*), precious medicine (Skt. *gorocanā*), yogurt (Skt. *dadhi*), durva grass, bilva fruit, right-turning conch shell (Skt. *dakṣiṇāvarta śaṅkha*), vermilion powder (Skt. *sindūra*), and mustard seed (Skt. *sarṣapa*).

5. Some modern linguists speculate that Tibetan language might have some relation to archaic Burmese. Whereas Chinese has thousands of characters, Tibetan has an alphabet like Sanskrit and other Indo-European languages such as English. The Tibetan alphabet has thirty consonants and five vowels.

6. Tib. *kun bzang bla ma'i zhal lung* of Dza Patrul Rinpoche. Published in Tibetan by Sogan Rinpoche, Pema Lodoe (New Delhi: Archana, 2003). Published in English as *The Words of My Perfect Teacher* (Boston: Shambhala, 1998) ISBN 1-57062-412-7

7. The five sets of preliminary practices (Tib. *sngon 'gro*) consist of (1) 100,000 prostrations to the Buddha and the assembly of enlightened beings; (2) 100,000 recitations of the refuge and bodhicitta (i.e., pure attitude of the bodhisattva) formulas; (3) 100,000 Vajrasattva purifications; (4) 100,000 mandala offerings; and (5) 100,000 guru yoga practices. Each session of any of these practices is concluded with a dedication of merit to universal enlightenment.

8. There is an alternate reading of the last two lines due to the ambiguity of the Tibetan in poetic constructions. These lines could read:

> And like the elements gold and silver,
> His mind will never change.

I did not manage to question the lama on which meaning he intended. Perhaps both meanings were meant to be understood.

9. The "two teachings" are commonly described as indicating the verbal teachings as contained in the Buddhist canon, and the realization of those teachings in the hearts of those who effectively practice them. "Two teachings" can also indicate the older translations from the canon, as presented in the Nyingmapa lineage and elsewhere, and the newer translations as presented in the Gelukpa, Sakyapa, Kargyu and so forth. Bayan Monastery was known as a non-sectarian institution where both lineages were taught and practiced together.

10. The Chinese authorities were concerned that no evidence of Tibetan monastic culture remained. They destroyed Tibetan institutions so thoroughly, it seems, so they could then even deny that these institutions had ever existed. Their vision was the complete obliteration of Tibetan culture in Tibet, and its replacement by Han Chinese culture. Even the ruins of monasteries and shrines were unacceptable. In Golok and surrounding areas, this destruction without a trace largely succeeded. In other places, as in Central Tibet, the monasteries were too large and numerous to completely obliterate.

11. The three sets of vows are the pratimokṣa, bodhisattva, and tantric systems of vows, commitments, and practices.

12. Do Khyentse Yeshe Dorje (Tib. *mdo mkhyen brtse ye shes rdo rje*, 1800–1866) was the rebirth of Rigzin Jigme Lingpa (1729–98), and was known as the emanation of Jigme Lingpa's mind. He was renowned as the son of the powerful mountain god Nyenchen Tanglha. His root lama was the First Do Drubchen Jigme Trinlay Özer (1745–1821), and he himself was the root lama of Dza Patrul Rinpoche (1808–87).

13. Wangchen Gyerab Dorje (Tib. *dbang chen dgyes rab rdo rje*) was a teacher of Jamgön Ju Mipham (1846–1912).

14. The three foundations of monastic training (Tib. *'dul ba gzhi gsum*) are (1) the summer retreat (Tib. *dbyar gnas*; Skt. *varṣā, varṣika*), (2) the ceremony that concludes the summer retreat (Tib. *dgag dbye*), and (3) the monastic purification practice (Tib. *gso sbyong*) that is held in monastic communities on the new moon and full moon of each month since it was instituted by Buddha Shakyamuni.

15. Khewang Lozang Dongak Chökyi Gyatso (Tib. *mkhas dbang blo bzang mdo sngags chos kyi rgya mtsho*, 1903–57) was also known as Nyen-gön Sungrab Tulku (Tib. *snyan dgon gsung rab sprul sku*).

16. Sechen Monastery in Kham is the main Eastern Tibetan branch of Mindröling Monastery of Lhasa.

17. Of the 6,436 monasteries in Tibet before the Chinese invasion, the Chinese Communist Party ordered the complete destruction of 6,423 monasteries. Thirteen large monasteries have been kept as museums and Tibetan cultural "theme parks" with skeleton crews of disempowered monks.

18. The Machu River flows down from the Tibetan plateau and east across China to the Pacific. It is known there as the Yellow River (Ch. *huang he*). It is the sixth longest river in the world, flowing 3,395 miles from the Bayan Har mountains in Tibet to the Pacific Ocean. Historically, the Machu River basin is known as the "cradle of East Asian civilization."

19. The term "wheel protector" (Tib. *'khor lo'i mgon po*) refers to the authentic lama's ability to protect the disciple's inner wheels (Skt. *cakra*) that are the inner mechanisms of an individual's life and destiny. The wheel-protecting lama is also called the "root lama."

20. The *three types of kindness* shown by an authentic lama are the kindnesses of bestowing the tantric initiation, the lineage transmission, and the precepts and detailed instruction required for effective practice of the sublime Dharma.

21. A *lha reg kha btags* is a white silk greeting scarf of the type suitable to be offered as a gift to gods and goddesses.

22. The First Do Drubchen Rinpoche Jigme Trinlay Özer (1745–1821) born in the Do region of Golok.

23. Drimé Özer (1308–1364), also known as Longchen Rabjam or Longchenpa (Tib. *klong chen pa*). As an enlightened being, he sends emanations (Skt. *nirmāṇakāya*) such as wise and compassionate teachers as needed for the benefit of beings.

24. The all-conquering realization of spontaneous presence (Tib. *lhun grub thod rgal*) is the superior of the two main practices of Dzogchen, the other being Cutting Through to Primordial Purity (Tib. *ka dag khregs chod*). Its superiority is described by way of seven unique features described in Jigme Lingpa's text.

25. Tib. *bar do'i smon lam dgongs gcig rgya mtsho*. The text that was so helpful to Lama Rinpoche when it was smuggled in a bottle of yogurt into the Darlag Dzong death camp where he was on death row.

26. *Tong len* (Tib. *gtong len,* Lit. "bestowing and taking") is a Buddhist meditation where one cultivates the ability to bestow all good things upon others, and take from them all their troubles, pains, and obstacles.

27. A tertön (Tib. *gter ston*) is a lama who reveals special teachings given by Padmasambhava for use in later centuries.

28. Do Drubchen Kunzang Shenpen (Tib. *rdo grub chen kun bzang gzhan phan*) lived from 1745 to 1821. He is also known as Do Drubchen Jigme Trinlay Özer (Tib. *'jigs*

med phrin las 'od zer), was the First Do Drubchen Rinpoche, and the main disciple of Jigme Lingpa (Tib. *'jigs med gling pa*, 1729–98).

29. Khenpo Jigme Phuntsok (Tib. *mkhan po 'jigs med phun tshogs*) (1933–2004) was born in the Water Bird year of 1933 in the Lhonor district of Serta, in Kham (Eastern Tibet). He was the founder and head of the great monastery and university of Larung Gar in Serta and died in Chinese police custody in Chengdu, 2004.

30. Khenpo Münsel Rinpoche (1916–93).

31. Magic wisdom body (Tib. *ye shes sgyu ma'i sku*). This is one of the ways in which those on advanced stages of enlightenment manifest themselves to elite meditators and yogins in order to teach and inspire them.

32. The eight worldly concerns are the ordinary worldly obsessions with gain and loss, pleasure and pain, fame and disgrace, praise and blame. These worldly concerns motivate ordinary people and cause them to accumulate bad karma and wander endlessly from lifetime to lifetime in the samsara. They are the hope for pleasure and the fear of pain, the hope for gain and the fear of loss, the hope for fame and the fear of disgrace, and the hope for praise and the fear of blame.

33. Dissolved into suchness (Tib. *dbyings su zhi*).

34. In the state of perfect, complete enlightenment (Skt. *dharmakāya*), there is no need for any further practice or training, so it is called the meditation-free zone of the dharmakāya (Tib. *sgom med chos sku'i klong*).

35. English descriptions of the Nyingma tradition of Buddhism in Tibet are widely available. The following is a brief description of Nyingma history based on information provided in an article that appeared on a web site of His Holiness the Dalai Lama. The origins of the Nyingma are associated with the work of an Indian yogin, Padmasambhava, also known as Guru Rinpoche. He came to Tibet at the invitation of the Tibetan King, Trisong Detsen (742–797). At the suggestion of the sublime Indian scholar Shantaraksita, the King asked Padmasambhava to come to Tibet to overcome the local opposition to the spread of Buddhism. This opposition was from conservative elements of the Tibetan ruling classes, and, according to tradition, from local divinities and demons who, like their human counterparts, feared that their privileged position was under threat. Shantaraksita was feared throughout India as the greatest debater, who could overcome any intellectual opposition to the spread of Buddhism. But the Tibetan opposition was more visceral and less intellectual. Padmasambhava's special yogic and mantra powers were needed. It is said that he vanquished the divinities and demons with these powers, and forced them to swear fidelity to him, the King, and the Three Jewels. The human followers of these divinities and demons then fell in line.

With these obstacles cleared away, King Trisong Detsen, Shantaraksita, and Padmasambhava joined together to complete Samye, the first Buddhist monastery of Tibet in the year 810. Once established and consecrated, Samye became the home for Tibet's first native Buddhist monks, and the center of Buddhist culture in Tibet. Soon the tremendous task of translating the Buddhist canon from Sanskrit to Tibetan began in earnest at Samye, and continued for many centuries.

Padmasambhava gathered many Tibetan disciples, in particular his twenty-five main disciples. He transmitted to them many teachings, in particular the esoteric system of the Dzogchen. These disciples were assigned tasks consistent with their abilities, to spread the teachings and to take rebirth in the centuries to come as tertöns (i.e., Dharma treasure revealers). As tertöns, they appeared from that time to the present and gave the hidden teachings of Padmasambhava as relevant in each new place and time. Each of these disciples possessed special powers. For example, Vairocana was renowned for his penetrating insight, Khandro Yeshe Tsogyal for her ability to frighten away the lord of death and remove all obstacles of a long and successful life, Jñana Kumara for his magical abilities, Namkai Nyingbo for his ability to cross the sky on beams of light, and Kawa Peltsek for his ability to read the minds of others.

Padmasambhava was joined by other important Indian Buddhist scholars, yogins, and *siddhas* such as Dharmakirti, Vimalamitra, Buddhaguhya, and Shantipa. Gradually both the yogic traditions of the siddha and the canonical traditions of the scholars spread through the land. In particular, the Dzogchen tradition took a central place in the early centuries of Buddhism in Tibet. It was brought by Padmasambhava and others. They are said to have received it from a lineage that included Garab Dorje, Shri Simha, Jñanasutra, Vimalamitra.

While the oldest Nyingma monastery is Samye, there were no other major Nyingma monasteries built until Nechung Monastery was established in the twelfth century by Chokpa Jangchub Palden, and Katok Monastery was built in Eastern Tibet in the year 1159 by Kadampa Desheg (1112–92). Later, in 1676, Mindröling Monastery was established by Rigzin Terdag Lingpa (1646–1714). He was also known as Minling Terchen Gyurmed Dorje. Dorje Drag Monastery was established by Rigzin Ngagi Wangpo in 1659. Palyul Monastery was established by Rigzin Kunzang Sherab in 1665. Dzogchen Monastery was built in 1685 by Dzogchen Pema Rigzin. Zhechen Rabjampa established Zhechen Monastery in 1735. Other important monasteries in Amdo (northeast Tibet) include Do Drubchen Monastery, Awo Sera Monastery, and Tarthang Monastery.

After the holocaust of the 1950s and 1960s, major Nyingma monasteries that were destroyed in Tibet were re-established in India. These include Tubten Evam Dorje Drag in Simla, Thekchok Namdrol Shedrub Dargye Ling in Bylakuppe (Karnataka), Nechung Drayang Ling in Dharamsala, Ngedon Gatsal Ling in Dehra Dun; and Evam Gyurmed Ling and Palyul Chökhor Ling in Bir.

One of the distinguishing differences between the Nyingma and the other Buddhist lineages in Tibet is that the former divides all Buddhist teachings into nine vehicles, whereas the latter divide them into three sutra vehicles and four tantric systems. The nine consist of the three sutra vehicles (shravaka, pratyeka-buddha, and bodhisattva vehicles); three common tantra vehicles—Kriya tantra (external practices and rituals), Upa tantra (external practices combined with meditations), Yoga tantra (mostly meditation); and three inner tantras—Mahāyoga (generation stage practices), Anuyoga (completion stage practices), and Atiyoga (identified specifically with the Dzogchen).

Within Dzogchen lineages there are three philosophical systems: Vairochana and Shrisimha's mentalist system (Tib. *sems sde*); the space expanse system (Tib. *klong sde*) of Shrisimha, Vairochana, and Longde Dorje Zampa; and the precept system (Tib. *man ngag sde*) attributed to Padmasambhava's inner essence lineage (Tib. *snying thig*) and systematized by Manjushrimitra.

The Nyingma transmission of canonical literature consists of three types of teaching: oral traditions, treasure texts, and pure vision. The oral traditions include the tantras of the Mahāyoga, the Anuyoga, and the Atiyoga (i.e., Dzogchen). The treasure texts include the works (or discoveries) of lamas over the centuries including the so called "Five Kings of the Treasure Texts," whose teachings include meditations related to Avalokiteshvara, Padmasambhava practices (Skt. *sādhanā*), Dzogchen teachings, the Kagye teachings, Vajrakila teachings, and teachings on medicine, transmigration, exorcism, and magic. The Five Kings are Nyangral Nyima Özer (1124–92), Guru Chowang (1212–70), Dorje Lingpa (1346–1405), Padma Lingpa (b. 1405) and Jamyang Khyentse (1820–92). These and many other tertöns (i.e., "treasure text revealers") keep the Nyingma lineages lively and relevant in each generation by giving new teachings to meet the needs of changing times and circumstances. This is also done by the "pure visions" which are teachings given by teachers whose level of realization allows them to directly perceive ultimate truth and find ways to lead ordinary people to that realization.

While the Nyingma lineages accept the same *Kangyur* and *Tangyur* (i.e., the canon of sutras, tantras, and shastras) as other Tibetan schools, they also have an exclusive canon of *Nyingma* tantras as compiled by Longchen Rabjampa (1308–63) and Tertön Ratna Lingpa (1403–73), as well as the *Treasury of Precious Termas* (Tib. *rin chen gter mdzod*), which consists of sixty volumes compiled by Kongtrul Yonten Gyatso (1813–99) and an extensive library of the collected works (Tib. *gsung 'bum*) of many influential Nyingma teachers, yogins and scholars such as Rongzom Chökyi Zangpo (1012–88), Do Drubchen Jigme Trinlay Özer (1745–1821), Patrul Rinpoche (1808–87), and Jamgön Mipham Gyatso (1846–1912).

The Nyingma lineage continues into the twenty-first century as a dynamic school of Buddhist thought and practice. Its dynamism comes from its ability, developed over so many centuries, of adapting ancient truths and practices to the changing needs of different generations.

36. Lungtok Tenpay Nyima (1829–1902) was the lama of Khenpo Ngagchung (1879–1941), who was Lama Rinpoche's own lama.

37. Tib. *drang srong skyo glu* (Full title: *drang srong skyo glu nges pa'i mt shang 'don mgon po'i skul 'debs spro dga' bskyed cing bgros su gdams pa*).

38. The detailed explanation (Tib. *khrid*) is the instruction on the meaning of a text. The spiritual transmission (Tib. *lung*) is where a lama reads the entire text, sometimes exceedingly quickly, to his disciples in order to transmit to them a textual teaching he himself has received from his lama. In this way, the blessings and powers of the teaching are transmitted from master to disciple in generation after generation. A lama may choose to give the khrid and the lung separately, on different occasions, or to give both together, or to give just one or the other.

39. The Five-Fold Preliminary Practice consists of the accumulation of 100,000 full prostrations to the Three Jewels and the Buddhist pantheon, 100,000 refuge rituals, 100,000 bodhicitta generation practices, 100,000 Vajrasattva purification practices, and 100,000 mandala offerings.

40. Lhotsen was my father's cousin. However, in Tibet we refer to any close relative of our parents' generation as "uncle" or "aunt".

41. Although my mother's terminal illness lasted almost a year, and I was able to send medicines and help to arrange for medical care from my new home in America, my many attempts to receive permission to visit my mother were blocked by the Chinese regime.

42. The special spiritual bond is requested upon encountering a spiritual teacher in whom one has faith. A brief encounter with a respected teacher is made meaningful by gaining some sort of individual guidance. A Buddhist person will ask a lama for a special spiritual bond and may leave the exact form to the lama's discretion. For example, the lama may give a teaching or some precepts tailored to that individual's unique needs, abilities, and predispositions. He may recite certain prayers or mantras. He may present the person with a sacred substance, or read them a particular scripture. Others will request the special spiritual bond as a teaching on a particular subject or a recitation of a text that they have brought.

43. The actual substance (Tib. *dngos 'byor*) mandala is the offering of all of one's valuable property. It is often presented in the form of gold, silver, jewels, textiles, livestock, etc. The mental manifestation (Tib. *yid sprul*) mandala is the offering of non-material substances produced through the power of meditation.

44. Tib. *gzhi khregs chod skabs kyi zin bris bstan pa'i nyi ma'i zhal lung snyan brgyud chu bo bcud 'dus*. This text has not been published to date.

45. A Dharma treasure (Tib. *gter chos*), also called a treasure text, is a special tantric or Dzogchen teaching given by Padmasambhava (700's) to his disciples to be used in future times as needed, such as when they take rebirth in later centuries. These teachings are crafted to be of special benefit to the beings of the times and places where they appear, and to the lineages of masters and disciples who follow them. The Dharma treasure may suddenly come to the teacher who is called a tertön (i.e., "treasure revealer"), and who is recognized as having been, centuries earlier, a disciple of Padmasambhava. Typically the tertön would then recite the teaching and a disciple or disciples would make an authorized transcription that would subsequently become part of the Nyingma canon.

46. The hair and nails are the insensate parts of the body, and therefore are not pervaded by the mind of the highly adept practitioner of the Dzogchen who leaves them behind at death while dissolving the rest of the body into the clear light of the mind.

47. The rainbow body (Tib. *'ja' lus*) is the dissolution of the body into rainbowlike light at the time of death by one who has realized the ultimate and therefore can no longer be obstructed by anything in either samsara (i.e., ordinary existence) or nirvana.

48. Tib. *bar do bzhi*; Skt. *caturantarābhava*. The four states of existence are (1) the natural state (Tib. *rang bzhin bar do*; Skt. *jatyantarābhava*); (2) the state at the moment of death (Tib. *'chi kha'i bar do*; Skt. *mumūrṣāntarābhava*); (3) the state of reality itself (Tib. *chos nyid kyi bar do*; Skt. *dharmatāntarābhava*); (4) the state of becoming (Tib. *srid pa'i bar do*; Skt. *bhāvāntarābhava*).

49. The manner of producing such texts at that time was limited by circumstance and technology to hand copying by people like Sogan Rinpoche. Gradually, in the years that followed, copy machines became available in the larger towns of his remote district. In 2011 Sogan Rinpoche and his associates managed, with the backing of the Tsadra Foundation, to publish this and other texts by Lama Rinpoche in one volume, *mkhan chen mun sel mchog gi zab gsung phyogs bsdus* (*The Collected Works of Khenpo Münsel*). 1000 copies were printed privately. This text is reproduced in Tibetan as chapter 6 of this volume.

50. This text is reproduced in Tibetan as chapter 5 of *mkhan chen mun sel mchog gi zab gsung phyogs bsdus* (*The Collected Works of Khenpo Münsel*).

51. An important and influential lama such as Khenpo Ngagchung may choose to emanate more than one body. Having attained the powers of control over rebirth, and being motivated by the bodhisattva's vow to guide all beings to liberation, a lama may be reborn as three or more individuals. These may be designated respectively, the lama's body emanation, his speech emanation, and his mind emanation. In addition, he may send an emanation of his qualities and another of his activities.

52. Tib. *ye shes bla ma* (Full title: *Rdzogs pa chen po klong chen snying thig gi khrid yig ye shes bla ma*).

53. The Sanskrit term *vikalpa* (Tib. *rnam rtog*) in general means "confusion," but more precisely it is any conceptual process such as discursive thought, preconceived ideas, interpretative concepts, habitual thinking, thought construction, conceptualized reflection, imagination, conceptual understanding, conceptual division into subject and object, superstition, dualistic thought, clinging to duality, etc. This is the true enemy, the true evil that must be eliminated according to the Buddhist perspective because it confuses and obstructs the mind, preventing the direct perception of ultimate reality (a.k.a. the supreme ultimate, the nature of mind).

54. The lineage of actuality refers to the first of the three types of lineage in the Dzogchen. The three types of lineage of the wisdom holder of the Dzogchen are (1) the lineage of the inner thought of the Buddha himself (Tib. *rgyal ba dgongs pa'i brgyud pa*), (2) the lineage of the symbolic words of the wisdom holder (Tib. *rig 'dzin brda yi brgyud pa*), and (3) the lineage of that which can be heard by an ordinary person (Tib. *gang zag snyan khung brgyud pa*). The lineage of actuality is the innermost reality, the essence of the thought of the Buddha himself. It is something beyond the grasp of words or expression. Its full realization is what distinguishes one as an enlightened being. It is the ultimate essence of the Buddha's own realization, and the precious nectar of supreme realization that is handed down from bona fide master to authentic disciple.

55. Dzogchen maintains the essential continuum of its practice (Tib. *nyams len gyi ngo bo rgyun skyong rgyu yod pa*) means that Dzogchen practice consists of maintaining continual awareness of one's direct realization of profound emptiness. That is, once one has directly experienced the true nature of one's mind (also called clear light or profound emptiness), one allows the mind to remain in this non-dual state of integration wherein it gradually becomes fully habituated.

56. Experience (Tib. *nyams*) and realization (Tib. *rtogs pa*) can get confused as one strives in meditation. In the practice of meditation, one may experience various visions, thoughts, and ideas that may or may not be of value or validity on the path to the realization of higher truths. The valid experiences must be nurtured and developed. The false ones must be abandoned. It is easy to be confused and to think that certain visions or thoughts are of true importance when in reality they are just delusions and mistakes. Only one who abides at a higher level of realization can sort out the true from the false. This is the function of the authentic spiritual teacher, the physician of the mind.

57. The five types of worldly desirables are the objects of the five senses—visual, auditory, olfactory, gustatory, and tactile.

58. The common path is understood as either the thorough knowledge of the sutras and shastras by a scholar who also possesses deep faith and devotion toward the Dzogchen, or else the experiential preparation gained through authentic engagement in the specific preliminary practices of the Dzogchen, including the five sets of 100,000 repetitions (i.e., prostrations, refuge, bodhicitta, mandala offerings, confession/purification).

59. A dakini (Skt. *ḍākinī*) is a goddess, angel, or demoness who, depending upon her particular orientation and level of spiritual attainment, may protect and assist Buddhist practitioners or may attack them, consume them, or create various obstacles for them. When they are affiliated with the Dharma and have themselves attained high stages of realization on the bodhisattva path, their help to human yogins is incalculably great. They then become an object of refuge, one of the three general tantric refuges, and facilitate the attainment of siddhis, and the accomplishment of various enlightened activities. The dakinıs associated with the Dzogchen are generally of this latter type, and figure prominently in the transmission of the Dzogchen lineage from the beginning.

60. The four stages of perception (Tib. *snang ba bzhi*) are a Dzogchen analogue of the five paths (*pañcamarga*) of the Mahayana. They are (1) the direct perception of ultimate reality (Tib. *chos nyid mngon sum gi snang ba*); (2) the perception of increasing meditative experience (Tib. *nyams gong 'phel ba'i snang ba*); (3) the perception that reaches the limit of awareness (Tib. *rig pa tshad phebs kyi snang ba*); and (4) the perception that ceases the clinging to reality itself (Tib. *chos nyid du 'dzin pa zad pa'i snang ba*).

61. Tib. *bka' yongs rdzogs bsdus pa*.

62. Tib. *lam rim chen mo* (Full title: *mnyam med tsong kha pa chen pos mdzad pa'i byang chub lam rim che ba*).

63. Welshul (Tib. *dbal shul*), also Washul (Tib. *wa shul*), is the ancient name of the Serta region of Kham. The first Sogan Rinpoche was the ruler, as well as the head lama, of this entire region.

64. Bayan Serthang Gön Tennyi Dargye Ling (Tib. ba yan gser thang dgon bstan gnyis dar rgyas gling) is on the slopes of Mt. Bayan, a 14,000+ foot mountain on the banks of the Machu, across the river from the town of Darlag Dzong). Its name means the golden space monastery of Bayan—the abode of the two aspects of the sublime doctrine. The two aspects of doctrine are explained in two ways: (1) the early transmission (associated with Padmasambhava and the Nyingmapa lineages), and the later transmission (associated with the Gelukpa, Sakyapa, and Kagyupa lineages. (2) the twofold division of the Dharma, viz., the verbal doctrine enshrined in the Buddhist canon; and the internal realization of the doctrine that is acquired through study and meditation.

65. The Tibetan calendar cycle is 60 years long and has twelve animals and five elements. For example, the Earth Mouse year of the sixteenth Tibetan calendar cycle began in early 1948 and ended in early 1949. The Iron Tiger year of the seventeenth Tibetan calendar cycle began in February of 2010.

66. The Fourth Sogan Rinpoche, Natsok Rangdröl, being a tertön (i.e., "treasure revealer"), was in regular communication with both gods and lamas. He was known for his access to transcendent deities in various pure lands, and to the greatest of lamas both in this world and in the worlds beyond.

67. The ten virtues are the abstention from killing, stealing, sexual misconduct, lying, slander, harsh language, senseless talk, covetous attitudes, malicious attitudes, and wrong views.

68. Natsok Rangdröl and ḍākinī Dekyong Wangmo were fellow disciples of both Tulku Drimé Özer (Rigzin Sang-ngak Lingpa) and Jigme Lingpa. However, she was disadvantaged in her early life by her quiet humility and, to some degree by being a woman and therefore unable to enter the monastery as a monk. Later she was accepted by Natsok Rangdröl as a bona fide ḍākinī and therefore was allowed to enter the monastery.

69. Sera Khandro's biography is available in the Tibetan original, and has been translated into English: Sarah H. Jacoby, *Love and Liberation, Autobiographical Writings of the Tibetan Buddhist Visionary Sera Khandro* (Columbia University Press: New York, 2015).

70. As is the case with many sacred mountains, the name of the mountain is the same as the name of the resident god whose presence is the criteria whereby the mountain is called "sacred." The faithful come to Drongri Mukpo Mountain and make offerings to the god Drongri Mukpo.

71. Gyatrul Rinpoche was a close friend of Choktrul Thubga and recounts an occasion when he brought a dead fish to life.

72. Sera Yangtrul Rinpoche is the rebirth of Drimé Özer (Tib. dri med 'od zer) the main teacher, the root lama, of the Fourth Sogan Rinpoche. Drimé Özer's biography is a large text well known in Tibetan literature. As for Sera Yangtrul Rinpoche, he was arrested for the crime of being a Tibetan religious and cultural leader by the forces of the Chinese regime when they invaded our country. He was subjected to years of torture in the prison camps, but like Lama Rinpoche, his pure internal powers of loving kindness and profound wisdom prevailed, and he survived to lead a hidden Buddhist renaissance in his homeland.

73. The five aspects of perfection are: 1) the perfect teacher; 2) the perfect time; 3) the perfect audience; 4) the perfect teaching; and 5) the perfect place.

74. The wise lama would be one who knew the former birth of the lama who is thought to have been reborn as this child. He or she may have received instructions from the former birth of the lama regarding place and circumstances of

the rebirth, and will also be able to create a series of tests to see if the child recognizes objects and people closely associated with the former birth. Gods who are recognized to have insight into these types of issues are typically consulted through human oracles or mediums, and by way of various techniques such as visiting sacred sites associated with them, such as a sacred lake, where the signs and portents of the new rebirth may be divined.

75. In the Tibetan system, there are certain years, such as one's twenty-fifth year, that bring various types of obstacles.

76 Palyul (Tib. *dpal yul)* Monastery is in Kham. It is the main monastery of the Nyingma Palyul lineage. It has many branch monasteries such as Tarthang Monastery in Golok where Tenzin Zangpo was the senior abbot.

77. Sangye Tsering is one of the two rebirths (Tib. sprul sku, Pron. tulku) of Khenchen Ngagi Wangpo, also known as Khenpo Ngagchung, who was the root lama of my own Lama Rinpoche (Khenpo Münsel). His other rebirth is the renowned Tulku Nyima Gyaltsen, abbot of Dokho Monastery in Derge.

78. The *Treasury of Precious Termas* (Tib. *rin chen gter mdzod)* is a 111-volume compilation of treasure texts revealed by influential and beloved Nyingma teachers. This vast collection was edited and arranged for study and for initiations by Jamgön Kongtrul the Great (1813–1899). For a lama to give initiations for the entire collection takes several months of intensive daily teachings and ritual.

79. The ceremony of final departure takes place at the end of the forty-ninth day after a person dies. At death one enters the bardo if liberation has not been attained in the death process. The length of this intermediate state can be as short as an instant if one's propelling karma (Tib. *'phen pa'i las)* is particularly good or particularly bad. Otherwise it can take days or weeks to complete the intermediate state either by attaining liberation, or as is typically the case, entering a womb (or egg) in preparation for rebirth. In no case, however, does the intermediate state last more than forty-nine days. Therefore, at the end of the seventh week after death there is a big ceremony of final departure that concludes the period of transition.

80. *The Tale of a Youth Who Learns Wisdom* (Tib. *gzhon nu blo ldan gyi gtam)* tells of a haughty youth who has been raised with little education or discipline. One day on the road he sees an elderly man with balding head and long white hair and beard. The elder is making his way slowly with the help of a long staff. The youth looks at him and laughs, "It's not snowing, so why is your hair so white? There are no dogs to beat, so why the long stick?"

The elder looks at the youth and says, "Young lad, you must learn that it is not sensible to taunt an old person just for being old. Even a fierce tiger loses his luster with age, even a fast horse hobbles with age. You too will need a stick to walk before you even reach my present age." Slowly the lad begins to think about what he has been told, and at length humbly asks for further instructions. The elder then teaches him about the transitory nature of life, the inevitability of death, and the importance of cultivating qualities that transcend physical death.

81. The concept of the four endings is:

    1. the ending of all birth is the arrival of death

    2. the ending of all coming together is separation

    3. the ending of all building up is falling apart

    4. the ending of all collecting is dispersal

    The concept of these four endings is the frequent topic of many oral and written teachings on the transitory nature of the world, meant to inspire diligence and to encourage an orientation that strives to make the best use of available time, but is not surprised when time comes to an end.

82. A human life is said to be fully qualified (Tib. *dal brgyad 'byor bcu shang ba'i mi lus*) if it possesses the eighteen aspects of freedom and opportunity as follows:

    1. freedom from birth in the hells

    2. freedom from birth as a *preta*

    3. freedom from birth as an animal

    4. freedom from birth as a long lived god

    5. freedom from birth as a barbarian

    6. freedom from wrong views

    7. freedom from birth where the Buddha has not been

    8. freedom from birth as a deaf mute

    9. opportunity of birth as a human

    10. opportunity of birth in a civilized area

    11. opportunity of birth with intact faculties

    12. opportunity of having a lifestyle compatible with Dharma practice

    13. opportunity of having faith in the Dharma

    14. opportunity of birth where a Buddha has appeared

    15. opportunity of birth where a Buddha has turned the *Wheel of Dharma*

    16. opportunity of birth where the Dharma still abides

    17. opportunity of birth where the Dharma can be practiced

    18. opportunity of birth where spiritual friends are available

83. The song is in six-syllable Tibetan verse: each line of verse having exactly six syllables. It can be sung with any melody that is based on six-syllable lines.

84. The most famous of all Buddhist sacred images is the Jowo Rinpoche. Embodying the actual presence of the Lord Buddha Shakyamuni, it was sent by a wise Dharma King in India to a King of China over 1800 years ago in order to spread the teachings of Buddha to that land. For those whose minds were open, the Jowo Rinpoche always speaks directly in that person's language, bestowing whatever aspect of Dharma teaching is most beneficial. In the early seventh century,

during the Tang dynasty, the Tibetan Dharmaraja Songtsen Gampo extended his military and political control through Nepal and the upper Ganges basin of India all the way east to Chang'an (Xian), the capital of Tang China. The Tang emperor Taizong, a.k.a., Li Shimin, sued for peace, and in exchange for being allowed to keep his throne, sent his greatest treasure, the Jowo Rinpoche, and his second greatest treasure, his daughter Princess Wen Cheng, together with 10,000 loads of lesser treasure, to King Songtsen Gampo in Lhasa. He also dispatched his greatest Buddhist prelate, Xuanzang, to Tibet and Tibetan affiliated parts of India to learn Mahayana Buddhism. Xuanzang traveled through Tibet and into India with his illustrious disciple Sun Wukong, and his other main disciples Zhu Bajie and Sha Wujing.

85. Amdo Lungtok (Tib. *a mdo lung rtogs*) overcame the opposition of some neo-conservative elements who had gained administrative control over the Jokhang in those days, and were not interested in the addition of the Guru's image.

86. The full name of Tarthang Monastery is "The Palyul Tarthang Monastery—the Dharma realm where the sutras and the tantras are studied and realized" (Tib. *dpal yul dar thang dgon mdo sngags bshad sgrub chos gling*). As one of the largest monasteries in the region, Tarthang has many tulkus and many khenpos. Khen Rinpoche Tenzin Zangpo was one of the greatest in the century in both categories.

87. Tib. *tshe ring ljongs*

88. Tib. *padma 'od gsal theg mchog gling*

89. Tib. *gsang chen 'od skur grol ba'i gnas mchog*. This refers to the rainbow body attained by practitioners of the tantras, especially the Dzogchen, when they finally transcend the limits of samsara.

90. Forest of the Trees of Enlightenment (Tib. *byang chub ljon pa'i nags t Shal*) suggests a forest of bodhi trees (i.e., *ficus religiosa*). However, this area has no bodhi trees, nor anything much in the way of trees. It has alpine grasses, small shrubs, and some moss. More importantly, it does possess the qualities that make for an ideal venue for a meditative retreat such as that found by the Lord Buddha under the bodhi tree. It is very quiet, isolated, peaceful, and is alive with the fine savors of the earth and the rare essences of heaven.

91. Tib. *'phags pa sems nyid ngal gso*.

92. For the concise form of this text, in English and Tibetan, see: Sogan Rinpoche and Robert W. Clark, *Treasures of the Nying T'ik: Preliminaries and Auxiliary Texts* (San Francisco: Trilobite Publications, 2009). ISBN 978-0-578-04617-4

93. This guru yoga practice by Lama Rinpoche, Khenpo Münsel, is called *Invoking the Lama from Afar* (Tib. *bla ma rgyang 'bod*). It is presented in Tibetan and English translation in Chapter IV of the above referenced book: *Treasures of the Nying T'ik*.

94. This would be in January or February of 1990.

95. The five desires are the desirable objects of the five sense powers.

96. Khyentse Özer (Tib. *mkhyen brtse'i 'od zer*) is the personal name of Jigme Lingpa (Tib. *'jigs med gling pa*) (1729–1798).

97. The Great Secret is the Dzogchen. The body of light is the dharmakāya.

98. Padma Mati is the Sanskrit for Pema Lodoe.

99. My homeland in Amdo is at too high an altitude for most types of agriculture, so I never before witnessed the process of cultivating crops.

100. The pure essence of truth is the Great Secret meaning of the Dzogchen.

101. To cultivate true compassion in your heart means to generate the bodhicitta.

102. Dzogchen meditation requires different postures according to the nature of the practice. Commonly the mouth is just slightly open, rather than tightly closed, and the spine is completely straight.

103. These four lines and the following twenty six lines each begin with a letter of the Tibetan alphabet, in the correct order of the alphabet. Two additional lines repeat the last two letters of the alphabet. In this manner there are eight quatrains, each expressing a complete thought or theme. As with all the quatrains in this section, each line within a quatrain has exactly the same number of syllables, usually eight or nine, but some quatrains may have only six syllables, and others as many as eleven.

104. The Tara mantra: *Om tare tutari ture svaha* is recited by most everyone in Tibetan culture, even the least educated. However, the Dzogchen retreat makes is own strict demands on the participant, requiring constant unremitting focus on the mind itself, and constant criticism of any self-cherishing of the loathsome vagabond "self" that wanders endlessly in the samsara, seeking illusory pleasures and engaging in senseless and untoward actions.

105. The view of the Dzogchen is taught in the texts of transcendent wisdom such as the *Heart Sutra*. In the Dzogchen tradition, it is said that once one has been definitively shown the nature of mind, one attends to that direct realization. The term "attends to" (Tib. *bskyang*) is used rather than the term "meditates on" (Tib. *bsgoms*) as it is mere attention to a manifest reality rather than a focus or analysis of an abstract object.

106. In Mahayana texts, living beings are referred to as one's "old mothers" (Tib. *ma rgan*) because each person has had countless former lives, and in each life benefited from and relied upon the loving kindness of a mother for body, life, and nurturance. Therefore, no living being can be excluded from the circle of one's own kind mothers to whom a tremendous debt of gratitude is now owed. This is the basis for the bodhisattva's pursuit of buddhahood.

107. Tsari (Tib. *dpal gyi tsa ri tra; tsa ri sgang*) also is one of the most sacred mountains of Tibet along with Mt. Kailash (Tib. *gangs dkar ti se*), Lachi Gang (Tib. *la phyi sgang*), Amnye Machen (Tib. *a myes rma chen*), and others. Tsari is the home

of various local deities and autochthonous divinities, among who is the god Zhingkyong Kunga Shonu (Tib. *zhing skyong kun dga' gzhon nu*). However, Sogan Rinpoche's agenda did not include these mountains, but focused rather on the sacred meditation sites of many masters in the Dzogchen tradition.

108. The Tibetan gazelle (Tib. *rgo ba; Procapra picticaudata*).

109. AH (ཨ) is the Dzogchen symbol for ultimate reality, i.e., the true nature of one's mind.

110. These are the three prerequisites of Dzogchen practice. In order to be motivated to make continual diligent effort and not procrastinate, one must realize that all composite phenomena, such as one's own body, are impermanent, constantly changing, and will soon end in death. In order to proceed toward liberation, one must have the attitude of profound renunciation that sees through the vacuous pleasures of samsara and desires only true freedom. In order to transcend the self-cherishing attitude that keeps one bound to the cycles of birth and death, or at best seeks a limited nirvana for oneself alone, one must generate bodhicitta that pursues the ultimate happiness and welfare of all beings without exception.

111. This verse was written in the autumn, when strong winds strip the dry leaves from the trees and blow them everywhere together with the dry and dusty earth of this region.

112. In general the antidotes to the kleśhas (greed, anger, delusion, pride, envy, etc.) are specific meditations on such things as generosity, patience, wisdom, compassion. However, the ultimate antidote needed to completely eliminate all *kleśas* is the supreme realization of ultimate truth such as is attained through the completion of the Dzogchen. Therefore, the term "antidote" on this occasion refers to the Dzogchen.

113. The stable state of Dzogchen perception (Tib. *lta stangs*) is a special state of a type of non-dual unification within a one-pointed meditative focus. On this occasion there was a lunar eclipse. In Buddhist tradition such an occasion is considered the most powerful time for accomplishing Dharma practices. It is said that the power and benefit of one minute of practice at this time is equivalent to more than 100,000 minutes of practice during ordinary times. After entering this special meditative state, I remained within it through the entire night until after the sun rose the following morning.

114. Bayan Mountain is called a "water mountain" because it has many productive springs that supply water to the monastery and surrounding communities. A volcano, for example, is called a "fire mountain."

115. The Tibetan words at the beginning of each of these four lines, "kye, kye-hoo, a-tsi, & o-o," express different degrees of surprise and dismay. "Kye" is mostly surprise. "Kye-hoo" is surprise and a little dismay. "A-tsi" is a little surprise, but mostly dismay. "O-o" is almost all dismay.

116. These syllables, *DZA HUM BAM HO* (ཛཿ$\frac{2}{3}$ཿ$\frac{2}{3}$ཿ), are a mantra used in esoteric tantric practice associated with arrival and activities of a deity in one's personal space.

117. The first letters of these four lines are *"'di, phyi,* and *bar do."* This spells out "this life, next life, and the bardo."

118. The name "Pema Lodoe" ("Lotus Intellect") is not written separately in the Tibetan text. By Tibetan poetic convention, the syllables that spell "Pema Lodoe" are indicated by special dots.

119. As in the last quatrain, the name "Sherab Gyatso" ("Ocean of Wisdom") is not written out, but is embedded in the text and indicated by special dots. Sherab Gyatso ("Ocean of Wisdom") was the ordination name bestowed on Sogan Rinpoche when he first became a Buddhist monk.

120. The terms in this quatrain are from the esoteric Dzogchen lexicon. The "innermost nature of your original mind" translates the terms *"shes rig gnyug ma'i rig pa,"* and "the vast expansiveness like endless space" translates *"rab yangs mkha'."* The "precious oceanic jewel" is the goal of Dzogchen meditation.

121. Khyider ("dog's claw"), as explained in the beginning of this account, was the childhood nickname given to Sogan Rinpoche by his parents. Here it is embedded in the text.

122. Basic provisions for the retreat are supplied once a month, as noted before. But these unsolicited gifts of various kinds of food, clothing, and other offerings were not needed. Whoever gave them must certainly have meant to help. However, the effect of accepting gifts is to be indebted to the donor. This was an unwelcome complication, so Sogan Rinpoche left a note for the anonymous donors to cease the donations.

123. A lama is called upon to guide the living to what is propitious in this life, and the dead to good fortune in the next life. Until he has truly found his own way, he should not be claiming the ability to guide others.

124. The sound of profound emptiness (Tib. *grags stong*) is embodied in the sacred syllable A (ཨ).

125. The ordinary speech of humans, animals, and other non-humans is known as the "sounds of attachment and discord" (Tib. *zhen rgud*).

126. This is the definition of the supreme practitioner of Dzogchen, "a yogin whose mind is like endless space without any point of preoccupation (Tib. *gtad med nam mkha'i rnal 'byor*).

127. Here it is the worldly attachment to friends and relatives that causes difficulties for the Dharma practitioner in this life. When the Dharma practice reaches a high level of accomplishment, such worldly attachments have been eliminated and no longer create obstacles.

128. Accepting offerings from the faithful to perform prayers and rituals for those in need, or for those who have died, is suitable only if one truly has the power

to benefit them. Otherwise it is an evil deed that is said to cause rebirth in a hell realm.

129. The Kadampa is a lineage of Tibetan Buddhism founded by Atiśha Dipankara Shrijnana (980–1054) and developed by his main disciple Dromtonpa (Drom-tön Gyal-we Jungne, 1005–1064) and his main disciples, known as the Three Noble Brothers: Geshe Potowa (Potowa Rinchen Sal), Geshe Chengawa (Chengawa Tsultrim Bar) and Geshe Puchungwa (Phuchungwa Shönu Gyaltsen).

Dromtonpa founded Reting Monastery (Tib. *rwa sgreng*) in 1056 in the Reting Tsampo Valley north of Lhasa, which became the main center for Kadampa culture. The Kadampa masters were distinguished by their devotion to the simple lifestyle of the Buddhist ascetic, avoiding honors and pretence, and focusing only on the essential principles taught by the Lord Buddha, such as renunciation, bodhicitta, and the wisdom realizing profound emptiness. The last famous master of the Kadampa was Je Tsongkhapa (1357–1419), the founder of the Gelukpa lineage. With Je Tsongkhapa, the Kadampa became merged with Gelukpa and was no longer identified as a separate lineage.

130. The "seven treasures of the Noble Ones" (Tib. *'phags pa'i nor bdun*) are faith, generosity, discipline, learning, modesty, sense of shame, and wisdom. An *ārya* (Tib. *'phags pa*) is one who has transcended the world of ordinary beings by achieving a direct (i.e., non-conceptual) realization of profound emptiness (Skt. *śūnyatā*). Such a realization is attained by continuous reliance on these seven treasures.

131. Dzogchen meditation entails both secret transcendence (Tib. *khregs chod) and* penetrating vision, also known as the "original purity of secret transcendence" (Tib. *ka dag khregs chod*) and "spontaneously arising penetrating vision" (Tib. *lhun grub thod rgal*). This quatrain refers to the three unique postures and three unique modes of perception of penetrating vision. The postures are compared poetically to the unique activities of the giant Himalayan condor, who majestically soars among the high mountain peaks, glides easily to his precipitous perch, and looks out upon a vast expanse with visual perception far beyond the limited and restricted vision of ordinary humans. The three unique postures are the majestic lion posture of the dharmakāya, the resting elephant posture of the sambhogakaya, and the elegant rishi posture of the nirmāṇakāya. Just as the condor sees everything nearby and far off with incredible precision, the Dzogchen meditator's perception goes far beyond the abilities of the ordinary person. Gazing upward, he emulates the perception of the dharmakāya. Looking sideways, he emulates the vision of the sambhogakaya. Lowering his gaze, he emulates the view of the nirmāṇakāya.

132. The five poisons are desire, aversion, delusion, pride, and envy. They represent all the afflictive mental states, as the 84,000 afflictive mental states are subsumed in these five.

133. A celestial yogin (Tib. *nam mkha'i rnal 'byor pa*) is a yogin who has attained direct realization of the nature of reality. A yogin who has abandoned all worldly deeds does not necessarily have such realization. Therefore, the aspiration expressed in this verse is to be a yogin who has both attained realization and has abandoned all worldly deeds.

134. There are five unseemly modes of livelihood (Tib. *log 'tsho*) that are commonly noted: relying on hypocrisy and pretence (Tib. *tshul 'chos*), on flattery (Tib. *kha gsag*), on deceptive solicitation/hustling (Tib. *gzhogs slong*), on expropriating the property of others (Tib. *thob kyis 'jal ba*), and on acquiring things by deceit (Tib. *rnyed pa 'dod pa*).

135. The twelve ascetic practices (Tib. *sbyangs pa'i yon tan bcu gnyis*) are:

    1. Eating only alms (Tib. *bsod snyoms pa*)
    2. Eating the day's food in one sitting (Tib. *stan gcig pa*)
    3. Not eating after the noon meal (Tib. *zas phyis mi len pa*)
    4. Owning only three robes (Tib. *chos gos gsum pa*)
    5. Using a simple umbrella or poncho (Tib. *phying ba pa*)
    6. Making clothes from discarded rags (Tib. *phyag dar khrod pa*)
    7. Dwelling in isolation (Tib. *dgon pa ba*)
    8. Dwelling among trees (Tib. *shing drung ba*)
    9. Dwelling in the open, without a roof (Tib. *bla gab med pa*)
    10. Dwelling in cemeteries (Tib. *dur khrod pa*)
    11. Sitting up at night without laying down to sleep (Tib. *tsog bu ba*)
    12. Sleeping at night wherever one happens to be (Tib. *gzhi ji bzhin pa*)

136. Uncreated, self-existent emptiness (Tib. *a don skye med*) is the primary meditative focus of Dzogchen.

137. The popular Tibetan ritual of the smoke offering (Tib. *bsang*) is concluded with all the people taking a measure of roasted barley flour (Tib. *tsam pa*) in their hand and tossing it into the air with shouts of Lha Gyal Lo! (Tib. *lha rgyal lo*) which means literally "may the gods be triumphant" which is a wish or prayer that goodness in general, and the virtues of the buddhas and bodhisattvas in particular, flourish throughout the world. While this is an admirable sentiment, it is not necessarily associated with diligent application to the difficult and often austere practices whereby universal goodness can actually be accomplished.

138. Achak, also called Akyong Bum (Tib. *a skyong 'bum*), is the locality in Golok where Sogan Rinpoche was born and raised.

139. The fifth path is the bardo, the intermediate period between death and rebirth. The five paths are (1) birth, (2) sickness, (3) old age, (4) death, (5) bardo.

140. Although one may pass through the bardo in much less time, the maximum duration of the bardo before rebirth is 49 days. Therefore, this is the usual period of mourning and merit dedication for the deceased.

141. The Buddha taught that all composite phenomena (Tib. *'dus byas*; Skt. *saṃskṛ-ta*) are impermanent. However, phenomena that are not composites, like pure space, true cessations, and meaning generalities, are permanent. Both permanent and impermanent phenomena are empty of true existence, that is, they do not truly exist.

142. This is probably the *megalaima faber*, known in Taiwan as the *five-color bird*. It ranges from Taiwan through parts of Southeast Asia and southern China, and is occasionally seen in Tibet. It is similar to the male painted bunting of North America.

143. "Ancient precepts" here refers to the Dzogchen oral tradition handed down from ancient times from master to disciples.

144. Whatever occurs in the course of meditation, any thoughts, images, emotions, etc., are not to be resisted or cut off by applying some antidote, as is done in other forms of meditation. Rather they are allowed to dissolve naturally. By doing this, they lose their power to disturb the mind, and thereby become part of the path of transcendence rather than an obstacle to it.

145. Tib. *sems kyi mthil du bzung.*

146. The Tibetan snowcock (*Tetraogallus tibetanus*).

147. In this composition, Jigme Lingpa refers to himself as "young man."

148. The three sets of vows are the individual liberation (Skt. *pratimokṣa*) vows, the bodhisattva vows, and the tantric vows.

149. Reflexive awareness, or transcendent apperception (Skt. *svasaṃvitti*) is the simultaneous and direct realization of the nature of mind and ultimate reality.

150. The Crystal Cave of Yarlung (Tib. *yar lung shel brag*) was one of the main mountain caves where Padmasambhava meditated and taught during his eighth-century C.E. sojourn in Tibet.

151. This stone image of Padmasambhava was taken out and hidden during the Chinese "Cultural Revolution" of the 1960s, and brought back in the 1970s when the official policy of the Chinese regime no longer required the physical destruction of Tibetan cultural treasures.

152. These caves are several hundred meters apart, but as they are high up on the mountain, the path is steep and difficult. These and the other caves where we went to meditate are famous landmarks. Each cave is readily identified by such things as ancient shrines, rock carvings, and accumulated offerings.

153. The account of Padmasambhava and the beer-drinking prodigy is repeated by the Indian progenitor of the Sakyapa lineage, Mahāsiddha Virupa (837–909), a renowned yogin and abbot of Nalanda University. In both cases a prodigious amount of alcoholic beverage was consumed with the promise to the innkeeper that the bill would be settled as soon as the sun set. Both, with their powers of siddhi, held the sun hostage in the sky while they continued to drink hour after

hour. The frightened innkeepers and villagers then paid the bar tab in exchange for the release of the sun.

154. Yarlha Shampo (Tib. *yar lha Sham po*) is a sacred mountain in the Yarlung valley where the first king of Tibet descended from the empyrean. It is also the name of the presiding deity of that mountain.

155. Machik Labdrön (Tib. *ma cig lab kyi sgron ma*, 1055–1149) is the founder of the Chöd Lineage. Her monastery and temple was called Zangri Kharmar (Red Citadel of Copper Mountain). It was built upon a high red sandstone outcrop at the southern end of Copper Mountain (i.e., Zangri), above the northern banks of the Tsangpo River. Machik Labdrön's meditation cave was on the cliff to the west of Zangri Kharmar Monastery, which was destroyed in the 1960's.

156. Geshe (Tib. *dge bshes*; Skt. *kalyānamitra*) is the highest possible academic degree in the main Gelukapa monastic universities (Drepung, Ganden, and Sera). It requires decades of study, contemplation, and meditation on the topics of the sutras and shastras.

157. The summer retreat is the traditional 45-day period during the summer when Buddhist monks, since the Lord Buddha founded the monastic order, gather for special practices of purification and in general to acquire further knowledge and insight into the Buddha's teachings. On the day of the full moon and the new moon, there are purification procedures (Tib. *gso sbyong*; Skt. *uposadha*) that involve practices and rituals to confess and purify downfalls, and to restore and renew vows. Khen Rinpoche and Sogan Rinpoche joined the other monks on these two days of the purification procedures. Otherwise they remained in their solitary retreat the entire time, except for the usual period on the second day of the Tibetan month, and in this case, also on the first day of the Tibetan month as it is the day following the new moon.

158. This letter to parents, friends, teachers and family is in the form of a poem whose meaning can be found by following metaphor and simile. A clear and explicit message could be understood by the occupation police, and could be a source of serious trouble.

159. The Sanskrit term *jina* ("victorious one") is a common epithet for a buddha. It indicates victory over the four mara devils who stand in the way of perfect buddhahood.

160. A vajra brother or sister is a person with whom one has received Dharma teachings, especially Vajrayana (i.e., tantric) teachings from the same lama.

161. This phrase, "flowers of pure gold will come to adorn your crown," is meant to have a variety of meanings suitable for the variety of its intended readers. It indicates that assiduous Dharma practice can result in the fulfillment of one's innermost wishes. For Tibetans this means the quick return of His Holiness the Dalai Lama to his seat of power in Lhasa. For monks at Bayan and Awo Sera

monasteries, it would also mean the return of Sogan Rinpoche himself. For tantric yogins, it can mean success in their internal energies and Dzogchen practices. In general, it indicates the coming of good fortune and success.

162. "Foot drinkers" (Tib. *rkang 'thung*) is a poetic term for trees, as they drink up their nourishment from their roots.

163. Mön is the warm, rainforest region in the border area of Tibet, Sikkim, Bhutan and Nepal between the Kosi and Teesta rivers.

164. Here the "circuitous and difficult passageways to the deep, cool waters of the vast ocean" would be readily understood as the dangerous journey out of Tibet, across the Himalaya, and into India, a land of freedom. The vast ocean is also a metaphor for His Holiness the Dalai Lama.

165. In the verse, "To the sun, the benefactor of all, in the sky of universal longing," the word for the sun is *kun phan* ("the benefactor of all"); this term also refers to His Holiness. The "universal longing" (Tib. *kun smon*) is readily understood as the longing of all Tibetans to be in the presence of His Holiness in the land of the Lord Buddha. These lines therefore clearly give reader an understanding of the destination.

166. Tarthang Tulku, *Ancient Tibet (Berkeley: Dharma Publishing, 1986), pp. 90–91*.

167. Namkhai Norbu estimates the date of Nyari Tsenpo's ascension as 414 B.C.E. Norbu, Namkhai. *Drung, deu, and Bön: narrations, symbolic languages, and the Bön traditions in ancient Tibet* (Dharamsala: Library of Tibetan Works and Archives, 1995) p. 220.

168. The names of each grouping of historical kings are popularly known by poetic designations such as "sky kings" and "earth kings."

169. The Jowo Mikyö Dorje image and the Ramoche Temple itself were both destroyed by the Chinese in the 1960s.

170. *Prayer to the Distant Lama*, also known as *Invoking the Lama from Afar*, was composed by Khenpo Münsel, and is found in English and Tibetan on pp. 10–24 of *Treasures of the Nying T'ik*, by Sogan Rinpoche and Robert W Clark (Trilobite Publications: San Francisco, 2009).

171. Ibid, on pp. 34–36.

172. Tib. *nor bu zla shel gyi se mo do.*

173. The *four types of enlightened activity* are pacification, increase, power, and wrath. These are the four ways of action by which an enlightened being benefits a world and all of its living beings.

174. This text is known in Tibetan as *tog mtha' bar gsum du dge ba'i gtam lta sgom spyod gsum nyams len dam pai snying nor*. It has been translated into English as *The Heart Treasure of the Enlightened Ones*. It has a commentary by Dilgo Khyentse Rinpoche and a foreword by His Holiness the Dalai Lama (Shambhala: Boston, 1992).

175. This is the *bka' brgyad bde gshegs 'dus pa* from the Fifth Dalai Lama's *dak snang gsang ba rgya can gyi chos skor.*

176. Tib. *ri chos bslab bya nyams len dmar khrid go bder brjod pa grub pa'i bcud len.*

177. *Guide for Pilgrims to the Sacred Sites of India* (Tib. *rgya gar gyi gnas chen khag la 'grod pa'i lam yig*). There is an English translation of this book by Toni Huber entitled *The Guide to India, A Tibetan Account* by Amdo Gedun Chöphel (Dharamsala: Library of Tibetan Works and Archives, 2000).

178. The twelve great deeds of a buddha are:

   1. Send an emanation from a Pure Land into a world's heaven
   2. Enter into a mother's womb
   3. Take birth
   4. Learn the arts and sciences of that world
   5. Take up a role in the world (e.g., marriage and social position)
   6. Point out the fatal flaws of worldly life (e.g., sickness, aging, and death)
   7. Renounce the ordinary world and engage in the spiritual path
   8. Take the vajra seat under a bodhi tree
   9. Defeat the four maras
   10. Manifest the attainment of highest, perfect, complete enlightenment
   11. Turn the Dharma wheel (i.e., teach the path to liberation and buddhahood)
   12. Attain nirvana after death (Skt. *parinirvāṇa*).

179. The Six Ornaments are the six most famous Indian pandits whose teachings and texts enhanced the Lord Buddha's teaching by providing detailed explanations. They are Nāgārjuna, Āryadeva, Asaṅga, Vasubandhu, Dignāga, and Dharmakīrti. Two Superiors are Gunaprabha and Shakyaprabha, who also provided much commentarial material.

180. The Eighty Mahāsiddhas are eighty of the most famous tantric practitioners of India. These include such luminaries as Nāgārjuna, Sāraha, Virūpa, Tilopa, and Nāropa.

181. "Tso" is the Tibetan word for "lake," and "Pema" is Tibetan for "Padma", and is the short form of the name "Padmasambhava." Tso Pema is known in Indian languages as Rewalsar.

182. Tib. *sdom gsum rab dbye* and *thub pa dgongs gsal.*

183. The twenty-four sacred sites are the locations on Earth where Chakrasamvara and Vajrayogini maintain their mandalas. These are Arbuta, Devikoti, Jalandhara, Godavari, Grihadevata, Himalaya, Kalinga, Kamarupa, Kancha, Kosala, Kuluta, Lampaka, Malava, Maru, Nagara, Oddiyāna, Ote, Pretapuri, Puliramalaya, Rame Shari, Shaurashtra, Sindhura, Suvarnadvipa, and Trishakune.

184. Tibetans, following the teachings of the Buddha, reckon the beginning of a person's life as the moment of entering the womb at conception, rather than the moment of exiting the womb at birth. Conception is the moment we enter this life and take up this body. As the moment of conception is difficult to specify

with any certainty, and in any case is rarely documented, it makes better sense to Tibetans to count one's age as starting on losar.

185. Note that the English alphabet has only 26 letters, but the Tibetan alphabet has thirty consonants and five vowels.

186. The poem makes the point that much must be accomplished in the practice of Dharma if this life is not to be wasted, as the end of life approaches without warning, worldly pursuits must be abandoned in favor of diligent Dharma practice. The last verses give the hint that Sogan Rinpoche will be going to the West to accomplish his destined path, and there will rely exclusively upon the King of All Dharma, His Holiness the Dalai Lama:

> The sun of my present life is going on, to set in the West,
> My sublime father, the King of All Dharma,
> To you alone do I turn for all answers now and in the future.

187. The activity of the Dharma here indicates such things as the building of monasteries, the erection of stupas, and all other actions that contribute to the infrastructure of Buddhism that facilitates its ongoing practice in this world.

188. Ghantapa refers to the mahasiddha Ghantapada (Tib. *dril bu pa*) who meditated on Chakrasamvara in a cave on this mountain. He was accompanied there by his consort/wife. The people of the region became aware of this arrangement and considered it to be bad form for a monk/yogin not to be celibate. He then appeared before the people flying through the sky above their heads. His consort at that moment transformed into a *ghanta* in his hand. A *ghanta* is a ritual bell with a *vajra* handle. This mountain is very famous and is an important site of pilgrimage.

189. Tib. *sgrub skor rnam gsum.*

190. The title of my manual is: *Lha brag gter byon ma ha guru gsang mtshan thugs kyi sgrub ba'i sngon 'gro gzer snga nas brtsoms bsnyen sgrub nyams len bya tshul bskyud byang du bkod pa kun gsal me long.*

191. Khen Rinpoche and I flew by helicopter from Katmandu to Phablu. We waited there for two hours while the helicopter went to pick up Trulshig Rinpoche at his retreat place, then the three of us flew in the helicopter to his monastery for the Drubchen.

192. Asura Cave (i.e., Yangleshö) in Kathmandu Valley is known as a sacred place visited by Padmasambhava.

193. Sera Khandro is also known as Kunzang Dekyong Wangmo. She was the heroine, or (consort) of Natsok Rangdröl, the Fourth Sogan Rinpoche, as noted about in chapter 8. For more on her life see: Sarah H. Jacoby, *Love and Liberation, Autobiographical Writings of the Tibetan Buddhist Visionary Sera Khandro* (Columbia University Press: New York, 2015).

194. This quatrain refers to Sogan Rinpoche's lama, Thubten Tsultrim Gyatso Münsel (Khenpo Münsel). His name is embedded in the Tibetan text, and the syllables spelling out his name are marked by tiny sun and moon figures in accordance with literary tradition.

195. These are: 1) all meeting ends in parting; 2) all construction ends in destruction; 3) all accumulation ends in dispersal; 4) all birth ends in death.

196. The Lord of the Potala is Avalokiteshvara/His Holiness the Dalai Lama. The Ganden Podrang is the historic government of Tibet, now in exile in Dharamsala.

197. The fivefold degeneration (Skt. *pañcakaṣāya*) is (1) the decline of lifespans (Skt. *āyuḥ*); (2) the corruption of views (Skt. *dṛṣṭi*); (3) the increase of afflictive mental states; (4) the decline of sentient beings (Skt. *sattva*); and (5) the systemic degeneration of the era (Skt. *kalpa*).

198. The two types of *siddhi* are the common *siddhis* such as clairvoyance, flying, elixirs of longevity, etc., which are shared with various non-Buddhist yogas, and the supreme *siddhi*, buddhahood, which is attained only through Buddhist yoga.

199. Mahāyoga, Anuyoga and Atiyoga.

200. This is Sogan Rinpoche's name for his hermitage in Dharamsala.

201. This is in the autumn of 2002.

202. These are the three great stupas in the Kathmandu valley: Swayambhunath, Boudhanath, and Namo Buddha stupas.

203. Tib. *sems nyid ngal gso*. This was translated into English by Herber V. Guenther as *Kindly Bent to Ease Us*, Vol. 1.

204. The Pleasure Garden of Full Knowledge—A Tibetan Language High School/ Junior College in Golok (Tib. *mgo log bod yig mtho rim slob 'bring kun gsal skyed t shal khang*) opened in August 2007.

205. Centro Cian Ciub Ciö Ling in Polava di Savogna (UD) Italy.

206. Supreme liberation (Skt. *bodhi*) is the true benefit of self and other.

Indexes

Cited Texts